PRESS AND CONTEMPORARY AFFAIRS

by Sidney Kobre Ph.D.

Professor of Journalism, Director
Bureau of Media Research,
Florida State University

Florida State University

Distributed through
Bookstore,
Florida State University,
Tallahassee, Florida

Table of Contents

NEWSPAPER JOB

Today the job of the newspaper is to bring news from all over the world, combine it with local news to make it readable and understandable.

Toward this end newsmen are seeking to co-ordinate the news, and through depth reporting to background it for the reader, giving the "spot" news events greater meaning.

Chapter 1

Vital Role of Press in Democracy

In our democracy to be a good citizen is to be a well-informed citizen. In order to make decisions and to vote intelligently on men, parties and issues, John and Mary Smith have to keep abreast of the current news and understand its significance and meaning. In other lands, where dictatorships or small cliques operate the government, such understanding by the public is not essential. For the making of decisions is left to the inner circle. The elections and the voting are confirmation of what the party leaders have decided already.

Not so in a democracy. On election day John Citizen and Mary Citizen march to the polls and enter the little booth. They pull a lever or mark a ballot to register their approval of a school bond issue or the municipal program proposed by the Republicans or the Democrats. They may decide for or against the international political program, or the national economic measures advocated by one or the other of the parties. Every four years the ceaseless, irresistible rotation of men in office takes place--mayor, city councilman, governor, senator, even the president must go before the voters for confirmation or rejection. When the citizen makes the little mark "x", or pulls the lever behind the curtain in the polling cubicle, he registers an opinion based on his understanding of the men and issues.

And this opinion, built up item by item, cell by cell, is constructed from his reading of the newspaper during the previous year, months or weeks. Thus it may be said that democracy depends on the free flow of news. This news must be presented accurately, objectively, fully. But its significance must also be understood.

Surveys of public opinion have shown, however, that we have a long stretch to travel before we get a generally well-informed citizenry. Although the newspaper reading public is vast, and a knowledge of current news is obtained by millions, only a small percentage of the public has an essential understanding of the national and international developments. A large number do not have any opinions at all, George Gallup has shown this repeatedly in his polls for the American Institute of Public Opinion.

The newspaper thus plays an important role in the operation of our government. Newsmen and newswomen are on the front line providing a supply line of news, "the food

1

of a democracy." If the public fails to understand or is indifferent to the news, part of the responsibility rests on the newsworkers. They have not done the job of making the news clear, meaningful and vital.

Newsmen in the past have concentrated largely on the spot news, the five w's of the news. The reporters have given the who, the what, the where, the when and sometimes the why of the happening. Such news is obtained quickly with the modern high speed means of communication. It is presented interestingly and factually, and, in most instances, objectively. But the significance of the event has too often been lost, because the happening has been presented as an isolated occurrence. Today's news is not tied up with previous incidents, it is not fitted into any trend or pattern.

Today more newsmen are recognizing the limitations of the traditional but necessary spot news story. By expanding the news story coverage more completeness is given the event, so that the reader gets a better understanding of it. Newsmen write background news-features which go below the surface and place the news in its context. They write more explanatory editorials which explain rather than condem or praise or urge action. Some write enlightening columns which give body and significance to the inner meaning of events. Larger newspapers devote entire pages and sections to the co-ordination of the news. These include the New York Times, the New York Herald Tribune and the Philadelphia Bulletin, among others. The trend toward fuller explanation of the news is destined to grow according to all signs. The persistent march of more students towards the high schools and colleges and universities will tend to raise the educational level of the reading public. As this level is highered, greater demands for informative, enlightening news stories and articles will be made.

Newsmen of the future face a challenging situation. The reporter and feature-writer and editorial writer must deal with complicated news. They can't rely entirely on their ready skill as writers, their ability to cover the police beat and city hall. Newsworkers must have a grasp of local, national and international affairs.

They have to cover the spot news. But today editors also want men who can understand these developments. They need newsmen who can explain this news, put it into focus. It is essential that the investigator be able to present it as interestingly, as dramatically as he does the explosive spot news event.

To do this job effectively the reporter requires a thorough grasp of the social sciences--history, political science and economics. For these disciplines bear directly on contemporary affairs. The newsman needs to learn to apply this knowledge for explaining and giving proper perspective to current news on various levels.

2

The news writer can write better news stories, news-features and produce more enlightening columns and editorials if he can apply this subject matter to current events. He sees more deeply and has a better appreciation and knowledge of the factors and forces which have shaped and are shaping the news. He develops an understanding of the solutions to various current problems which the specialists suggest.

Many students get such knowledge in the various departments of the university or college. They need more than just the knowledge. It is necessary for them to apply such useful information to the news. They have to learn to utilize immediately source materials which throw an incandescent light on the flow of the rapidly moving events. They should learn, above all, to write this material for presentation to a mass audience, using all the journalistic devices to make the data readable, vivid. At the same time they must exercise the caution and use the qualifications of the scientist to keep within the bounds of truth.

This book is designed to aid the student-reporter in this learning process. It aims:

1. To keep the newsman abreast of current local, national and world events.
2. To show how spot news can be given background and focus for the reader.
3. To provide models for the writing of effective news and news-feature articles.
4. To point out useful sources for pertinent information from printed and human resources.
5. To show how certain social sciences, history, political science, economics and labor economics, may be employed usefully by news writers.
6. To furnish specific information on contemporary affairs which will supply background for the news worker.
7. To provide specific assignments which may be carried out by student-reporters.

It is clear that a volume which is geared to page one's fast changing news events cannot be entirely current. By the time the book has been printed, the news situation has changed. We have sought, however, to counteract this difficulty by pointing out certain long-continuing problems which persist in the news--those which have been going on for some time, are with us today and will probably boil up in the news tomorrow. Other standard types of news-features are classified to aid the student perceive the problems he will face. Provision is also allowed for the adaption of assignments to current immediate news-breaks.

Chapter 2

News Is Contemporary History

1. Importance of History to Newsmen

News is closely related to history. Actually, news
is contemporary history in the making. The news being reported today will be the events described by the historian
tomorrow. That is why, with a knowledge of the history of
an event--an international, state or local happening--the
newsman can understand it more adequately and report it
more fully. Further, he can correlate the present news
happening with what has gone before. The news investigator
does not regard the present event as an isolated or unre-
lated happening.

Quick Reaction: Newsmen must be able to react quickly to news events whenever they break. It is the peculiar
characteristic of news that much of it is surprising and
unpredictable. It just happens without forewarning. Newsmen, therefore, must have at their command knowledge of the
past events which led up to the current happening.

World War I is an example of unpredictable news. When
the Austrian Archduke, the heir apparent to the throne, was
shot in 1914, this was the outward incident which ignited
the war flames. Newsmen were caught unprepared. Similar-
ly, the attack on Pearl Harbor in 1941 was unexpected, and
few anticipated the outburst in Korea in 1950. Newsmen,
therefore, had to prepare themselves quickly to furnish
facts and information about the little country called Korea.
They had to search the encyclopedias and other reference
manuals for material on the previous incidents in the history of Korea to describe how the country came to be the
focal point of news.

Expected News: A considerable part of the news, however, is expected, with many small stories and forewarnings
appearing before the news occurs. The state prepares to
celebrate the 200th anniversary of its founding long before
the event actually occurs. The bill to provide for the
extension of the boundaries of the city is fought months
prior to its final passage. The Soviets latest move is but
one recent chapter in the story of the cold war. In these
and other news-instances the reporter, editorial writer or
special feature writer can anticipate and prepare for the
historical background feature or the editorial.

Likewise, after the first sensational story, many

important news-breaks leave a trail of stories. They are
not one-day flashes, but continue for weeks. The public
is constantly bombarded by a series of headlines and news
developments. Readers are ready for background historical
facts to supply them with fuller information.

2. Approaches to History

Newsmen should remember that history is more than the
development of government. History is the sum-total of the
activities of people, recorded and interpreted, according
to the modern historians. Newsmen, seeking background information, should be aware of the many phases of American
life which specialists have investigated and written about
in historical magazines and books. Knowing the area in
which their investigation falls, reporters can move more
quickly towards gathering the pertinent facts.

You will observe below the wide variety of specialized histories available:

Political History

> is concerned with the rise of democratic ideals
> and governmental machinery and the role they
> played in the development of the nation.

Economic History

> deals with production and distribution and the
> development of group interests related to these
> activities, and is concerned with their influ-
> ences on political and cultural life.

Diplomatic History

> studies the relations of the United States with
> foreign countries.

Constitutional History

> studies the importance of the constitution and
> the interpretations placed upon it by various
> Presidents and the Supreme Court at different
> times.

Agricultural History

> emphasizes the changing agricultural situation
> and the farmer's problems and how they affected
> economic, political and social history.

Cultural History

> deals with the educational, literary and artist-
> ic factors in American life and their signifi-
> cance.

6

Section

2

TWELVE PAGES

POLITICS
EDITORIALS—STAMPS
EDUCATION—MARINE

NEW YORK

Herald Tribune

SUNDAY, MARCH 1, 1953

FINANCE
THE WEEK IN BUSINESS
BUSINESS OPPORTUNITIES

TWELVE PAGES

Section

2

History in the Making: A Summary of World News

TRAINING CHINESE FLYERS IN THE UNITED STATES—The Nationalist air force on Formosa has no jet planes as yet, but thirty-five Chinese officers are learning how to fly them at Williams Air Force base in Arizona. At the right: Learning how a jet plane's ejection seat works. At the left: Pilot and American instructor study map of the Far East

The Red Probes

The problem of how to combat Communist Infiltration without stifling freedom of thought and speech was much on the minds of Americans. At President Eisenhower's press conference six out of the twenty-four questions bore on that topic—more than on any other single topic.

Various phases of the central problem were under discussion not only in Washington but throughout the land. Will Congressional probes into our schools and colleges tend to frighten educators into meekness on topics even faintly controversial? Should there be rules of procedure for Congressional investigations to guard against unfairness?

These and similar questions came to the fore as Congressional investigations were burgeoning. Sen. Joseph R. McCarthy, R., Wis., has been giving the State Department no peace, even though it is now controlled by his own party. The House Un-American Activities Committee launched an investigation of subversion in education under the chairmanship of Rep. Harold H. Velde, R., Ill. The House approved $300,000 for the committee, which was the largest lump sum it ever has received.

The Ford Foundation announced a grant of $15 million for a study of the entire field of freedom and civil rights in the United States. The study will reach into the Communist menace can be met with least danger to our liberties. Among the subjects to be considered are: Restrictions and assaults on academic freedom; censorship, boycotting and blacklisting activities by private groups; guilt by association.

Paul G. Hoffman, retiring president of the Ford Foundation, will be chairman of the board of directors of the new agency, the Fund for the Republic, which will conduct this study.

McCarthy Vs. 'Voice'

Sen. McCarthy, head of a Senate investigations-subcommittee, has been concentrating recently on the Voice of America. His familiar techniques have been in full swing, with the help of television. He and his staff have questioned present and former employees of the Voice, including subordinates, in a series. Then McCarthy has used television those whose testimony he considered most useful to his purposes.

Derogatory testimony about Troup Mathews, editor of the Voice's French section,

Voice propaganda beamed behind the Iron Curtain is based on the writings of Communists. Sometimes they are caught in found another professor who would not talk absurd contradictions; sometimes Ameri- —Dr. Barrows Dunham, head of the phil-

of the 1930s were named, but only Furry still connected with the university. The two ex-Communist witnesses who named him agreed that Communist activities on campuses had dwindled in the last fifteen years to the point of being very slight. One of the witnesses, Granville Hicks, who now is an active foe of the Reds, said the emphasis should be on "how little" Communist infiltration there is instead of "how much." He thought Congressional investigating committees were encouraging "an irrational apprehension" about Reds in the educational system.

In a closed hearing Friday the committee

is Communist persecution of other minority groups. This was done at the suggestion of the State Department, which did not wish Russia to label it a pro-Israel document and circulate it as propaganda among the Arab countries.

The resolution condemned "outrages" such as the persecution of Greek Orthodox congregations, the imprisonment of Roman Catholic prelates, the harassment of Protestants, the suppression of Moslem communities and "most recently the increasing persecution of people of the Jewish faith."

Statehood for Hawaii?

Since the 1930s there have been nine tries into the Union as one of the Representatives of the Republican in 1952 urged Interior subcommittee another the Republican surprised and skip

Linking History to News

The New York Herald Tribune seeks to give historical background to the news in its Sunday section, "History in the Making: A Summary of the World News." The section covers international and national events.

Science History

>is concerned with the development of the physical and social sciences as they influence and were influenced by other institutional developments.

Religious History

>places stress on the factor of organized religion from the colonial era to the present day.

Labor History

>stresses the rise of the labor movement, the changing status of the worker and his struggles to win and hold employee rights.

Biographical History

>points to the leaders in political, economic and cultural life, and stresses the contributions they made.

Social History

>deals with what people ate, what clothes they wore, what songs they sang, what games they played.

Local History

>is concerned with how the national trends shaped local developments and the peculiar characteristics which grew out of the local conditions.

3. Dynamic American History

U.S. History Colorful: Many students sidestep American history in college because they believe they have had enough of it in high school. But the student who expects to be a competent newsman or newswoman should learn as much about the development of American life as he possibly can.

The value of history as a working tool has been pointed out, but beyond that, the story of the American people is colorful and dramatic. Studied from the standpoint of a nation's development, U.S. history becomes a fascinating subject, especially if you read and watch the interaction of economic, political, technological forces. What can compare with the drama seen in the expansion of a small and scattered people huddled on the Atlantic seaboard to a mighty nation stretching from the Atlantic to the Pacific Ocean? From thirteen tiny colonies to a world power in a little more than one hundred and seventy-five years!

8

Into this story is woven the spread of democracy, the rise of industrialism, the diffusion of education, and the application of science. These are the great forces which have molded the modern world, and we can observe them all in our nation. Here, too, can be observed the struggle to make democracy have significance, and we see before us the eternal fight for civil liberty and religious freedom. America, too, has long been a melting pot of nationalities, where peoples from all over the world came, and out of their amalgamation developed a new people. It is a strange destiny that made this little experiment in democracy begun in the eighteenth century become the bulwark of democracy for the world in the twentieth century.

Threads and Patterns: As the news-breaks occur, the newsman must recognize the historical roots of the event and he must be able to trace its pattern through United States history. A ready knowledge of such history is to be desired. But a knowledge of available sources which can be referred to quickly for background information is also highly essential. This applies even to the newsman well-trained in history. New situations arise constantly for which he could not possibly have acquired sufficient and exact background unless he were a specialist in American history.

Too frequently for the student in journalism, United States history is taught in terms of epochs, with little effort made to trace through the individual threads from their beginning up to the present. The procedure of presenting history by periods is understandable from the standpoint of the historian, because he is teaching all kinds of students with all varieties of majors. But the student who expects to be a newsman and has special problems if he is to use and apply history. When a news-break occurs, he must be able to trace one historical thread back into the past. To background a current news event involving civil liberty, for example, the reporter would have to know the story of civil liberty in American history, rather than the historical facts in one particular era in our development.

It is true, of course, that the newsman needs to understand the epoch out of which the root-thread grew. The threads alter and change color and significance as they weave in and out of various parts of the historical pattern. But the newsman's emphasis must be on threads. It will be found that the historical strands are, generally, continuous. They may disappear for a time, but they re-appear later in issues which become news.

The New York Times
Magazine

April 15, 1956   SECTION 6

Editors of the New York Times seek to give
a background and understanding of current affairs
by means of its attractively-printed and well-
edited New York Times Magazine, issued as a
supplement in the Sunday edition. Excellent
articles written by reporters and experts in
specific fields cover international and national
events, report over-all surveys and trends.

COMMUNIST CHINA TODAY
—A PICTURE REPORT
[See Page 6]

Section 4 | REVIEW OF THE WEEK | EDITORIAL CORRESPONDENCE | WEEK-END CABLES

The New York Times.

EDITORIALS | SPECIAL ARTICLES—SCIENCE | LETTERS—EDUCATION | Section 4

E © 1956, by The New York Times Company. SUNDAY, JULY 15, 1956. E

THE NEWS OF THE WEEK IN REVIEW

Still Running

Word From Gettysburg

Four weeks from tomorrow the Democratic convention opens in Chicago. A month before the conventions in 1952, there was tremendous stir and excitement. The Eisenhower and Taft forces were battling mightily over disputed delegates and hurling epithets—"thieves," "shysters," "hypocrites"—back and forth. On the Democratic side, Kefauver and Harriman were counting their delegates and—like everybody else—wondering whether Adlai Stevenson would finally say yes.

Last week, by contrast, the political winds blew softly. The President, at casual second hand, let it be known he was still going to run. Republican Senator Dirksen said: "Spell it out in caps—WONDERFUL." Democratic Senator Humphrey said the news was like "Macy's announcing that Christmas was coming." In the Democratic camp, there was brave talk of winning—but the talk did not have a ring of conviction.

'Why Shouldn't I?'

White House press secretary James C. Hagerty has sedulously impressed on newspapermen that the President's abdominal operation had nothing in common with the coronary thrombosis last September. He has emphasized that ation was really routin like an appendectomy; t cuperative period this ti involve any testing of dent's physical function merely "a routine convale ation"; and that consequ was really no question of dent's reconsidering his run.

Nevertheless, those clo President knew that the evitably public specu whether the President h second thoughts on run because he had said he w draw if he felt his healt low par, his advisers kn tion looked for some from him. But in keepin impression they wanted they opposed a dramatic ment like that on Feb. Tuesday the announcement came. Reporters agreed that it was a masterful job—as The New York Times correspondent said—of "calculated nonchalance."

THE G. O. P. TICKET IS SET—AS THE PRESIDENT CONFIRMS HIS DECISION

Thorough Historical Backgrounding In its section "News of the Week in Review" the New York Times presents a summary of the international, national state and local news in highly readable style. (top) On inside pages special articles giving perspective to these events and trends are written by its special correspondents. (bottom)

EISENHOWER: Meeting with Congressional leaders, he says he will run.

NIXON: Back from world tour, he says he is still willing.

The New York Times (George Tames). Associated Press

CAMPAIGN: Hall and Hagerty discuss plans with reporters.

ness of the implications of the reported plans for U. S. foreign and domestic policy.

Under present operations the Army maintains about 40 per cent of its troops overseas. There are five divisions in Europe under NATO command, two in Korea and one division in Japan. A reduction of 450,000 men in ground forces strength, such as is contemplated in the Radford plan, would mean withdrawal by 1960 of 180,000 men from overseas bases. The ability of the ground forces to defend Air Force bases where B-47 bomber wings are stationed and which would be essential for refueling of B-52 intercontinental bombers would be seriously opened to question.

Obviously a reduction in the ground forces of such magnitude, leaving only token forces abroad, would involve a drastic modification of U. S. foreign and defense policy now based on joint efforts with our allies. In fact, there was a feeling that such cuts would mean a "fortress America" policy much as was advocated by former President Hoover and the late Senator Taft during the "troops for Europe debate" in 1950.

While President Eisenhower supports the shift in defense emphasis from ground forces to an air-atomic base, he has also strongly supported the whole concept of mutual security as a vital segment of U. S. defense planning. In 1953, in a speech in Minneapolis, he rejected as "dangerous" the "fortress theory of defense" which he said would leave the United States to "stand by itself."

Questions on 'Risks'

Criticism of the Federal Government's loyalty-security program has been steady ever since its inception under President Truman and its revision under President Eisenhower. Among the complaints about the Eisenhower program have been these: that the standards for judging security risks are vague and negative; that there is no uniformity among departments in administration of the program; that procedures are unfair to employes; that the scope of the program is unnecessarily broad, making for cumbersome and excessively costly administration.

In response to such criticism, the Administration has made some change in procedure and appointed a bipartisan commission to study the whole security program. Hearings on the program are in progress before a Senate committee ...

FOUR CARTOONISTS ASSESS THE POLITICAL SCENE AFTER THE MINNESOTA PRIMARY

Shanks in The Buffalo Evening News

"Say! This is fun!"

Herblock in The Washington Post and Times-Herald

"Remember those Davy Crockett caps you had on sale?"

Yardley in The Baltimore Sun

"Of course, there's always me."

Hudson in The Cleveland News

Campaign song.

NOW THE DARK HORSES ARE MORE IN RUNNING

Stevenson Defeat in Minnesota Has Brought Five to the Front

By W. H. LAWRENCE

Special to The New York Times.

WASHINGTON, March 24—Democrats widened their search this week for a Presidential nominee.

Non-participants were perhaps the chief beneficiaries of the bruising Minnesota primary which ended in a stunning upset victory for Senator Estes Kefauver of Tennessee and a crushing defeat for Adlai E. Stevenson of Illinois.

The post-mortem political discussions which began in Washington early Wednesday morning turned not so much on Senator Kefauver and Mr. Stevenson as they did on dark horses who would not admit they were candidates at all and others, like Governor Averell Harriman of New York, who rated themselves "inactive" candidates.

Certainly the dark horses had new hopes in their own prospects, which had been pretty much discounted when the assumption was general that Mr. Stevenson, the 1952 nominee, ...

... ator Symington did not have Mr. Truman's support when later he sought the Democratic nomination for Senator from Missouri. He has hit the Republicans hardest on charges they needlessly endangered national defense by reducing the Air Force and other defense appropriations for a domestic political end.

Senator Johnson—As majority leader, the Texan has been highly praised for the direction of the Democratic strength in the Senate and for minimizing the public display of differences between Northern liberal and Southern conservative Democrats.

Now proposed as a "favorite son" from Texas, Senator Johnson would be a natural candidate around whom Southern delegates could rally as they did in 1948 and 1952 around Senator Richard B. Russell of Georgia. This could be accomplished either in a serious bid to win the nomination for Senator Johnson, or ...

Dobbins in The Boston Post

"Wha' hoppen?"

... at any rate, is that he has been as independent as his voting support. He has admitted publicly that he voted for the late Senator Robert A. Taft in 1950, and has highly praised President Eisenhower. So far, he has concentrated on running for Senator from Ohio in 1956 while sewing up that state's Democratic convention delegation, for a while at least, as a "favorite son."

Religious Question

Like the late Alfred E. Smith, Governor Lausche is a Roman ...

FARM VOTE AGAIN SEEN PLAYING DECISIVE ROLE

Minnesota Worries Republicans as Fight Over Farm Bill Goes On

By WILLIAM M. BLAIR

Special to The New York Times.

WASHINGTON, March 24—Since 1948 and President Truman's surprise Presidential victory Republicans have been hypersensitive about the Midwestern farm vote. Tuesday's Minnesota primary set G. O. P. political nerves jangling again.

Neither Republicans nor Democrats presume to answer the question of "what happened in Minnesota" at this stage. But there are public claims by Democrats that the big Democratic turnout reflected a revolt against Administration farm policies, and Republican counter-contentions that Minnesota reflected a revolt against Democratic "bossism."

It is significant that the Republican National Committee dispatched staff members to canvass the Minnesota situation, which heretofore has been regarded as poor but not hopeless. Similar assays will be extended to other farm states.

By any accounting, the Mid- ...

... votes and Henry A. Wallace, Progressive party candidate, handed the 74 votes of New York, Maryland and Michigan to the Republicans.

Four years ago, President Eisenhower swept the farm bloc. But since 1953, Democrats have made considerable gains in Congressional and local elections in this heartland of the Republican party. Two years ago, when the Democrats regained control of Congress, they showed vote gains in Illinois, Indiana, Iowa, Kansas, Minnesota, the Dakotas and Wisconsin, all states with a Republican history, and in Missouri, a normally Democratic state.

Democratic Gains

The 1954 election also gave the Democrats their biggest campaign ribbon when Democrats won nineteen of thirty-four gubernatorial races throughout the country, including Ohio and Minnesota. In state legislatures ...

Brett in The Miami Herald

"Getting there first."

... ests along strictly partisan lines. To hasten the bloc's departure from the political scene, the Administration played on the conflicts among commodities, not only in Washington but on the hustings.

Republican success was demonstrated in 1954 when the Administration won the fight for flexible price supports and again in the Senate this week. Special concessions were offered on cotton and corn which split the old corn-cotton-wheat coalition that once provided the base for farm-bloc power in Congress.

MINNESOTANS ALLERGIC TO BINDING PARTY TIES

State Has Independent Record and Often Changes Political Sides

By RICHARD J. H. JOHNSTON

Special to The New York Times.

MINNEAPOLIS, March 24—Minnesota has a long political record as one of the most independent and unpredictable of states in the Union.

• Nebraska and Minnesota are the only states that do not require party designations for candidates to the Legislature. On the local levels judicial, municipal and county positions are also without party label.

In the Nineteen Thirties the Farmer-Labor party, with no national connections, took over control of the state's executive offices. It held dominion over the state in that branch for nearly ten years.

In 1944 the Farmer-Labor group joined with the Democratic party to form what is now the Democratic-Farmer-Labor party to further demonstrate political non-conformity.

Before 1952 the state gave majorities to five successive Democratic Presidential candidates. ...

... since slowed to a thin trickle the strong strains of German (the predominant original settlers), Swedish, Norwegian and Finnish still are in evidence. Those of Irish and Dutch descent are scattered through the state.

It was demonstrated last week that Minnesota's political activities do not present the sharp contrasts and clashes of the truly bipartisan political states.

Revolt Factor

Most astute observers here of the state's political history believe that this fact, coupled with what is now accepted as a "revolt" among D-F-L voters against what appeared to be a program of "dictation" from Gov. Orville L. Freeman and Senator Hubert H. Humphrey, top chieftains of the D-F-L, caused the voters of Minnesota to demonstrate once again their independence at the ballot box.

This has given pause here to ...

RECURRENT NEWS THREADS

These news-types appear regularly and have
their roots in the historical pattern.

1. News About Civil Liberty

2. News Concerning Religious Liberty

3. News of the Supreme Court: Activities and
    Attacks Upon It.

4. News Dealing with Economic-Political Pro-
    grams and Forces (Fair Deal, New Deal, New
    Freedom, Square Deal, Jacksonianism).

5. News Concerning Labor

6. News Relating to Agriculture

7. News About Third Parties

8. News of Anniversaries

        Independence Day
        Constitution Day
        Bill of Rights Day
        Armistice Day

9. News Concerning Social or Cultural Life

        News About Songs

            Sports
            Entertainment Forms
            Manners, Morals
            Scientific Development

    These news types appear again and again in
current news events, and each has historical
roots. In addition to studying history by epochs
or periods, the newsman must become acquainted
with these news-problems as historical units or
threads.

    In the following pages will be found some typical
news-events, or long-range recurring news-problems. Many
of the persistent issues today and tomorrow have roots in
the colonial period. Some of these issues are basic to American democracy -- civil liberty and religious liberty.

Civil Liberty in the News

The newspapers shout these and similar headlines in every generation:

> Congressional Investigation Committee
> Charges State Secretary is Red
>
> Ku Klux Klan, Active Again,
> Tars and Feathers Youth
>
> School Teachers Must
> Sign Loyalty Oath

To write an interesting and significant backgrournd news-feature for these events, you would have to investigate and present the story of civil liberties in colonial America and their earlier origins in England. An appreciation of the precious heritage civil liberty represents might be presented by means of a dramatic word-picture showing how hard the colonists fought for civil rights. The problem of civil liberty has recurred as a persistent theme in the changing story of America. It emerged in the Alien and Sedition Acts of 1797. In every generation various political and economic groups, or a combination of the two, sought to demolish the foundations and destroy the safeguards of the individual which had been built up.

The reporter would reveal that especially during and after almost every war since the Revolution, organizations aroused public opinion to eliminate critical opposition. The background story would tell how these efforts usually spent themselves after a time, and the American public returned to its respect for the original democratic principles. The issue frequently developed into a titanic struggle between those who believed the nation was in danger and those who claimed that the real danger was in the loss of civil liberty and the throttling of the non-conformists who furnished new and fresh ideas for a progressive democracy.

The background investigator, in his story, might point to the conclusions that the serious students of democracy have drawn about civil liberties. Civil liberties in the American view has come to mean:

1. An emphasis upon the worth of the individual.

2. The thought that democracy can work best if a free play of ideas and opinions exists. The unsatisfactory ones will be subjected to criticism and driven from the market-place of ideas.

3. The idea that democracy can work most efficiently if the individual has the right to speak his mind, to protest against wrongs and injustices of all kinds. Democracy needs a safety valve.

13

Chart No. 1

Historical Roots of Civil Liberty News
News Manifestations Today

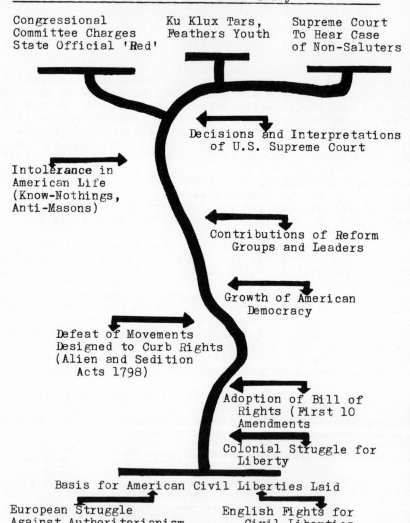

Congressional
Committee Charges
State Official 'Red'

Ku Klux Tars,
Feathers Youth

Supreme Court
To Hear Case
of Non-Saluters

Decisions and Interpretations
of U.S. Supreme Court

Intolerance in
American Life
(Know-Nothings,
Anti-Masons)

Contributions of Reform
Groups and Leaders

Growth of American
Democracy

Defeat of Movements
Designed to Curb Rights
(Alien and Sedition
Acts 1798)

Adoption of Bill of
Rights (First 10
Amendments

Colonial Struggle for
Liberty

Basis for American Civil Liberties Laid

European Struggle
Against Authoritarianism
(writings of Locke,
Rousseau, Voltaire)

English Fights for
Civil Liberties
Rise of Parliament;
Bill of Rights

Intent Reporters

Every competent newsman, it is evident, should know the story of American civil liberties, their origins, development and present status. When a new civil liberties issue appears again--as it undoubtedly will--he will recognize its significance, place the issue in its context, and write competently upon it.

Some Sources for Information

A number of stimulating books about the history of American civil liberties are available at most libraries. Leon Whipple wrote a readable account, The Story of Civil Liberties in the United States. Another popular account of the historical development is Lucius B. Swift's How We Got Our Liberties. Carl Carmer presents the history of civil liberties through the leaders in his Fighters for Freedom. Cornell University, in Ithaca, N.Y., has established a center for research in civil liberties and has issued Safeguarding Our Liberties, a series of stimulating lectures on current problems in civil liberties. A very readable book is T.V. Smith and Edouard C. Lindeman's The Democratic Way of Life. To Secure These Rights is a report of President Truman's Commission on Civil Rights, dealing with contemporary issues. An interesting series of articles by various authorities was published in the Annuals of the American Academy of Political and Social Sciences in the issue titled, Essential Human Rights, comprising volume 243, issued January, 1946.

Marshall Field's Freedom is More Than a Word is of particular interest to newsmen as it deals with freedom of news distribution and freedom of the press. In Let Freedom Ring Arthur Garfield Hays recounts the battles for civil

15

ENQUIRER STAFF WRITERS INTERPRET THE NEWS

The Washington Scene

Glenn THOMPSON

Vice President's Silence Is Loud Indeed.

WASHINGTON: With the House grinding to a halt in the form of three-day recesses that will keep that chamber empty until September 12 and with the Senators talking on last week in their interminable fashion, also mostly to empty seats, we have an opportunity today to check up on a few minor items, to wit:

Vice President Barkley's readiness. The genial Kentuckian chooses his words well. One becomes good at that after 38 years in the Congress. It is not quite so easy, however, to keep from saying things when you say it with silence or by saying something else.

This sounds complicated. It is. The Vice President, however, said two important things this week by just such a round-about methods.

For one, he said he was ready to run on the national ticket in 1952. He said this by saying something else. Asked in a magazine interview about his own political future in view of his age (73), his words were:

"I have ahead of me lots of years—whether they will be years of public service may depend on the American people—that's something I can't control. But, as you know, in the last 50 years the average span of a man's life has been increased by about 25 years. A man who is 70 now is supposed to be about what the man 50 years old was 50 years ago."

People like **Governor Lausche** and **Sen. Estes Kefauver**, if they had their eye on the vice presidential nomination, now might look around for something else.

★ ★ ★

THE VICE PRESIDENT also said he took a dim view of the talk of **Chief Justice Fred M. Vinson** for President. He said this with silence.

On a television program, Meet The Press, last week, the Vice President was asked if he had seen a national poll which indicated that Justice Vinson would beat **Sen. Robert A. Taft** in a race for President. (The same poll, a month before, had shown that Senator Taft would beat **President Truman.**)

"Yes," replied the Vice President, "I saw that in the papers."

That was all. The clock on the wall ticked and ticked. People on the program waited. Nothing more happened. It was like a rock dropped into a country well: One plunk, and finished.

Speaker Sam Rayburn, Mr. Barkley's old friend, may favor Chief Justice Vinson, Mr. Barkley's fellow Kentuckian, for President. Reports say he does. Mr. Truman may even favor him. They take Sunday afternoon rides together. The golden silence of the Vice President, however, seemed to indicate he dissents.

★ ★ ★

SENATOR TAFT'S SLIP: Friends here of Senator Taft were chuckling last week and wondering if the Senator has announced his candidacy for President by accident. Some of them already were convinced that he was definitely a candidate despite his denials.

The Associated Press account said that the Senator, addressing Republicans at Portland, Maine, declared: "If Republicans get out, there isn't any doubt of my election." After there's a and laughter, he corrected: "I mean ... no doubt in my mind we can win."

against him, although he denies it. There was no doubt that **Joseph T. Ferguson** demanded an investigation, declaring that the Taft people spent too much money.

Well, the committee wanted to hire an attorney over here named **Robert Murphy** but it turned out that he does business with the government and, to hire him, a waiver would have to be voted by both Houses. **Sen. Homer Ferguson** (R., Mich.), opposed this in the Senate. **Rep. Clarence J. Brown** (R. Ohio), Taft's old campaign manager, not only opposed, but beat it, in the House. The committee had to hunt up another attorney. This delayed things.

Until Thursday, when the committee suddenly announced it expected to begin hearings September 24, it began to look like the thing would be delayed until the January session. That could have been bad. There was no doubt that the Taft people spent quite a sum. The figures would make good headlines right at the time people are filing for delegates to the national convention, possibly pledged to Senator Taft for President.

★ ★ ★

THE HUBER MATTER. The House meanwhile last week closed its books on another Ohio investigation, this one into the congressional election last fall in Ohio's 14th District (Akron).

There young **William H. Ayres,** war veteran and automobile dealer, defeated **Rep. Walter B. Huber,** Democrat. Mr. Huber promptly cried "foul," filed a protest, and presented evidence to show that his name was not rotated properly on ballots and this had been disastrous.

He could not prove, however, that Ohio election officials had not followed the law in the way they ran things. The result was that, after its subcommittee on elections (of House Administration Committee) had rejected the protest unanimously, the House itself rejected the protest on a voice vote.

Some Democratic politicians, interested in winning future elections in Ohio, heaved a sigh of relief at this. They pointed out that the last time they won a seat through a protest was in New Hampshire in 1936. Republicans have carried that district ever since.

★ ★ ★

BEST SENATOR. Pageant Magazine, which got itself quite a bit of publicity two years ago with a poll of Washington correspondents on who's the best and who's the worst Senator, came out with a new poll recently.

Two years ago, you remember, Senator Taft was named "best" and **Sen. John W. Bricker** "worst" giving Ohio some kind of distinction.

As pointed out here before, Senator Bricker was a victim of circumstances in 1949 and did not deserve the blow that fell. The correspondents themselves seemed to realize that this year. Senator Bricker is not even listed among the 11 "worst" Senators.

He is not among the 11 "best" either, it is to be admitted.

Sen. Paul H. Douglas (D., Ill.) was voted "best," **Sen. Joseph R. McCarthy** (R., Wis.), "worst."

Senator Taft was voted both fourth "best" and fourth "worst," a result which proves something but we are not quite sure what—maybe the uselessness of polls of correspond-

—FROM THE ST. LOUIS GLOBE-DEMOCRAT.

HOW LONG?

WEEK'S NEWS IN BRIEF

BY JACK RAMEY.

THE ORIENTAL MIND makes overbearing profit out of United Nations' adherence to rules of warfare concocted at Geneva, Switzerland. Orientals have proceeded for centuries upon the general truth later expressed in the Western maxim: "All's fair in war." The gentlemen's warfare rules stipulated at Geneva mean nothing to the Eastern minds directing Communist warfare in Korea. Just as gentlemanly conduct meant nothing to Chinese Nationalist feudal leaders perfectly willing to exact personal profit from U. S. loans and supplies intended for opposing the Japs.

When the United Nations forces were cutting into human ribbons the Commie forces north of the 38th Parallel, when Red morale in China and in the battleline was disintegrating, the Oriental minds were quick to throw their slyest decoy into UN's path.

They needed time for reorganization and reinforcement. By fighting, they could not mount another offensive. Most

On September 15 he goes to Ottawa for Atlantic Pact talks with 11 other foreign ministers.

In late October he flies to Rome for a second round of Atlantic Pact strategy meetings. From there he plans to go to Paris for opening sessions of the UN Assembly in November.

★ ★ ★

AMERICAN officials say there is evidence the Russians have reinforced their Eastern German garrison by more than 50,000 troops within the last three months.

This does not foreshadow a westward Soviet invasion, but it is being watched closely.

At the moment, the Russians are bringing their divisions closer to readiness—but not necessarily to the point where they can jump off in an attack.

★ ★ ★

THE USUAL QUESTION was asked **General Eisenhower** when he had lunch recently with a group of visiting American newspapermen at his headquarters at Marly, near Paris:

On Foreign Affairs

William H. HESSLER

We Need Greece, Turkey, Yugoslavia.

Mr. Hessler has just returned from a five-week tour of the Near East.

ATHENS, overcrowded Greek capital, one-third the size of Cincinnati with three times the population, is hot right now—climatically and politically. The sun beats down unmercifully through the day, turning up temperatures that have ranged above 100 degrees in recent days. And since Athenian Greeks are mostly all politicians by temperament, the imminence of general elections — September — has brought the political atmosphere to a boil also.

The most recent even to heighten the tension is the declaration of **General Papagos** that he will be a candidate for the presidency. Papagos, the man who moved into the leadership of the Greek armed forces, cleaned out the politics, and whipped the guerrillas, is a sort of Greek **Eisenhower** but with far more political enemies than General Ike has to contend with.

★ ★ ★

THE MAIN RESULT of his entry on the political scene has been a closing of ranks among the almost innumberable political parties. As a result, there may be only a half-dozen parties in the coming contest; instead of 15 or more. By itself, this is clearly a good thing.

The United States continues to be a dominant force throughout Greece, as it has been since 1947. As nearly as I can reckon it, the United States has put about $1,800 million into Greece since the end of World War II. In contrast to Turkey, where military aid is the main story, Greece has received primarily economic assistance. It is a country that simply cannot support itself, even on a subsistence basis. The aid will have to go on indefinitely, if the Greeks are not to collapse again. And I suppose it will go on, in some guise, as long as Greece is considered, strategically, as important as it is now.

★ ★ ★

IN THE EARLIEST postwar phase, aid to Greece was mostly a matter of outright relief, with some funds for reconstruction of war-damaged roads, industries, port works and so on. In the next phase, it was chiefly a matter of long-term investment in production—agricultural above all else. In the third and present phase, it is more largely a teaching job, a task of showing the Greeks, right down to the peasant farmer, how to do more with the acreage and the animals and machinery at his disposal. Technical assistance, therefore, has loomed up larger with the passing years.

The toughest problem of the ECA in Greece has not been the administration of its program of economic aid, complex as that is. It has been and is today the diplomatic task of inducing the Greek government to make some basic reforms in its taxation and budget and monetary policies. There is some progress, some since I was there last autumn.

For years, wealthy Greeks have evaded virtually all taxation. They bought shares in shipping and other companies, anonymously. They paid no taxes. And there was no properly graduated income tax. The great bulk of revenue was extracted from the mass of desperately poor farmers and workers. The wealthy lived in Athens or New York or somewhere else and paid virtually no taxes to any government. Smaller businessmen got by almost as easily, refusing to keep books that would show their earnings.

Finally, some months ago, a law was passed requiring the open registration of stock ownership. And a progressive income tax was put onto the statute books. It may be hard to enforce compliance. But at least a beginning is being made. Ironically, it has fallen to the lot of the United States, one of the conservative countries of the world, to compel Itay, Greece and Turkey—to name but three benefiting countries—to set up the "leftist" reform of taxing the rich as well as the poor.

★ ★ ★

ECA'S CURRENT effort in Athens centers on a venturesome rationing system. Until now, only bread has been rationed. The new plan is to ration also olive oil, rice, sugar, coffee and one or two other basic foodstuffs, keeping the cost down to the lowest figure economically possible, and also insuring that the ration actually will be available to all. There will be price controls for numerous other items of consequence to consumers.

The gimmick in this program is the large initial appropriation from American funds, to accumulate a three-months' stockpile of the essential commodities, and thus to head off the speculation which has worked havoc there in an economy of recurring scarcity.

One must hope the scheme will work, for the people of Greece have had a rough time for many years. They deserve a better break; but they won't get it from their own "better classes," who are a grasping plutocracy conditioned by generations of national insecurity into focusing their entire energies on the quick buck—the exorbitant profit.

Despite its grinding poverty and limited hopes of escape from that, Greece remains a strategic asset of great importance. The Greek soldier is a good soldier, and the Greek sailor is a first-class man at his job. Rearmed in large measure, the Greek armed forces are small but capable of very rapid mobilization to more than double their current strength.

★ ★ ★

ONCE THE COUNTRY was cleared of Communistic guerrillas, more than a year ago, the effort of the American Military Mission was shifted to readying the Greek army, navy and air force to play an effective part in the common defense against the Soviet Union and its satellites—who are very close by.

Compared to that of Turkey, the Greek war potential is modest. But in combination, Greece, Turkey and Yugoslavia probably could put 2½ million men into the field fairly quickly. Set alongside the total of forces that General Eisenhower can hope to command even after another year, this is a stupendous figure. And these are tough, brave men out there.

Why all three countries have not been fitted into the main structure of Western defense, I am sure I don't know.

About Cincinnati

Today's World **The Philadelphia Inquirer** ***Page Three***

TUESDAY MORNING, AUGUST 2, 1955 h★

Why Red China Released U. S. Airmen

Mr. and Mrs. Frank W. Brown pray in church at St. Paul, Minn., after learning the Chinese Reds were releasing their son, Howard, one of the 11 airmen.

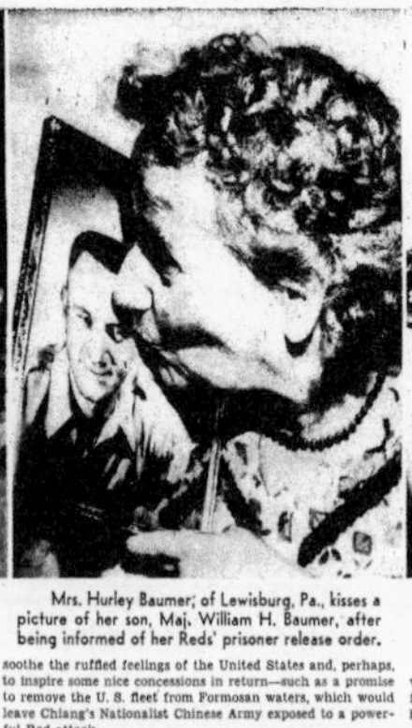

Mrs. Hurley Baumer, of Lewisburg, Pa., kisses a picture of her son, Maj. William H. Baumer, after being informed of her Reds' prisoner release order.

Mrs. Charlene Benjamin (right), wife of Worthington, Minn., airman Harry Benjamin, Jr., and her mother, Mrs. C. L. Hartman, read report of release.

AP Wirephotos

Mrs. May Arnold, of Montgomery, Ala., looks at a picture of her husband, Col. John Arnold, Jr., one of the captured American airmen being released.

By SAUL SCHRAGA

WHY did Red China suddenly decide to release the 11 American fliers, after insisting all along they had been justly convicted as spies?

The timing of the move was considered especially noteworthy. Although there had been reports for months that Chinese Premier Chou En-lai intended to free the captured Air Force men, he chose the very day—in fact, one hour before—meetings were to begin at Geneva between Communist China and U. S. representatives.

It was taken for granted that Chou's move was part of the new aura of friendliness displayed by the Russian Communists in the "summit" meeting of the "Big Four" that ended a week ago at Geneva.

But speculation as to the pinpointing of the timing and the manner of the release produced several theories. The most frequent was that the Chinese Communist government had scored for itself a juicy propaganda point.

Some sources suggested that Red China was after something much bigger than the 11 airmen, or probably even of the 40 civilians still being held.

Among these are the questions of a seat in the U.N. for Chou's government, and a free hand to go after Chiang Kai-shek and his army on the island of Formosa.

Release of the fliers, it was reasoned, was calculated to soothe the ruffled feelings of the United States and, perhaps, to inspire some nice concessions in return—such as a promise to remove the U. S. fleet from Formosan waters, which would leave Chiang's Nationalist Chinese Army exposed to a powerful Red attack.

The Chinese Reds realized, it was thought, that the United States would never stand for bargaining for the freedom of the fliers.

So, since any successful bargaining on this point would entail the eventual release of the fliers, why not let the men go without acrimonious haggling, and get off to a good start on the talk? If the United States refuses to concede anything, then holding the men would do no good, anyway. So runs the speculation on Chinese reasoning.

The announcement over the Peiping radio came an hour before the Chinese and American emissaries—U. Alexis Johnson, U. S. Ambassador to Czechoslovakia, and Wang Ping-nan, Chinese Ambassador to Poland—sat down for their first session, a 45-minute affair, at Geneva yesterday.

Still to be discussed as one of the earliest items on the agenda is the release of 40 civilians, including John Thomas Downey, 24, of New Britain, Conn., cousin of singer Morton Downey, sentenced to life imprisonment as a "spy," and Richard George Fecteau, 27, of Lynn, Mass., sentenced to 20 years.

It was considered that in Red China's present mood, there was a good chance that everybody would be freed in the near future, to clear the decks for what the Reds regard as the real business of the meeting—agreement on the Far East.

The 11 airmen were among the crew of 14 on a B-29 shot down by the Communists on Jan. 12, 1953, while on what this Government insists was a "purely routine" mission of dropping propaganda leaflets.

The big ship, carrying a crew of 14 officers and men, was in permissible territory when attacked, the United States had consistently maintained—either over Korea or international waters.

The Chinese, who stuck to the fiction that they were not taking part in the Korean War—and technically they were not—said the B-29 was nine miles inside Chinese territory, in Manchuria, when it was brought down. Three of the crew died in the crash.

Few Americans were aware of all this, however. They learned about it, to their shock and indignation, on Nov. 23, 1954, when the Peiping radio blared out the news that the 11 fliers had been tried and convicted of spying, along with the two civilians, Downey and Fecteau.

The six officers, it was announced, got sentences ranging from four to 10 years.

The United States officially reacted with one of the stiffest denunciations ever visited on a "friendly" nation in its history.

The Defense and State Departments joined in a note accusing the Chou En-lai government of using "trumped-up" charges to jail the Americans; violating international law, and called it guilty of "bad faith," and "amorality."

On Christmas Eve, Dag Hammarskjold, Secretary-General of the United Nations, took off on a flight to China, to talk over the matter. He returned with indications that the situation was not beyond salvaging.

Meanwhile, Senator William F. Knowland (R., Calif.) called for a naval blockade of the Chinese mainland in retaliation, but the Administration refused to be stampeded.

Early in July, Premier U Nu of Burma, on a visit to the United States, offered to mediate the issue of the captured fliers.

Meanwhile, since the conference of the 29 Asian and African nations, held in March at Bandung in the Indonesian Republic, there had been reports that Chou En-lai was about to release the Americans. He was only, so some of the reports said, waiting for the right moment.

Apparently this was yesterday.

MAJ. WILLIAM H. BAUMER
A Second World War combat pilot in the Pacific, Maj. Baumer, 32, whose home is in

HARRY M. BENJAMIN, JR.
Airman 2/C Benjamin is from Worthington, Minn. This is one of the pictures taken by

LT. JOHN W. BUCK
Waiting for him at their home in Armathwaite, Tenn., are his

DANIEL C. SCHMIDT
Airman Schmidt, 22, of Redding, Calif., wrote his family

SGT. HOWARD W. BROWN
Sgt. Brown, whose home is at St. Paul, Minn., is shown being

JOHN W. THOMPSON
Airman 2/C Thompson is from Orange, Va. He was one

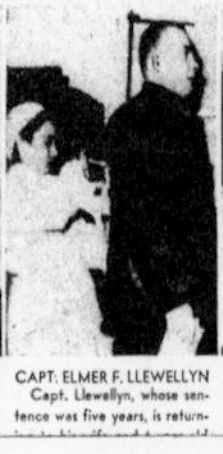

CAPT. ELMER F. LLEWELLYN
Capt. Llewellyn, whose sentence was five years, is return-

STEVEN E. KIBA
Airman first class Kiba, from Akron, O., was radioman

liberties in various parts of the United States which he fought as a lawyer during the past few decades.

Headquarters for the effort to protect civil liberties in the United States is the American Civil Liberties Union, located in New York. Pamphlets, brochures and various other literature on civil liberties may be obtained from this organization.

HISTORICAL MAGAZINES:
A SOURCE OF INFORMATION

The professional historical journals offer some of the best sources for the investigation of specific topics. Their articles are ordinarily quite readable, requiring little or no technical vocabulary. Most of the journals are well indexed, and their indexes therefore serve as valuable guides to articles and book reviews in the various areas of history.

The American Historical Review. Contains articles on European as well as American history. Both annual and decennial indexes have been prepared. In 1945 a Guide to the American Historical Review (1895-1945) was published by the United States Government Printing Office, Washington. This presented a topical index to the articles with a brief statement of the gist of each article. The Mississippi Valley Historical Review. The magazine issues annual indexes and has also published a topical guide.

Democracy vs Communism

Since World War I news about the various forms of government and their struggle for survival and supremacy have been paramount in the news. First it was Hitler's fascism, then it was Soviet communism versus democracy. It would be natural that the live news of today and tomorrow will grow out of the conflicts in view-points and principles between democracy and other systems of government.

To place democracy in its context, to present a fuller appreciation of its contributions, democracy's roots must be investigated and its development traced. We have mentioned two of democracy's basic freedoms. The third is representative self-government. This concept, too, was won after many bitterly-fought struggles with English kings, with colonial proprietors, and even with other colonists who gained and held control.

Writing a news-feature on democracy, the reporter would indicate that government through elected representatives did not arise full-blown in the colonies. As other institutions, it was an English heritage granted after bloody contests with English rulers during the centuries before the colonies were founded. Here, the reporter would show, the representative principle shaped by local self-government was eventually secured in the colonies, and that it was a denial of these rights of the colonial assemblies that helped to stoke the fires of revolution.

The reporter would tell how the principles of representative government became a part of the democratic plan, incorporated into national, state and municipal frameworks of government. Full, free and unqualified participation in citizenship still was not granted for some years. The religious, property and sex qualifications were cast off slowly. Now a drive is being made to eliminate the color qualification. Democracy, the reporter would point out, was a step forward in the march of human progress, but a step which was learned slowly and could be lost easily.

Supreme Court Issue Is Front Page News

Every generation produces conflicts and hence news-issues relating to the Constitution. In the 1930's it was the so-called court-packing program of President Franklin D. Roosevelt. In the 1910's and 1920's the news on page one concerned the United States Supreme Court's interpretation of social and welfare legislation. In the 1890's the news about the Court related to injunctions against labor. In the pre-Civil War era the Court's interpretation of the slavery issue made news which stirred the nation. In 1954 and 1955 the Court's decisions on desegregation became a center of controversy.

To write about the Supreme Court the newsman needs to know where to get information regarding the history of the Court to be able to trace its development and the changes in its viewpoint. At times the guardian of previous and hard-won liberties, at times called by some the last refuge of die-hard conservatism, the Court has played a varying but ever important role in the development of American democracy.

Sources: A number of writers have addressed their attention to the significant place of the Supreme Court and have discussed the trends of its decisions. Irving Brant wrote the provocative Storm Over the Constitution, and Robert H. Jackson, later associate justice of the Supreme Court, produced The Struggle for Judicial Supremacy, which some authorities consider as having top-rank because of its analysis of the function of the court and its insight into the decisions.

Other useful books are Charles Gordon Post's Supreme Court and Political Questions, Charles A. Beard's Supreme Court and the Constitution. The more recent development of the Court is given in Ten Years of the Supreme Court 1937-47, edited by E. S. Corwin. It is a reprint of material which appeared in the American Political Science Review in the December, 1947, and the February, 1948, issues.

Reference Works Useful For Investigation
Of Historical Backgrounds of the News

These standard reference works should be familiar to all:

Encyclopedia Britannica

The Encyclopedia Americana

Of especial use for the newsman searching for the historical roots of the news:

The Dictionary of American Biography

This work comprises 2o volumes, index volume and supplements. It contains biographical sketches, from half a page to a dozen pages in length, about hundreds of persons in American history. Particularly valuable for backgrounding in preparation for articles on Washington's, Lincoln's and others' birthdays.

Dictionary of American History

In six volumes this dictionary has brief articles on a large number of topics,

---

presented in alphabetical order. The
articles are concise and factual.

Encyclopedia of the Social Sciences

In 15 volumes this encyclopedia presents
interpretative essays on topics over the
fields of the social sciences. Material
is not limited to the United States, and
in many instances the essays compare American developments with those in the rest
of the world.

4.   Social History In The News

The history of America is not always told in terms of
the economic and political developments. An essential element, for a complete and accurate account, is the social
development of the nation. What songs people sang, what
clothes they wore, what books, magazines and newspapers
they read--all help to make up the complete story. The
changes in the form of entertainment provide a fascinating
series. News events furnish the springboard for background
features. With the coming of television, for instance,
many newspapers had the opportunity to print lively, picturesque articles on the types of entertainment enjoyed by
Americans during various periods, and the possible social
significance of television. Often song cycles are repeated
and they suggest features using the history of popular
music in this country.

Such articles treating the lighter side of a nation's
life are not necessarily limited to superficial treatment.
The news-investigator can develop a story of an art and
throw light on the present. A background series on popular
songs would trace the development of creation and distribution of songs from the Stephen Foster period to the machine
like creation, mass-production and mass-distribution tactics
of today, involving name bands, radio and television facilities.

The wide variety of specialized volumes on different
aspects of social history may be seen in the following
brief list:

Frederick Lewis Allen   Only Yesterday

an informal history of the
1920's. The fads, foibles,
dresses, social habits, recreational activities re-
counted.

	Since Yesterday
	a social history of the 1930's, similar to the above.
Winton J. Baltzell, ed.	A Complete History of Music
David L Cohn	The Good Old Days
Aaron Copland	Our New Music
Hilaire Hiler	From Nudity to Raiment (the story of clothes)
John J. Martin	American Dancing
Robert B. Weaver	Amusement and Sports in American Life

5. Anniversaries Give Opportunities:

Reporters and feature writers frequently make use of the opportunities provided by various national anniversaries to write interesting background features. Such anniversaries include Independence Day, Constitution Day, Bill of Rights Day and other celebrations. The birthdays of Washington, Jefferson, Lincoln, Robert E. Lee, Wilson and other leaders also become newspegs by which the newsman may review the lives of the great Americans and present their peculiar qualities as men and their contributions as leaders.

While these features and editorials often become overstandardized, newsmen should seek to make them pertinent and fresh with new tie-ups to present-day news. Newsmen have access to early publications, they sometimes report events in national history, such as the original signing of the Declaration of Independence. From the newspaper files the news-investigators derive the facts, then re-write the slow-moving stories of the earlier reporters in today's tempo. An opportunity is also provided to tell about the changes in reportorial methods and speed of news production and transmission since the pioneer days.

The seventy-fifth anniversary of one of the most interesting incidents in American history prompted this **AP** article which appeared in many newspapers.

Hayes-Tilden Race Closest in History

Washington, Nov. 8 (AP)-Republicans and Democrats ran their closest race for the Presidency-with a margin of one electoral vote-on Election Day 75 years ago.

The Hayes-Tilden contest of 1876 touched off the most prolonged and bitter election dispute in American history. There were threats of another Civil War during the four months that elapsed before Hayes was finally decreed the winner.

It was a particularly hard blow for the Democrats because newspapers at first generally reported that Democrat Samuel J. Tilden of New York had been elected. He had an unchallenged plurality of popular votes and an apparent 203 electoral votes to 166 for Republican Rutherford B. Hayes.

But on November 8, the day after the election, reports of vote disputes began coming in. Republican politicos quickly contended that, contrary to Democratic claims, Hayes had won in South Carolina, Louisiana and Florida. They said he had received 185 electoral votes to 184 for Tilden.

Those three southern states were under Republican "Carpetbag" rule. They were in the process of transition from negro to white government and both sides made charges of fraudulent election practices.

Louisiana at first reported more than 6,000 majority for Tilden, but the Republican-controlled vote canvassing board threw out returns from several parishes (counties). The board charged white intimidation of negro voters and declared Hayes had carried the state by 3,437 majority.

Two sets of returns were sent in from South Carolina, one by Republican electors and one by Democratic electors. South Carolina Democrats complained that detachments of Federal troops stationed near the polls had prevented a free and fair election.

Republicans claimed Hayes carried Florida by a majority of 75 votes. Democrats contended Tilden had won by a 90 majority.

The Democrats also challenged the validity of one of three Republican electoral votes in Oregon.

Congress decided to create an electoral commission to settle the disputes. This commission was to be composed of five senators, five members of the House, and five justices of the Supreme Court.

The House at that time was controlled by the Democrats. The Republicans had a majority in the Senate. Chosen for the electoral commission were three Republicans and two Democratic senators and two Republican members and three Democratic members of the House.

Then four justices were designated, two Republicans and two Democrats. These four were to choose a fifth justice.

It was understood they would select Justice David Davis, an independent in politics, so that the commission would have seven Republicans, seven Democrats and one neutral member.

However, while the bill providing for the commission was pending the Illinois State Legislature chose Davis to fill a U.S. Senate vacancy.

The remaining Justices were Republicans. Justice Joseph Bradley, described in one newspaper as "an able and honest fervid Republican," was selected.

Congress started counting vote returns February 1. When it referred the Florida, Louisianna, South Carolina and Oregon dispute to the commission, composed of eight Republicans and seven Democrats, each dispute was decided 8 to 7 in favor of the Republican claims.

Some Democrats in Congress accused the Republicans of "stealing the Presidency" and of "bayonet rule in the South", but more moderate Democrats decided to abide by the ruling of the commission they had helped to set up.

Finally, after a stormy night session of Senate and House, Congress reported at 4 o'clock the morning of March 2 that Hayes had received 185 electoral votes to 184 for Tilden.

The popular vote was 4,284,885 for Tilden and 4,033,950 for Hayes.

Hayes took the oath of office on March 3 because March 4, official inauguration date, fell on Sunday.

It was reported that southern Democrats were induced to accept the decision awarding the election to Hayes by promises from Republican bigwigs that Hayes would withdraw Federal troops from the southern states.

Hayes did withdraw the troops and generally was friendly toward the South. Republican extremists in Congress, however, denounced his conciliatory attitude.

Unsuccessful moves were made by several members of Congress to provide for the election of a President by a plurality of popular votes doing away with the electoral votes.

Ten years later Congress passed the electoral count act of 1887. This act holds that presidential electors are state officers and aims at having the states settle their own disputes over electoral vote certificates.

If a state is unable to settle such disputes, and sends conflicting election certificates to the Senate, the law provided that the two houses of Congress, each acting independently, shall decide which certificate is to be accepted.

If the Senate and the House are unable to reach an agreement, the law provides that the electoral returns which have been certified by the state's governor shall be favored.

If the governor certifies none of the electoral returns, the state loses its electoral vote. No contest has as yet developed to test the electoral count act.

In 1889 Democrat Grover Cleveland recived 96,000 more popular votes than Republican Benjamin Harrison, but Harrison was elected President. Harrison, however had 233 electoral votes to 168 for Cleveland.

Next to the Hayes-Tilden contest, the closest Republican-Democratic electoral vote race was between Woodrow Wilson and Charles Evans Hughes in 1916. Wilson received 277 electoral votes   to 254 for Hughes.

Jacksonville, <u>Flori-</u>
<u>da Times-Union.</u>

6.   Local History Is Essential

Many opportunities present themselves to the reporter
or editorial writer to utilize his knowledge of the history
of the city. If he is a newcomer to the town in which the
newspaper is published, the newsman should lose no time in
beginning his study of the development of the community and
area in which it is located. This may involve trips to the
library as well as talks with old residents to reconstruct
the history of the community. Frequently the newsman who
has been a resident of a particular city all his life lacks
a fundamental knowledge of the economic, industrial, social
and population trends and developments there. Fragmentary
information based on a few highlights or incidents previously published or read about make up the sum-total of the
newsman's knowledge. His fund of information might be filled in with a thorough-going study of the evolution of the
community. For out of this study will come a grasp of the
past as well as an understanding of the roots of many of
the current problems residents face.

A knowledge of the beginnings of Baltimore more than
two hundred years ago helped the writer once in a campaign
for the improvement of the transportation system in that
city. The newspaper with which he was connected backed
the efforts for various civic groups which desired   to secure crosstown bus service, travelling east and west. The
transportation company refused to install the needed service.

A study of the history of the city indicated that in
the 1700's and 1800's the city of Baltimore was connected
with towns in western Maryland and Pennsylvania by a series
of roads over which the carts and stage coaches travelled.
These routes extended largely in a north, northwest and
northeast direction. Residents, as they pushed out from
the harbor, settled along these roads which stretched out
like five fingers. When the trolleys were introduced in
the late 1800's, they followed these old routes. By 1920,
however, the population picture had begun to change. Thousands of families settled in the newly-developed areas between the old routes at the northern end of the city. The
proper bus system was not provided for them. In the 1930's
still more thousands poured into the northern suburbs.

In a series of articles the writer pointed that the
trolleys were following the historic ox-cart and stage
coach roads, running on north and south routes. The city's
population had now filled in the intervening areas and,
therefore, an east-west connecting transportation link was
needed. If a person wished to travel from northeast Baltimore to northwest Baltimore, he required three trolley

rides and two transfers. The tiresome journey consumed an
hour and a half. The short route across town required
twenty minutes.

The historical background illuminated the entire case
and played an important part in securing a final victory
and the installation of the needed east-west bus service.

7. Newspaper Anniversary Editions:

A knowledge of national, state and particularly local
history proves invaluable to the newsman in producing anniversary editions of his newspaper.[1] A basic comprehen-
sion of the trends and developments of the community can be
woven into the history of the particular press for a stimulating special edition. The influence of the newspaper
upon its locality, and, in turn the shaping of the press by
the changing social and economic conditions can produce a
fascinating picture of the times. Here is the news about
the one hundredth anniversary edition of the Portland
Oregonian.

OREGONIAN CELEBRATES

CENTENNIAL FOR MONTH

By Claire Lyon

Portland,Ore. - An anniversary without band, spotlights, a gala open house or
a 3oo-plus-page edition, marks the Oregonian's
100th birthday, Dec. 4.

In the words of Managing Editor Robert C. Notson, the Oregonian
"did not desire to mark such a mile-
stone by issuing a paper noticeable
mainly by its bulk." Instead, the
aim is to give a bit of the centennial flavor to the readers every day
in December.

General Manager M.J. Frey stated: "Breaking away from tradition
in observing such events, we decided
to pioneer a new idea-a month-long
observance of 100 Years of Headlines."

Device:
"A Century of Head-
lines"

"In this way only," he explained
"could the full brilliance of the
region's century, its events and the
people be adequately covered."

As a result, all editorial,
circulation and promotion efforts
were directed toward making December
a Centennial Month.

[1] See Wibur Peterson, Newspaper Anniversary Editions,
          Iowa City, Iowa, State University of Iowa, 1955.

During this month readers will
find a daily 100-year picture page,
plus special features and flashbacks
recapturing the drama of events head-
lining the century. With a total of
some 1,500 news pages planned during
December, the month becomes a vivid
encyclopedia of history and human interest...the theme was "Relive-100
years of headlines." Live and trans-
cribed copy flooded radio stations
during the latter part of November.

Recapture drama of
regions history

The Theme:
"Relive-100 Years
of Headlines"

The story of the Oregonian is
the story of the pioneer Oregon country itself. From a two-man force -
the founding editor, Thomas J. Dryer,
and his assistant, Henry L. Pitock,
in 1850 - the paper has multiplied to
a staff of nearly 700, more people
than there were in Portland a century
ago.

From scarcely 200 subscribers
circulation has climbed to a few
under a quarter-million, making it
the largest newspaper north of Los
Angeles. - Editor and Publisher,
          Dec. 2, 1950.

The newspaperman assigned the job of writing the history of the newspaper would first make a thorough study of
the early newspaper files. He would then check other printed materials in the morgue and in local libraries, searching for information about the development of the paper.
Old residents, former employes, publishers and advertisers
may furnish additional facts about the journal. For local
history which would have to be woven into the articles, the
following sources are described.

Sources for Local History: Newsmen need to know the
sources where they may find information about local history.
No essential spot should be overlooked. Libraries are the
best sources for facts about the past of any community.
There books about the local scene, a newspaper clipping file
and old maps are kept. Annual reports from all the city
departments are usually sought and placed on shelves by
libraries. Such reports frequently contain invaluable histories of municipal departments and of the city.

Many libraries make a determined effort to secure all
city directories and telephone books, which often tell the
story of the town in any particular period. The study of
these volumes will reveal how far the city has progressed
in any period. A number of towns and cities are covered in

special histories. Maps are usually a neglected source, but they give a graphic picture of the changing population trends. Some of the metropolitan libraries have special sections or departments devoted to local history.

The morgue or reference department of the newspaper will furnish facutal material and books about the development of the community. A particularly helpful source for the backgrounder of local history is the special anniversary editions of newspapers, mentioned before.

Active historical societies prove valuable to many newsmen exploring the past of their communities. Books, newspapers and magazines and other material may be found on their shelves. In some communities the only source for local history is the chamber of commerce which may be able to furnish pamphlets, books and statistics.

Many states have historical magazines containing material which may be used for backgrounding. Some of the articles might be converted into readable newspaper features. The magazines are usually issued by state or local historical societies and universities. Such magazines include the Journal of Southern History, Mississippi Valley Historical Review, the Pacific Historical Review, and the Southwestern Historical Quarterly. The student should check with the librarian for historical publications devoted to the area in which the university is located. A magazine dealing with his home state may be available.

8. Cautions For Newsmen

While the newsman should not let up in his effort to discover interesting, dramatic materials which will lend color and flavor to his lead and the development of his article, it is essential that for accuracy and truth he indicate the dramatic situation he is describing is only one phase of the complete story.

Too often the historical feature or the article which backgrounds a current event historically is merely a superficial, routine, done-a-thousand-times piece. The writer might have developed it into a strong historical article showing the various economic, political and social forces and accidental events which produced the historical happening.

Effective news writers seek to invest the background historical article with new meaning, with fresh ideas and with modern slants. Such articles then take on added vital significance and importance for the reader.

The newsman should consult both personal and printed sources for needed information and explanations to fill out the historical picture. Librarians, state archivists and historians on the staffs of state universities, colleges and high schools usually will prove helpful to the reporter, furnishing information and pointing to official and other printed sources for facts. Sometimes well-trained historians are found in active historical societies. We shall mention a number of printed sources in later pages.

9. Interviewing Techniques

In interviewing historians and other scientists for information, reporters must be particularly careful. The reporter is dealing here with scientists, who, as specialists, are aware of the complexity of human beings, and the scientists therefore shy away from simple, pat statements about incidents or people who appear in the news. They are afraid, too, of reporters' exaggerations and mis-statements about their sciences and research. Qualified scientists are cautious about making broad claims for specific research which applies only to a limited area or group.

To get full co-operation and assistance in writing his news or feature article, and in checking his facts, the newsman must be aware of this situation and be cognizant of the attitude of the scientist on the other side of the desk. At the beginning of the interview, the reporter must assure the historian or other social scientist of his desire to get an accurate account, rather than a garbled version of the story. The reporter, too, must be certain to state clearly that confidential material will be regarded as such, and that anonymity where imperative will be kept. Often if rapport is established first and the scientist is not high-pressured, he will yield more significant information for the reporter.

10. Writing The Feature

In writing the special historical feature, great care, of course, must be taken to avoid exaggeration. Scientists, as we already remarked, are wary of reporters because of the newsmen's lack of understanding of scientific method and their often uncontrollable desire to sensationalize any kind of story. Happily, this is being overcome now, especially in the natural science field . William Laurence of the New York Times, the late Howard W. Blakeslee, of the Associated Press, and Watson Davis, of Science Service, have gone far in establishing the confidence of science in reporters and newspapers.

In this type of feature story the selection of the lead would be determined by the character of the material and the type of public toward whom it is directed.

The following are suggestions:

    1. Use the newspeg, based on some incident in the news.

2. Select the strongest and most striking state-
    ment made by anyone during the course of the
    investigation.
3. Focus on a dramatic aspect of specific inci-
    dent.
4. Give a graphic portrayal of a scene in which
    an historical incident occurred.
5. Write a strong, lively lead which would compare
    an historical event with a current happening.
6. Present a summary of the highlights of the
    article in brief, concise style.

The body of the story should unfold the facts in natural order, once the lead is written, If the reporter, before writing his article, outlines the material, he will
give the story a firm structure and will eliminate all un-
neccesary details.

Translate the Technical   Every trade, profession
and science has developed short-hand vocabularies and lang-
uages of its own, The psychologist talks about Gestalt
psychology and about psychotic personality; the sociologist
discusses ecological patterns as well as the social lag;
while the political scientist argues about power politics
and the commission form of government. Likewise, the phy-
sicist deals in protons and nuclear fission.

Don't forget that journalism, too, has its special
vocabulary--crop a picture, stickful of type, bulldog
edition. To the specialist each one of his own terms carries a wealth of meaning. He associates many ideas with each
technical words he uses. He is able to give exact, rather
than loose, meanings to specific ideas and situations.
He thus converses with others in his profession more quickly.

Fact and Discussion Questions
for Chapter II, "News is Contemporary History"

1. Discuss the value to the newsman of knowing history.
    Illustrate.

2. Is all news unexpected? Explain.

3. What are some of the pitfalls newsmen fall into in us-
    ing historical materials? How would you overcome them?

4. Why are historians sometimes uncooperative with news-
    men? How would you handle such a situation?

5. List some of the techniques for writing interesting
    leads on history stories.

6. (a) Discuss the statement: "newsmen must know the
    threads and patterns of history." (b) List four re-
    current news threads.

7. Outline an article you might write on civil liberties
    in America.

8. List three basic ideas of democracy a newsmen should
    remember.

9. Outline an article comparing democracy and communism.

10. List three historical magazines of value to a newsman.

11. What reference books would you consult for an article
    on George Washington?

12. What is social history?

13. Discuss the statement, "anniversaries provide opportun-
    ities for the newsman to use history." Illustrate.

14. How would you make a traditional Fourth of July story
    interesting and readable?

15. Discuss the important points in the AP article on the
    Hayes-Tilden race.

16. How did the reporter use history in writing the trans-
    portation campaign stories in Baltimore?

17. List some sources for local history.

News Clipping Assignment

Read your local newspaper for four days, clipping some important local events which would have historical angles.

(a) Did the news articles carry their own historical background?

(b) Do you know of the events which led up to the present news?

(c) Outline the steps you would take in securing further history about the events.

Written Assignments

1. Write a news-feature on the historical background of some local news event current now in your community.
    (a) Where would you get the information?
    (b) Explain how the preceding events throw light on the present situation.
    (c) Make full use of the library and interview public officials and others who might know the history of the event.

2. Write three news-features, "Six Acts in the Drama of....................(your community)".
    (a) Make this a strong historical series on the development of the town or city.
    (b) Check the library for books on the history of the community, and for previous magazine and newspaper articles as any reporter would who went to the newspaper morgue for material.
    (c) Pay particular attention to the economic development, the spread of the population, the coming of the railroads, trolleys and busses and planes.
    (d) Did you find out anything about the changing political scene?
    (e) Weave this into a colorful series, integrating all the materials by eras, such as I "Pioneer Period", II "Expansion Era."

3. Write a news-feature on "Background for Civil Liberties."
    (a) Assume some problem relating to the civil liberty issue has arisen, such as the denial of civil liberty rights for certain individuals in your community.
    (b) Develop an interpretative feature telling the story of the origin and development of civil liberty in the United States.
    (c) Bring out the facts which show how this issue is related to basic democracy.
    (d) Check at the library for books and pamphlet material relating to this question.

(e) If time permits, write to the American Civil Liberties Union, in New York, for further facts, current and annual reports.

4. Write a news-feature on Independence Day, or the Fourth of July.
(a) Assume you are writing the article for a newspaper which has published such features many times before.
(b) How would you make it fresh and interesting? What devices would you use to dramatize the story? To make it seem real and significant today? What personalities would you weave into your article? How?
(c) Weave into your story the significance of certain parts of the Declaration of Independence today. This will require you to read the document carefully.
(d) Do you know the significance of the Declaration for the peoples of the world at the time it was written. What effects did it have on other nations? What were the sources of its ideas?
(e) What pictures would you use for illustration?
(f) Examine the best sources for facts at the library.

5. Write a series of short news-features on one of the anniversaries in American history which recur each year.
(a) Examples might be Constitution Day, Bill of Rights Week, or Anniversary of adoption of any of the constitutional amendments.
(b) Other types might be the anniversary of Washington's, Jefferson's, Franklin's, Hamilton's, Wilson's, Theodore Roosevelt's birthday or death.
(c) See section 7 above for suggestions.

6. Write a news-feature giving the background of the struggles for religious liberty in America.
(a) Assume an issue has arisen in your community or Congress relating to the question.
(b) Make the incidents relating to the history of religious liberty forceful.
(c) Trace the roots of the issue and its later development.
(d) How would you relate it to the growth of democracy?
(e) What pictures would you use?

7. Write a three-part series on Freedom of Press.
(a) Begin with colonial period dramatizing the situation. Bring in the Peter Zenger trial.
(b) Tell about the Alien and Sedition Acts of 1792.
(c) Refer to recent efforts to block newspapermen from getting news.

8. Develop a series of two special articles about the Supreme Court.
   (a) A national issue has developed over the powers of the United States Supreme Court. It is on the front pages of nearly every newspaper. The issue is controversial and many readers discuss it among themselves .
   (b) Develop an effective series for your newspaper on the Supreme Court under various strong justices.
   (c) Weave into your articles some of the important decisions of the court which have influenced the direction American life took.
   (d) Fit into your series the proposals of Franklin D. Roosevelt to expand the membership of the Court in 1937.
   (e) In addition to those references cited in the text, the student might find a capable summary of the development of the Supreme Court in Curtis D. Mac-Dougall, Covering the Courts.

9. Write a two-part series on "Third Parties: A Factor in American Politics."
   (a) A third party has made its appearance in an American presidential election.
   (b) Tell the history briefly of some of the important third parties which have appeared on the American scene.
   (c) What conditions produced them? Who were their leaders. What effects did they have on the dominant parties?
   (d) What tentative conclusions have students of the subject drawn about such movements?

10. Write a strong news-feature backgounding some current national news event.
    (a) You may use New York Times "News of the Week in Review", New York Herald Tribune "History In The Making". Christian Science Monitor special feature.
    (b) You may consult Time, News-Week, U.S. News & World Report.
    (c) Check with encyclopedias, Facts on File.

11. Write an informative explanatory article on a current national news situation with a professor of United States history, or a professor of political science based on an interview with him.
    (a) Acquire some backgound at the library yourself before going for the interview.
    (b) Write out prior to the interview a series of 10-12 questions which you can ask about the issue.
    (c) Feel free to ask others as the conversation develops.

Here are some historical series of value to the newsman making special historical investigations for articles.

Edward Channing	History of the United States (6 vols. and index) New York: Macmillan: 1905-25. An older work, factual rather than interpretative, but still one of the best accounts of American history to 1865.
Allen Johnson (editor)	The Chronicles of America, 5o vols. New Haven: Yale, 1921; Allan Nevins (editor, vol. 51-56) Small volumes popularly written on periods and developments.
Arthur M. Schlesinger and Dixon R. Fox (editors)	History of American Life, 13 vols., New York; Macmillan, 1927-29. Planned from the point of view that history is the sum total of human activities. Special attention to socio-economic problems and culture.

CALIFORNIA
SUN
1956 MAGAZINE

MODERN SOCIETY:
WHAT DOES IT OFFER?

Creditable Job   A student laboratory newspaper, the
California Sun interprets current problems in the news. A
highly creditable publication, it is issued by the Department
of Journalism, University of California at Los Angeles.

THE MICHIGAN JOURNALIST

Published for the Department of Journalism by the Ann Arbor News, Ann Arbor, Michigan.

Experimental Laboratory Newspaper of the Department of Journalism, University of Michigan

Vol. 23, No. 7   ANN ARBOR, MICHIGAN, JUNE 2, 1950   Four Pages

Fee System For Parking Under Study

Charge In University Lots Would Prevent Abuses, Declares Watkins

NO EXPANSION SEEN

Present Facilities Limited; Demand Continues High, Points Out Gwin

By Kenneth E. Miller

Better Conditions Cited As Cause Of Increasing Student Travel Abroad

By Connie Lee Jones

Mao Regime Called Better Than Chiang's

Chinese Peasants Satisfied With Communist Policies, Declare Observers

MILITARY AIDS FARMER

Political Land Redistribution Among Working Class Cited As Popular

By Jack Vandenberg

County Child Delinquency Reported Below Average

Standing Based On School Enrollment Statistics, Not 1940 Census

By Robert J. Bailyn

Japan Policy Termed One Of Strategy

Hall Says U. S. Action Not Based On Liberalization Along Western Lines

SEES WITHDRAWAL

Believes Cost Of Occupation Too Great For America To Stay Much Longer

By Yat-chi Tze

Counter Charges Thrown In Fight Over Quad Food

Shiel Denies Bias In Food Policies

Economics Professor Sees No Unfair Competition In New Snack Bar

OLD ISSUES RAISED

Efficiency, Costs Called Only Relevant Factors In Restaurant Case

By Robert J. Bailyn

The Tallahassee Sun

VOL. 1 — NO 2   TALLAHASSEE, FLORIDA; TUESDAY, NOVEMBER 1, 1955   LABORATORY NEWSPAPER

Top News Events Interpreted By FSU Students

Bob Aldrich Is An Ardent Fisherman

By Pat Wiesner

Journalism Classes Issue Experimental Paper

by Sidney Kobre
Professor of Journalism
Florida State University

TALLAHASSEE — Commissioner of Agriculture Nathan Mayo takes part in the formal acceptance of the mobile laboratory designed to give the Dairy Division of the State Department of Agriculture quicker and more scientific analysis of all dairy products. Standing at the side of the 25-foot trailer are C. G. Wyatt of Wyatt Trailer Sales, Ocala, manufacturer of the unit; Alex G. Shaw, Gainesville, Chief Dairy Supervisor; and Commissioner Mayo. Shaw will be in charge of the trailer unit which will conduct statewide tests with Gainesville office as headquarters.

Fla. Supreme Court Rules Against Union Picketing In Miami

by Howard Hartley

Employee Relations Best In Nation At Union Carbide

By William P. Branson

DEPTH REPORTING

These laboratory newspapers carry depth reporting articles by journalism students. The Michigan Journalist is a publication of the School of Journalism, University of Michigan, at Ann Arbor. The student-reporters at Florida State University, in Tallahassee, wrote the copy for the Tallahassee Sun.

Chapter 3
Global News

1. World Is Shrinking

The world is shrinking.
We live in one world.

These are two new concepts which have become part of the thinking of many in this country. They represent ideas which have come to the front since World War I, and they reflect the public's interest in world affairs and the increasing attention newspapers are paying to international views. In the colonial period the settlers were international-minded. They had close ties with Europe, especially England. Ships sailed more frequently between Boston and Liverpool than between Boston and Charlestown, S. C. Control over the economic and political life in the colonies was exerted by parliament. The colonial gazettes thus were dominated by the news of European and particularly English affairs.

After the Revolutionary War the people of the United States continued their interest in foreign affairs, especially English and French news and developments. Beginning about 1815 the United States became more national-minded, concentrating on the solution of many domestic problems rather than on external affairs. Newsmen turned their attention to these affairs. The people were concerned later with developing the vast agricultural regions in the West, building up a strong industrial system, battling the slavery issue. Then they tilted against the trusts. No time for foreign affairs.

By the 1890's the United States began to turn more aggressively to foreign markets for its mounting factory production. The thinking of some was turned to the establishment of colonies. While many businessmen were interested, the public could not be aroused to concern itself with foreign news and events. The middle west, with no coast line, was especially removed, felt particularly self-sufficient and so had strong nationalistic rather than international interests.

The tide of public interest changed after the Spanish-American War in 1898. Interest in international affairs was further stimulated by the Mexican border incidents of 1914.

The United States, however, was pulled into the international vortex, first economically with the shipment of armaments and food supplies, then militarily, when formal

36

to colonize its backward neighbors?

In 1901, an assassin pumped a bullet into McKinley in Buffalo, and the name of Roosevelt moved on to the nation's lips. New York politicians had thrown the vice-presidential nomination to the grinning man from Oyster Bay, hoping he would become obscure and let them run their state alone. But when he walked into the White House Teddy Roosevelt began waving a big stick, dynamically fought railroads and industrial monopolies, pushed the Panama Canal toward completion, and battled exploitation of natural resources.

In 1908, T.R. stepped down and boosted William Howard Taft to the Presidency, but the rotund Taft soon proved himself not quite the puppet T. R. thought he would be. The result, in 1912, was a new party-the Progressives-pushing Roosevelt for the Presidency against Taft and Democrat Woodrow Wilson. Thanks to the Republican split, ex-Princeton President Wilson proceeded into the White House.

By the time he left, a dying man, in 1921, America had broken irretrievably with its past. In 1912 we were virtually as unconcerned about Europe and its problems as it was possible for one nation on earth to be about another region. In 1914 the Old World's cannon began to roar and slowly the noise came closer. In 1916 Wilson was reelected because "he kept us out of war" but a year later another slogan became more important: "The world must be made safe for democracy." So the Yanks went over, and bled along the Marne and in the Meuse-Argonne, and Gen. John J. Pershing became the nation's hero.

Then came disillusionment - Europe kept pushing off payment of war debts to "Uncle Shylock" - and Americans fooled themselves into thinking they could leave the continent to its "age-old squabbles" and return to the traditional isolation.

Novelists, dramatists, songwriters have glamorized the '2os: Prohibition, jazz, hip-pocket flasks, raccoon coats, Trudy Ederle and the Channel swimmers, the big bull market and flowering prosperity. The nation kept cool with Coolidge put Herbert Hoover in the White House, and then sat back to wait for Utopia.

In October, 1929, the stock market crashed. The party was over. America did not know it then, of course, but it had had its last adolescent fling. Now it would have to face reponsibilities.

They came, fast: The most devastating depression in history, more than 15,000,000 unemployed, the panic of the hungry slowly moving over the country. And then, In Germany, arose a hateful ex-house painter who from a prison cell had callously blue-printed plans to rule the world.

war was declared in 1917. The shock of that war made a number of people, including President Woodrow Wilson, realize that whether we wanted to or not, the United States was bound up with world affairs. America had a stake in the fight for world peace.

During the post-World War I period, the unsuccessful efforts to build a strong League of Nations, the cynicism connected with the Disarmament Conference, all reflected the public's interest in a return to nationalism. The general feeling seemed to be that we had nothing to do with European squabbles.

But World War II brought us back into the sea of international events again. We could not turn our backs in the face of reality. The United States was going to be drawn into the world-wide arena whether she liked it or not. In the post-World War II era, the United States destiny was bound up with the solvency of democracy everywhere. This was especially true since the Communist officials in the Soviet Union had decided to extend their power and make it a fight to the last drop of blood between communism and democracy.

One invention, the airplane, contributed to the thought that we were an inseparable part of the world and that this was a shrinking world. Physical distance was trimmed because flying speed was increased. Instead of being five trans-Atlantic liner days away from America, Europe was only so many hours of airplane time. Improved facilities for communication, such as the radio, also stimulated globular shrinking.

John L. Springer wrote this informative news-feature for the Associated Press:

HOW U.S. GREW TO WORLD POWER

From second-rate power to mightiest nation on earth is the progress chalked up by the United States, taking inventory at the beginning of a new half-century.

The first 50 years of the 2oth century actually have seen a revolution. The country has virtually doubled in population (from 75,000,000 to about 145,000,000). Its wealth has trebled. Its scientific and inventive genius has made it the most and efficient nation in world history.

Foreigners say America's booming optimism is notorious. But even the most blatant prophets of 1899 could hardly have foreseen their country's sizzling course of progress in this half-century. Those were the days of President McKinley, of gaslights, 6o-hour weeks, rampant tuberculosis, and fearful infant mortality. Big issue of the times: Having mopped up weakling Spain, how far should the United States go in its 'manifest destiny'

With tradition-breaking Franklin D. Roosevelt
in the White House, the country threw out methods
of the past and enacted unprecedented laws to
battle the depression at home. The government
reformed the banks, probed the utilities, destroyed sweatshops, encouraged unions to grow to as-
tounding proportions, began a vast program of
social security.

Fighting the war at home, the nation watched the
steady growth of House Painter Hitler's Germany
abroad, together with the aggressions of his allies,
Japan and Italy.

Could America keep out of a new war? The new
"scientific" opinion polls said the public thought
the country should stay out. But when Hitler
sent his troops into Poland, they had their doubts.
Roosevelt ran for a third term and flatly promised
America's fathers and mothers their sons would
"not be sent to fight in any foreign war." But
the doubts remained.

They were justified. On the morning of Dec 7,
1941, a squadron of airplanes flying the insignia
of the Japanese Rising Sun flew over Hawaii, sent
bombs screaming down on Pearl Harbor, and pulled
America into the war.

This war speeded up-and dramatized-the revolution which had been moving slowly since the start
of the century.

It put 15,000,000 Americans under arms, sent
them to stalk down the Axis in every continent.
To supply them-and to supply the rest of a be-
leaguered world-America's factories and farms were
given "impossible" production goals. They met them
with new techniques, new machines, new know-how.
The machine age really began to flower. A good
indication of this flowering is shown in electricity. In 1900, the entire country used about one
billion kilowatt hours of electrical energy. This
year it will use about 300 billion kilowatt hours!

That increase of 300 times merely suggests how
power-cheap power-has taken over thousands of jobs
on farms, in factories and homes that formerly were
performed laboriously by human hands.

World War II likewise spurred a revolution in
government: It cast Washington's shadow over virtually every businessman and worker. In 1900,there
were 350,000 civilians in the federal employ; now
there are 2,000,000. At the turn of the century
there were but 15 executive agencies; now there
are 69, covering vast fields of conservation,
agricultural supervision, housing, veterans' and
social welfare that were considered the private
province of the individual 50 years ago.

The war likewise put an end to the belief that
America could be isolated from the rest of the
world. For the United States emerged as the almost
only "Have" nation in a sea of "Have-nots". Upon
American shoulders fell the job of rebuilding the

world. Upon America, too, fell the job of shor-
ing up the earth's democracies against the oppor-
tunistic advance of Communist Russia.

When the blast of the first atomic bomb reverb-
erated over Hiroshima Aug. 7, 1945, and signalized
the early end of the war with Japan, the United
States had become so deeply committed to world
cooperation that a return to isolationism was un-
thinkable. Participation in the United Nations
from its beginning was one proof of the change;
a second-and more dramatic-proof was the signing
this year of the Atlantic Pact obliging the United
States to aid other western powers which may be
attacked.

Since the end of the war, changes in American
life have been evident on all fronts. Statistic-
ally, the average American is far better off: he
earns more money, works fewer hours, enjoys far
more comforts than anybody, anywhere, in history.
Government taxing policies have made the very rich
poorer and the very poor richer. The idea once
hateful to a democracy of a peace-time drafted
army is now an accepted fact. The government is
stepping, more and more, into the field of public
welfare, housing and health.

Begun by Roosevelt, the "New Deal" has been
broadened and expanded by the piano-playing ex-
Senator from Missouri, Harry S. Truman, who became President when F.D.R. was felled by a stroke
in April 1945. In the past year Democratic candidates for office announced they fully favored
the idea of a "welfare state": in the past year,
most Democrats were elected.

Newsman has New Problems

Newsmen in the second-half of the twentieth century
were confronted thus with a new and rapidly shrinking world.
Big news today is news of the Soviet, of Germany, of England. Headlines about China, Korea and Indo-China are
hungrily awaited by the public because of their explosive
nature. All of the current international events have their
roots in the past, and the exploration of this past will
furnish the indispensable master keys to the understanding
and interpretation of world news today.

The newsman needs also an understanding of efforts to
develop an international peace organization, beginning in
recent decades with the League of Nations and coming up
through the United Nations Organization.

2. Spotlight on World Events

In the following pages will be found some of the highlights of world events since World War II which will provide background for the reporter. Certain broad fundamental, and somewhat revolutionary changes on the world stage
will be noted. These include:

(1) The rise of Soviet Russia as a world power
(2) The deep rift, or cold war, which developed be-
    tween the United States, as leader of the Western
    nations, and the Soviet Union and its Communist
    satellites
(3) The aggressive imperialistic tendencies of the
    Soviets
(4) The break-down of the balance of power of the
    nations in Europe, with England throwing her
    weight on one side or the other
(5) The weakening of France as a world power
(6) The drive of colonials in Asia, the Middle East
    and Africa for independence.
(7) The efforts by Western Powers and by Soviets to
    re-align countries leading to the formation of
    new political, economic and military alliances
(8) The development of several world regions of con-
    flict and trouble - (a) the Western Europe, cen-
    turing around Germany, (b) the middle East, (c)
    Indonesia, (d) Far East China, Japan, Korea
(9) The establishment of the United Nations

Peace Negotiations
Even before the guns were quieted and World War II ended, diplomats of the Big Three - the United States, Great
Britain and Soviet Russia began to lay the goundwork for
peace and the conditions of surrender.

Moscow Conference   The Western allies met in Moscow
on Nov. 1, 1943 to accomplish this end. They agreed to
co-operate on negotiating a peace which would be permanent.
They declared there would be no military occupancy of the
conquered nations unless by consent of the other allies.
They intended to restore democracy in Italy and give independence to Austria.

Teheran Conference   At the end of November Joseph
Stalin, Winston Churchill and Franklin D. Roosevelt met at
Teheran, in Iran Russia. Again plans were made for bringing an end to the war. It was agreed that a general international peace organization should be established. Meanwhile, allied troops in July, 1943 began to invade Itlay
from Africa and move north.

The first step in the final phase of the war began in
June, 1944. Following extensive preparations and planning,
the American, British and Canadian troops breached the German wall at Normandy, on the coast of France. This was
D-Day, June 6, 1944. More than 250,000 air, sea and land
troops took part in the greatest invasion in history. The
German troops were stunned and surprised, but began to
fight back.

Yalta Conference   With victory in sight, at least in
Europe, the Big Three met again at Yalta, in the Crimea, in
February, 1945. They agreed to restore to rights of self-
government in those nations which Hitler and Japan had over-

41

Events Marking World War II End,
Launching UNITED NATIONS

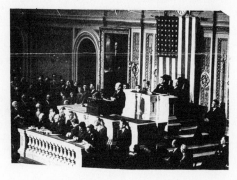

Potsdam Meeting From the conferences of the Big Three
at Potsdam came the ultimatum to Japan to surrender
at once or be destroyed. Prime Minister Clement
Attlee and President Truman were newcomers to the
top level of statesmanship. Soviet Russia's
Joseph Stalin had participated before.

Significant Conference Prime Minister Churchill,
President Roosevelt and Joseph Stalin meet on the
palace patio at Yalta to decide what to do at the
end of World War II. Signal Corps photo.

Signs U. N. Charter President Truman signing the United
Nations Charter in Washington, completing ratification of
the document by the United States. Secretary of State
James F. Byrnes shared in the historic occasion.

AP photo.

Harmony Plea British Prime Minister Clement C. Attlee pleaded
for harmony among all nations in addressing a join session
of the United States Congress.

run. The Big Three, in an amicable mood, decided to divide
Germany, when defeated, into occupation zones, with
each of the four nations, Britain, the United States,
France and Soviet Union, occupying and controlling a different section, Germany was also to pay stiff reparations
for losses. Soviet Russia was to enter the war against
Japan. In return, Russia got various possessions and what
amounted to political and economic rights in China and in
industrial Manchuria. The Big Three representatives again
agreed that the establishment of an International Peace
Organization was badly needed. The concessions to the Russians at Yalta produced a hurricane of controversy later.

By April, 1945 the German people and the generals knew
they were beaten. Plans were made by various generals to
assassinate Adolph Hitler, but this did not succeed. While
the Russian guns were firing at Berlin, Hitler and his mis-
tress. committed suicide. Germany surrended April 29, 1945.

The cost of the war was immense. More than 10,000,000
were killed. An equal number of soldiers were disabled.
The United States lost 150,000. The civilian population
suffered. Cities were in ruins. Industry was crippled.
As soon as Germany surrendered, the four allies moved in to
occupy the country. They began to take away the arms and
arrest all leaders in the Nazi movement.

Postdam Conference   The terms for defeated Germany
were fixed at the Postsdam Conference in July-August, 1945,
This involved the complete disarmament of the country and
the dissolution of Hitler's National Socialist Party. Germany was to be democratized. The allies declared they
would try the "war criminals", the generals and those in
charge of the concentration camps where millions had been
burned and gassed to death. At the conference, it was
agreed that a Council of Foreign Ministers would be established to negotiate peace treaties with the other defeated
nations.

The allies also issued an ultimatum to Japan with which
they were still at war. They demanded Japan to surrender
immediately, but this was rejected. To shorten the war,
U.S. planes flew over Hiroshima, Japan on August 6, 1945
and dropped an atomic bomb - which killed 80,000 and practically destroyed the city.

Three days later a second atomic bomb was dropped on
Nagasaki. An almost equal destruction and loss of life
resulted. Japan surrendered.

Meetings of Council of Foreign Ministers   The peace
negotiations were not easy to complete. For the first time
Soviet agressiveness began to assert itself. The London
conference in September and the Moscow Conference in December 1945 ended in disagreement. One of the questions at
issue was the degree of French and Chinese participation,
another was the spreading of the Russian influence in the
Balkans. At the Paris Peace Conference in July-October,

43

1946, the conflict between the United States and the Soviets became more pronounced. But treaties were signed, provisionally, with Italy, Hungary, Rumania, Bulgaria and Finland. A meeting in Moscow in December sought to salvage some unity.

Cold War Followed Hot War

The amicable Soviets of wartime now became unfriendly. They sought to engage in a world-wide expansion program. Its ultimate aim was the domination of as many countries as possible, establishing Communism everywhere on the globe. The gap separating the Soviet Union and her former allies grew wider. It developed into an open conflict on various fronts. The Soviets by various means sought to penetrate into surrounding nations and to win them over to the Soviet bloc. The United States, as leader of the Western bloc made efforts to check this expansion and contain the Soviet Union. The basic conflict took various forms in various regions -- Western Europe, where Germany was divided, Central Europe, the Middle East, and the Orient. Immediate settlement of the German and Austrian peace treaties were delayed for a more appropriate moment.

Cold War Fought on Several Fronts   The fight for nations to join either the Western or the Soviet bloc was waged on various fronts -- political, economic, military and propaganda. The old political system of getting alliances which would checkmate your opponent and which would balance the international weight in your favor was revived again. Germany, as we will see, was one of the prizes. Each group sought to win her favor.

China, which overthrew its old regime and became Communistic, turned to Soviets. But Japan and Yugoslavia drifted to the Western bloc. Occupied by Russian troops at the end of the war, Poland was made a part of the Soviet satellite system. Lithuania and others fell into the same orbit. When Soviet Russia attempted to move into Iran, the United Nations, established by this time, objected and forced Russia to withdraw her troops. The Kremlin also was opposed when it sought to penetrate into Greece and Turkey. President Harry S. Truman was responsible for this step to keep Greece and Turkey independent.

United States leaders saw that it was necessary to help rebuild economically European and other nations whose economy was devastated by the guns of World War II. It was also essential to assist the backward countries, struggling to gain their independence and raise their standards of living. Millions were on a starvation level. Health conditions were poor. People needed money, food, machinery. As yet not affected by the Industrial Revolution, they required technical assistance and know-how. Unless these nations were strengthened economically, they would be ripe for Communist penetration. It was pointed out that Communism takes root and grows in economically depressed and disorganized nations.

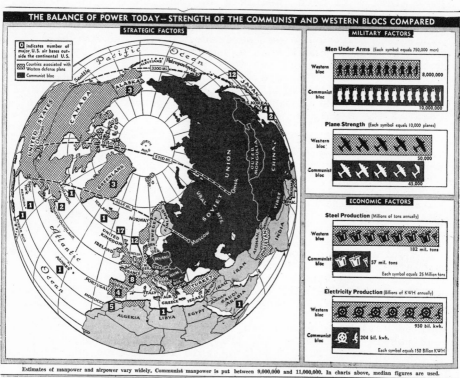

THE BALANCE OF POWER TODAY—STRENGTH OF THE COMMUNIST AND WESTERN BLOCS COMPARED

STRATEGIC FACTORS

Ⓞ indicates number of major U.S. air bases outside the continental U.S.
▨ Countries associated with Western defense plans
■ Communist bloc

MILITARY FACTORS

Men Under Arms (Each symbol equals 750,000 men)

Western bloc — 8,000,000

Communist bloc — 10,000,000

Plane Strength (Each symbol equals 10,000 planes)

Western bloc — 50,000

Communist bloc — 45,000

ECONOMIC FACTORS

Steel Production (Millions of tons annually)

Western bloc — 182 mil. tons

Communist bloc — 57 mil. tons

Each symbol equals 25 Million tons

Electricity Production (Billions of KWH annually)

Western bloc — 950 bil. kwh.

Communist bloc — 204 bil. kwh.

Each symbol equals 150 Billion KWH

Estimates of manpower and airpower vary widely. Communist manpower is put between 9,000,000 and 11,000,000. In charts above, median figures are used.

THE NEW YORK TIMES,

In the post war years the United Nations Relief and Rehabilitation Administration (UNRRA) supplied funds. The Marshall Plan, initiated by Secretary of State George Marshall, on June, 1947 proposed full co-operation with European countries in their efforts at reconstruction. More than $12,000,000,000 was spent to help them rebuild. Other plans were evolved and billions of dollars and goods were sent by the United States. Eventually, Soviet Union began to make favorable trade agreements with potential allies and satellites.

The Western bloc made an effort to consolidate the political military strength of its members. The North Atlantic Treaty Organization was born in April 1949 as a political and military alliance to head off the threat of the Soviet expansion. It was composed of twelve original members: Great Britain, France, Belgium,Netherlands, Luxemburg, Norway, Denmark. Also Ireland, Italy, Portugal, Canada and the United States were members. They agreed armed attack on any one country would constitute an attack on all. In August 1949 the Council of Europe was formed to establish a single parliament.

Economic Agreements   Other agreements, largely economic, were formed. The Benelux Customs Union, composed of Belgium, the Netherlands and Luxemburg, was signed in 1947 to control trade. The Brussels Pact was represented by Great Britain, France, Belgium, Luxemburg and the Netherlands. They agreed on a 5o year treaty to cooperate on economic, social, and cultural matters. The Schuman Plan, named after Robert Schuman, French minister of Foreign Affairs, proposed to put French and German coal and steel industries under international control.

Progress   In spite of numerous obstacles, progress was made in developing a Western bloc. At the end of the war Western Europe was wide open for invasion by Soviets. European production was at its lowest, military strength was weak. By 1955, fourteen nations had joined the Western Allies, for Turkey and Greece were added members of the original dozen. Militarily the west had become much stronger with forty-eight divisions ready.

The United States and Great Britain had atomic military advantages immediately after the end of World War II. The United States had developed the atomic bomb toward the end of the war and built up a stockpile of these weapons. The Russians, having brought over some of the German scientists in East Germany, made rapid advances in developing atomic arms. They set off both A-bombs and the hydrogen bomb.

On the propaganda front, both the United States and the Soviet Union made efforts to win "the minds of men". By means of printing presses, which produced newspapers and pamphlets, and by means of radio, the United States conducted a systematic propaganda campaign to reach those peoples

THE CHANGING FACE OF EAST EUROPE

U. S. S. R. and Soviet-dominated areas

A New York Times map

behind the Iron Curtain, which Soviet Union had thrown up.
This country spent millions of dollars on its "Voice of
America" program pointing to the advantages of democracy.
The Soviets retaliated, declaring America was capitalistic
and war-mongering.

German and Austrian Treaties Negotiated Nowhere was
the conflict more sharply seen than in the negotiations
over the German and Austrian peace treaties. The Soviets
at the Council of Foreign Ministers, which met in Paris,
in 1946, in Moscow in the Spring, of 1947 and in London in
the winter of 1947 would not give an inch. All efforts to
reach a compromise failed. At stake was Germany, which
had now been divided. Both sides realized the great economic and industrial potential of Germany, both saw her as
a block heading off military expansion of Soviet in Western Europe.

Seeking to have Germany regain her economic and industrial strength, the allies gave Western Germany a larger role in the European Recovery Program in 1948. The en-
raged Soviets replied with an economic blockade of Western
sections of Berlin in May, 1948. It was as though any U.S.
community was cut into two parts. How long could the resi-
dential zones survive? The United States was resourceful
and brought in supplies by means of an airlift. If the
Soviets had objected, this might have meant an open break.
They didn't want to risk a war. The Soviets lifted the
blockade after a year in May, 1949.

As the period of the occupation of Germany by U.S. troops
came to an end, preparations were made for the establishment of a democratic form of government. The German Federal Republic in Western Germany was formed in 1949, with
the University town of Bonn as its headquarters. American
military left. The Russians, not wanting to be left in a
bad position, countered with the establishment of the German Democratic Republic in East Germany, with Berlin as the
capital.

Schedule UN for Front Page
The United Nations Organization probably will be in
the news for some decades to come, because students of international relations and forward-looking governmental officials believe that some form of international organization
is neccessary for world peace. Wide awake newsman will
seek to understand the workings of this organization. They
will want to know its history, its great strengths and
shortcomings.

The United Nations is actually an outgrowth of the old
League of Nations. But the League had certain disadvantages which checked its successful growth. It was a part of
the peace treaties of World War I and thus it bore all the
hates associated with that conflict. The United States
senate because of internal political difficulties, rejected
President Woodrow Wilson's great dream of a world-wide cov-

Is New Charter Cure For Ailing UN?

By PETER EDSON
NEA Staff Correspondent

UNITED NATIONS—Revision of the United Nations charter adopted at San Francisco 10 years ago is possible in two ways:

Amendments to the charter may be approved at any time by a two-thirds majority vote in the General Assembly. This must be followed by ratification of the amendments by the governments of two-thirds of the members, including all the permanent members of the Security Council. These are the United States, United Kingdom, Nationalist China, France and Russia.

Any amendments now approved by the Soviet government could therefore never be adopted.

A general conference of UN members to review the Charter may be called at any time by a two-thirds majority vote in the General Assembly and any seven members of the 11-nation Security Council. A Russian negative vote cannot block this procedure.

The Argentine proposed a charter revision conference at both the second and third UN sessions in 1947 and 1948. It was defeated.

At the eighth UN session in 1953 there were three proposals for charter revision from the Argentine, Netherlands and Egypt.

A proposal to ask member countries for their views on charter revision lost 24 to 23. But a final resolution was adopted, calling for a compilation of unpublished San Francisco documents, a legislative history of the UN and all its specialized agencies.

This 10-year history of the UN was promised for 1954, but hasn't materialized yet. It is now scheduled for release in July, to prepare the UN members for consideration of charter revision.

The San Francisco charter provided that if no revision conference were called in the meantime, this subject shall be placed on the agenda for the tenth session of the General Assembly, which will meet in New York in September.

If charter revision is voted for, the conference might be held in 1956 or 1957 or even later. The past Russian view has been that no charter revision should be considered while there are world tensions.

Since the Russians could veto any amendments even if they were adopted by a revision conference, many UN experts op-

IN THEIR EARS, VISHINSKY: Secretary of State Dulles and Eleanor Roosevelt listen to an attack by Russia's late foreign minister at a 1947 UN session. The Red words were familiar.

SIGNING THE UN CHARTER: While President Truman watched, Secretary of State Edward Stettinius signed United Nations charter in flag-bedecked atmosphere of peace at San Francisco.

pose any attempt to change the charter now.

In spite of this negative view, U.S. Secretary of State John Foster Dulles has said that the Eisenhower administration will support the calling of a charter revision conference this fall.

Secretary Dulles has not announced any firm position which the U.S. delegation might take on charter amendments. But he has indicated some of the areas where changes might be considered:

1. Universality of membership. "Most of the United Nations," he says, "feel it is better to have even discordant members . . . than to attempt to confine the membership to those who hold the same views."

Soviet vetoes have denied membership to 15 countries, while seven Communist countries have been denied admission by majority vote.

Letting them all in would mean admitting Red China, which the United States has opposed.

The present charter provides for expulsion of non-co-operating members, but so far none has been expelled.

2. Security. "The greatest weakness of the UN," says Secretary Dulles, ". . . is the Security Council's inability to discharge its primary responsibility for the maintenance of international peace." A proposed remedy is to give more power to the General Assembly.

3. The Veto. Should the veto power be taken away from the Security Council on questions like admission of new members and questions involving the peaceful settlement of disputes?

"Presumably the United States itself would hesitate to go much further than this in now surrendering its veto power," says Dulles.

4. General Assembly voting: At the present time each country, large or small, has one vote. A suggested alternative is

"weighted voting" in which population, resources and contributions to the United Nations effort would determine the power of each vote.

5. Disarmament and Atomic Energy Control. The problems raised by nuclear weapons were not known when the UN charter was adopted at San Francisco 10 years ago. The possibility of a new UN agency to deal with control of world armaments and the applications of atomic energy, under President Eisenhower's plan, has been proposed.

A new disarmament role has been made all the more necessary since the United Nations has never been able to create the world police force to maintain peace, as envisaged at San Francisco.

6. International law. In the San Francisco charter, the General Assembly was called upon to develop and codify international law. It has made no progress, largely because the Communist countries do not recognize the application of moral law to human affairs.

What could be done about this by UN charter revision is a little difficult to see.

But if charter revision is not the answer for whatever is wrong with the United Nations, some of the alternatives sometimes suggested seem to offer little more hope. In fact, most of the alternative suggestions have been rejected by the U.S. government.

One group of extremists believes the United Nations is not strong enough. They propose

calling a conference to establish an Atlantic Union or a World Federation as a super-government.

At the other extreme are those who think that Soviet Russia and its satellites should be kicked out of the United Nations. Or that the United States should voluntarily get out.

But for either the United States or the Soviet Union to get out of the United Nations would, probably mean its end.

"With all its faults," says Secretary of State Dulles, "the United Nations as it is is better than no United Nations at all."

Tomorrow: The UN box score.

enant of Nations. He failed to consult with Republican
Senators. Led by Senator Henry Cabot Lodge, the Senate
turned its back on the first world league. This country
perhaps was not ready for the acceptance of its responsi-
bilities as a global power and wanted to forget the recent
horrors of international conflict. Since the United States
refused to join, the League was weakened. Its council met
three times a year; its assembly convened once a year. The
League could only recommend military action against an aggressor power. The League, which went into effect January
10, 1920, had some record of accomplishments. But it was
not able to stop Japanese and German aggressions in the
1930's, which led to World War II.

The great Western powers, during World War II, as indicated, saw and expressed the need for an international
organization which would keep the peace and settle disputes
between nations amicably. At a series of meetings held by
representatives of the Western nations, this desire resol-
ved into a definite organization.

Atlantic Charter Somewhere in the Atlantic Ocean Prime
Minister Winston Churchill and President Franklin D. Roosevelt met on a British battleship in August, 1941. Although
the United States had not declared war, it had ceased being
a neutral country. The Atlantic Charter contained the
peace aims of the Democratic countries. It amplified the
Four Freedoms passage in President Roosevelt's message to
congress in January, 1941. He declared we look forward to
a world founded on four essential freedoms...freedom of
speech and expression...freedom of every person to worship
God in his own way...freedom from want...freedom from fear.

Moscow Conference The Moscow conference in October,
1943 has been referred to in connection with the peace
terms. At the meeting the United States, Great Britain,
Russia and China agreed upon the fundamental principles of
an international orgainization.

Dumbarton Oaks Proposals The Dumbarton Oaks Confer-
ence held near Washington, D.C. between August 21 and Octo-
ber 7, 1944 offered several proposals for a world-wide or-
ganization. It was modeled, to some extent, on the old
League of Nations. It recommended a General Assembly, a
Security Council, an International Court of Justice, a
Secretariat. It also suggested an Economic and Social
Council and a Military Staff Committee.

Unlike the League of Nations, the Security Council
with the advice of the Military Staff Committee. was to
have at its disposal an international army to police the
world. Soviet Russia insisted that the Security Council
should have one vote. A minimum vote of seven of the
total of eleven votes would be necessary for procedural
matters. A similar vote was necessary in the settling of
international disputes, provided there was agreement between the United States, Russia, Great Britain, France and

China. The parties to the dispute, however, would be required to refrain from voting.

Yalta Conference   At this conference, the three great powers, Great Britain, Russia and the United States developed further the idea of establishing an international peace organization.

San Francisco Conference   At the invitation of President Roosevelt delegates from fifty nations on April 25, 1945 convened at San Francisco to make concrete the proposals of the Dumbarton Oaks conference and the Yalta Conference. The American delegation consisted of Democrats and Republicans. President Roosevelt wished to avoid the trouble encountered over the League. Unfortunately, President Roosevelt died on April 12. President Harry S. Truman opened the conference with a moving address. On historic June 26, 1945 the San Francisco Conference adopted the United Nations Charter, whose purpose was to insure international peace. It was a compromise between big nations and little nations. But it was the second general world parliament. The original 52 participating in the conference became members. Others were admitted later, but some were refused.

The all-powerful Security Council consisted of eleven members, of which five held permanent membership. They were Great Britain, France, the United States, the Soviet Union and China. Seven of the eleven were required for an affirmative vote, but all five of the permanent members had to agree. The great powers thus had the right of veto, a stipulation which caused great difficulty later, as the Soviets exercised this right repeatedly to block actions. On important questions the General Assembly which may discuss many matters, required a two-thirds majority of countries present. On other questions a simple majority was adequate. The Security Council, which was concerned with peace and security, was authorized specifically to employ land, sea and air forces supplied by the members to suppress aggressors. A trusteeship system was set up to supervise backward countries.

The United Nations Economic and Social Council (UNESCO) was designed to promote general welfare. The International Court of Justice was set up to settle disputes. Later the United Nations Atomic Energy Commission was established.

Some Strengths and Weaknesses   The U.N., which has permanent headquarters in New York City, represents an advancement over the League of Nations. It had a better start because the United States, which had become a global power, did not reject it, but played a significant role in its formation. It received the support of both the Democratic and Republican parties. Another advantage was the fact that the desires of the smaller nations were considered in planning the organization. Article 43, providing for a united military force, was an advancement, for it could

mean a stop to any aggressive action. The great weakness
was the power of veto which the Soviets exercised to prevent significant issues from arising and being discussed,
and to prevent quick settlement of disputes.

Editorial Research Reports furnished its clients with
a factual background story on the fifth birthday of the UN,
bringing together scattered facts about the organization:

UN Shows Strength as It Reaches Age of Five Years
EDITORIAL RESEARCH REPORT

The United Nations-which President Truman has
characterized as emerging from the Korean struggle
"stronger than it has ever been"-will be five
years old tomorrow. On that day in 1945, Russia,
last of the Big Five to do so, deposited her instrument of ratification of the U.N. Charter with
Secretary of State Byrnes in Washington. Russia,
Byelo-Russia, the Ukraine, and Poland all gave
notification on the same date. Thus the necessary ratifications of all five big powers and a
majority of the smaller powers - 29 out of 51 - had
been obtained.
     In the five years of its existence, the UN has
increased its membership by 18 per cent, from 51
to 60 nations. The League of Nations, which had
42 original members, grew in its first five years
to 53 members - or 26 per cent. One member Costa
Rica, had already given notice of intent to withdraw from the League.
     In five years the U.N. secretariat has grown
from about 2oo persons to 4117. The U.N. budget
for the first year was $21.5 million. The U.N.
budget for this year is $41.6 million; the esti-
mate for 1951 is $45.5 million.
     In its first year, the League spent $3,346,000.
In its fifth year, the League spent $4,371,963 -
slightly more than a tenth of the U.N. budget for
this year. The League had a secretariat of 411
in 1924, when it was four years old; 667 in 1927.
     The U.N.'s chief divisions are the General
Assembly, Security Council, Economic and Social
Council, Trusteeship Council, International Court
of Justice, Secretariat. Principal committees of
the Assembly are the General (steering); Political
and Security; Economic and Financial; Social,
Humanitarian, and Cultural; Trusteeship; Administrative and Budgetary; Legal.
     The Security Council's pendant bodies - all
stagnated by the East-West stalemate - are the
Military Staff Committee, Atomic Energy Commission, Commission for Conventional Armaments. Much
of the U.N.'s most constructive work has been
accomplished by such specialized agencies as
FAO, UNESCO, WHO, ILO, IRO, the International
Bank.

Although often criticized as ineffective, the
U.N. Assembly or Security Council has played a
formal or an informal role in settling the Soviet
-Iranian dispute, the Indonesia and Palestine
problems, the Greek-Albanian border troubles, the
Berlin blockade. Little has been accomplished towards
control of atomic energy, reduction of armaments,
establishment of an international police force,
agreement on World War II peace treaties. The
International Court's one judgement settled the
Corfu channel dispute between Albania and the
United Kingdom.

The U. N. has contributed two martyrs to the
cause of international peace. Count Folke Berna-
dotte of Sweden, U.N. arbitrator for Palestine,
and his French aide, Colonel Serot, were shot
in Jerusalem on September 17, 1948.

Since ratifying the U.N. Charter on September
8, 1945, the U. S. has reaffirmed adherence time
and again, despite the programs for economic and
arms aid to European and Asian nations negotiated
outside U.N. channels. Jacksonville, Florida
                                  Times-Union

In the following article the astute Edgar Ansel Mowrer
correlated the incidents which show the weaknesses and the
strenths of the UN by means of specific incidents. Each
of these incidents was published in the daily press at the
time it occurred, but this article sought to draw them altogether and to indicate their significance. It is a combination of factual background and editorial comment.

History of UN Can Decide Its Future
By EDGAR ANSEL MOWRER

What is happening to the United Nations?
I mean, is it developing slowly but steadily into an effective instrument of international law - or is it remaining just a political
or diplomatic instrument of those States which
are able to utilize it?

A look at its history should decide this.
In 1945, when it was created at San Francisco,
its makers obviously accepted the fact that
although its form was that of a political instrument (hence the introduction of the great power
veto in the Security Council and the inability
of the Assembly to do more than "recommend"
solutions), its purpose was to develop gradually into a law-making body.

Unhappily, owing to the unforeseen emergence
of the USSR's undeclared war on the non-Communist world, the UN developed quite differently.
The legal element was swamped by the political

element, that is, by diplomatic expediency.
When its members wanted to, they acted as though
the Charter were law. More often than not, they
preferred not to act.

The UN Security Council notoriously refused
to act in certain cases where, according to the
Charter, it seemed obligated to act. It failed
to enforce its own decision in the case of Palestine - and disgusted the Arabs. It then failed
to prevent open Arab aggression against Israel -
and disgusted the Jews and those who thought that
the Jews were in Palestine by right.

It failed to act in the case of alleged Pakistan aggression into disputed Kashmir - and disgusted the Indians.

As a result of this inaction, by June 24, 1950,
the world organization had almost ceased to count.
It looked almost as dead as the first League of
Nations. In Europe, where experience of the unhappy League had left behind much cynicism, people
had practically forgotten the UN. Even in the
United States, where the new institution had been
more effectively "sold" to the people its standing had slumped terrifically.

Then suddenly the U.S. decision to act in the
name of the UN against North Korean aggression
put new life into that organization. For the
first time in modern history, a very great power
was ready to fight in the name of world law and
order. UN prestige soared to the skies. The
1950 Assembly was as gay as the 1949 Assembly
had been dismal. Moreover, in recognition of the
fact that but for the absence of the veto-wielding
Soviet delegate from the UN Security Council meetings of June 26 and 28, that body could not have
acted legally, a majority of the Assembly adopted
(November 3) three related resolutions proposed
by the American delegation. These resolutions
practically remade the Assembly into a second
security body to act in cases where the Security
Council for any reason was unable or unwilling
to act.

This was indeed a big step toward creating an
institution of law.

Yet hardly had this step been taken when the
UN was faced with two new tests of its real nature. One of these is the request by Salvador and
by India to consider the question of Chinese
Communist aggression against(almost) independent
Tibet. The other is the demand by the Chinese
Nationalists that the UN examine the aggressive
role of the Soviet Union in creating and utiliz-
ing the Communist regime in China for aggressive
purposes.

Both these requests are legitimate. If the United States is willing to allow the Chinese Commun-

ists to come to this country to accuse us of
"aggression" in Formosa, it ought to insist that
the blatant imperialism of Communist China and
Communist Russia be looked into. So ought all
the other members of the UN, with the possible
exception of those accused.

This is, unfortunately, not the case. The
United States is publicly willing but privately
very dubious about accusing the Russians of aggressive purposes in China. It is opposed to looking
into the case of unfortunate Tibet. The reason
is simple. The United States considers the world
situation so grave that it wishes to extricate
our troops from Asia, not to involve them more
deeply.

The European nations also want U.S. forces to
remain free to be deployed, if necessary, in
Europe. They do not think that Communist expansion in Asia is dangerous enough over which to
risk a world war.

Non-Communist Asia is frankly frightened. It
fears (justifiably) that in case of major war,
it would be occupied by Communist hordes.

In consequence, all three elements are in
favor of placating, rather than of exasperating,
the Chinese Communists.

All three are reluctant to undertake further
action against them even if failure to do so
looks like appeasement.

Politically, this attitude is understandable.
But if it is taken, what happens to the UN Charter
and the legal character of the world organization?

That body, under that charter, was created to
stop aggression. Not just selective aggression,
all aggression. Not just when politically expedient, but every time. A sheriff who acts only
when he finds it convenient or expedient or without too great risk, is no true sheriff at all.
Law that is enforced only sometimes cease to be law.

At Lake Success, this week, the law-abiding
States face a dilemma: act under the Charter and
risk serious political consequences; fail to act,
and reduce what little legal character the UN Charter possesses.   Syndicated to Jacksonville Florida
                 Times-Union and other papers

Sources: Direct source of facts about the history and
operation and accomplishments of the UN may be obtained
from the United Nations, New York City. In addition to a
number of pamphlets and books on the UN, the information
bureau issues a magazine United Nations Reporter, which
presents interestingly current news developments. It also
publishes the U.N. Bulletin. The Courier, produced by the
United Nations Educational, Scientific and Cultural Organization (UNESCO), deals with the special problems of that
group.

The United Nations World is published by an independent company in New York and presents special background features on various issues which the U.N. faces. The editors concentrate on one big problem or one country connected with the organization. Readable sketches of various delegates and delegations brighten the publication's appeal.

COUNTRIES IN WESTERN BLOC

United States as a World Power

While much of the world had been economically crippled by the World War II, the United States attained greater prosperity than ever. Fears that demobilization would wreck the economy proved groundless. Industrially and commercially the United States leaped ahead. The economic system doubled its industrial output. Savings were quadrupled in five years after Hiroshima. Price controls, however, were withdrawn and the cost of living rose rapidly. The American people, for the most part, recognized that the United States was a global power and could not withdraw. Help was promised and given to the nations of the world. Following the death of President Roosevelt in 1945, Harry S. Truman, vice-president,completed the term and was elected in 1948. Dwight D. Eisenhower succeeded him in 1952, bringing back the Republican party to power for the first time in 20 years.

Great Britain

With 1,000,000 war casualties, with half of her foreign trade gone, with cities in ruin, England came out of the war broken. Her economy was shattered. England's overseas market was being captured by other nations. Her machinery for industrial production was old-fashioned. She depended on imports to sustain her economy, but now could not pay for them.

The British people voted the Socialist Labour Party in power in 1945. The Labour Party proceeded to nationalize the major industries. It embarked on a Welfare State and extended the nation's social services where needed. England was helped by the United States in this time of need for loans were given. Although the Conservatives won after six years of Labour rule, most of the Welfare services were continued. After Winston Churchill retired, Sir Anthony Eden, foreign secretary, became Prime Minister and head of the Conservative Party.

As a part of the world-wide movement toward liberation of colonials and allowing them to develop their own independent government, Great Britain slowly withdrew from her formerly-held overseas possessions in all parts of the world. Britain withdrew in 1948 from Israel, which she had controlled as a mandatory power under the League of Nations. She gave up some of her privileges in Egypt. Although granted independence, Burma chose to remain in British dominion. Great Britain made a significant move

when she withdrew from India, which she had ruled for so
many years. Two dominions, the Union of India and Pakistan were established. Mahatma Ghandi, who fought by means
of passive resistance the British rule, became head, but
upon his assassination in 1948, - Nehru became the Hindu
leader. The Irish people broke their last ties, ending
a long period of conflict.

French Republic Split
During the World War II Marshal Petain, the military
hero of World War I, and Pierre Laval collaborated with
the German invaders for four years. At the end of the
fight, the French people rejected the Vichy collaborators,
who ruled between 1940 and 1944. Petain was imprisoned.
Laval was executed. After the war, the French elected
Gen. Charles de Gaulle, but believing he might be a dic-
tator, or at least another Napoleon, the voters permitted
him only a year's rule. In September, 1946 they established the Fourth French Republic. The French government had
been characterized by a multiple party system, with no one
faction being able to win a majority of the votes. The
government operated effectively only when a successful
coalition of various parties was obtained. French governments did not last long. While in the United States the
successful party stays in for a four-year term, in France
unless the party in power gets a vote of confidence, it
goes out. From January, 1945 to July, 1954 France had 19
governments. The longest one lasted 13 months. Communists controlled a large bloc of votes. They represented
an economic protest, not the Kremlin line.

France was also beset by a multitude of economic woes.
It suffered a loss of foreign trade and inflation. Taxes
were paid by the industrial workers and consumers. French
industrial productivity was much lower than in the United
States. The country was upset by the uprising in Algiers,
where the nationalists wanted independence.

Germany, Defeated, Rises Again
The Germans paid a heavy price for Hitler. More than
10,000,000 men were killed; many were still missing.
7,000,000 were homeless. Cities were in shambles. Population was demoralized. Then in accord with the allied
agreements, 22 war criminals were tried at Nuremburg in
1945-46. Of these a dozen were sentenced to death, seven
went to prison and three were acquitted.

Under the Pottsdam agreement, Germany was divided into
four zones of control. Greater Berlin, as indicated, was
split, forming a fifth zone. Dr. Theodore Heuss was elected first president of the Federal Republic of Germany.
The new government embraced half the area of pre-war Germany, but contained three-quarters of the population. In
1951 Germany was invited to create a military force and
unite with the armies of the West. In May, 1952 she was
integrated with the North Atlantic Alliance. She signed a
peace pact with the Western powers which included her as

Germany in the Middle If War Comes

By JOHN L. SPRINGER

NEW YORK, Feb. 11—It used to be said that Germans would be much less war-minded if they ever had to fight on their own soil.

In World War I, they carried the fight into the lowlands and France; the war ended before Germany felt the tramp of Allied boots. In World War II, while they also took the initiative, their industries were blasted by Allied bombers, and in the closing months invading troops poured over the Reich from all directions.

Germans today probably are less war-minded than they have ever been. This indicates that the old axiom may be true. If so, after World War III—is one comes—the Germans probably will be the most pacifist nation on earth.

If war comes, Germany is in for it. She is in the middle. There is no escape. She will be devastated by retreating troops, rubble-ized by the artillery of advancing ones. She will know aerial war on a scale that pales all precedents.

Ever since they threw up their hands in 1945, Germans have dreaded a new call to arms. Some think a powerful Germany could be erected over the ashes of Communist Russia, but most shudder at the prospect of another war that would inevitably make Germany its battleground.

Control of Germany is, of course, necessary for control of Europe. To strike at Western Europe the Russians would have to drive across Germany's approaches to the Lowlands and France. To strike back at the Russians, a Western democratic force would have to sweep across Germany into Poland. Ironically, in either case the former allies would follow invasion paths set up by their former joint enemy, Hitler.

It was Hitler, seeking to carry war outside German soil, who made war inside Germany so attractive to mechanized forces. Hitler built broad auto highways throughout the Reich to facilitate troop movements. Germany's swift collapse in 1945 was due, in part, to the ease with which invading troops

could move over those roads.

If war comes, Germany will get it from the air no less than from the ground. Germany was Europe's No. 1 industrial nation before the war, and many of her top industries have been rebuilt. It is certain that the Russians will bomb them to render them useless to the Allies. Or the Allies will bomb them to keep them from the Reds.

Their possible future—as unlimited victims of World War III—is not very bright for the people who thought 10 years ago that they would rule the world for 1,000 years.

TIMELY FEATURE   The above background news-feature on Germany, caught between the millstones of the East and West, was very timely. John Springer told about some of the background of the German problem and the issues the people of that nation faced.

an equal power.

The United States and the Western bloc wanted Germany
to succeed in her recovery program and helped her. The
industrial know-how, mechanical ability and organizational
genius Germany exhibited before the war manifested themselves again. The factories began to hum again. German-
made goods flowed to all parts of the globe. The automobile industry was a good example of the success of the industrial recovery. The autoworkers had been scattered,
the factories dismantled or gutted in the war. But the
auto manufacturers in the post-war period began to build
cars again and they were shipped to many foreign countries.
Assembly plants were even exported to South America to
produce cars for Brazil and the Argentine. The Volkswagen
became internationally known as a cheap, dependable family
auto.

In the Eastern sector, the People's Republic was set
up, and controlled by the Soviets. It contained 27 per
cent of the Germany's population and 31 per cent of its
area. Non-communists parties were allowed a token existence, but could not oppose the dominant Communist organization. A People's Police was set up. Thousands of German residents sought to cross over into the Western section.

Pro-Fascist Italy
Political chaos prevailed in post-war Italy. Its
economy was shattered. Italy lost its empire and source
of income in Africa. In 1946 Italy voted to abolish mon-
archy and set up a Republic. Communists were gaining a
stronger foothold. The Marshall plan helped Italy, and
efforts were made to speed the industrial and commercial
recovery.

Soviet Union Expands
Although not generally known, the Soviet Union suffer-
ed greater casualties than all other nations combined in
World War II. More than 12,000,000 Russians died. The
Soviet Union also lost $100,000,000,000 in property damage.
In order to strengthen her industry and agriculture, Soviet
Russia continued her 5-year plans. Old plans were mechan-
ized, new ones were built.

The Communist Party continued to control the lives and
minds of the Russians. Concessions were made in the
church and in family life, with large families being encouraged. Education, art, literature, music, science were
all integrated into the work of the Soviet Union.

In foreign policy, the Soviet leaders, as indicated,
changed their tactics. They dropped the outward friendly
sentiment to their former allies. They objected to the
capitalist system everywhere. They charged the allies
with stirring up war and hate, and with the exploitation
of backward peoples. They saw the nations of the world,
after the war, were crippled and that it was a superb

opportunity to establish communism.

Since 1939 the Soviets brought under domination nine
previously independent European nations. Also they made
satellites of parts of Germany and Austria. The Soviets
occupied and incorporated into their orbit: Poland, with
its 70,000 miles, Latvia, Lithuania, Estonia, parts of Finland. It added 1,000,000 population in the Baltics. Other
additions included Subcarpathian, Ruthenia, Moldana, Bess-
araoia, East Prussia and the Kurile Island and Southern
half of Sahalin. The latter were given by the Yalta agreements.

Soviet agents penetrated into Czechoslovakia, Albania,
Hungary, Rumania and Bulgaria, placing them under the Kremlin influence. In Asia, the Chineese Communists became
Red allies. Attempts to expand into Iran, Turkey and Greece
and Korea were blocked.

By mid-century Soviet Russia had become a hub of a
gigantic communist wheel. It embraced more than one-third
the population of the Earth. About one-fifth of the land
of the world came under the Kremlin's domination.

Russia also built up a formidable military power. It
acquired 175 divisions, 40,000 tanks, 20,000 planes, 300
submarines and atomic weapons.

Death of Stalin   The man who helped shape the policies of Yalta and who was responsible for spreading the
doctrine of communism in all parts of the world, died on
March 6, 1953. Joseph Stalin, called a combination of
Ivan the Terrible and Adolph Hitler, had ruled for 29
years. He stayed in power by various ruthless means, en-
slaving millions and tricking opponents. Although it
changed its mind later, the Communist Party portrayed him
as a great leader and Soviet hero. A vicious struggle over
the successor to Stalin developed, but Georgi Maximilian-
ovich Malenkov was appointed chairman of the Council of
Ministers. His powerful opponent, L.B. Beria was executed.

ASIA IN CONFLICT

With the ending of World War II, the teeming populations of Asia sought independence. Although beset by a
multitude of economic, political and health problems, they
wanted to govern themselves. Asia was vastly overpopulat-
ed. More than 1,200,000,000 persons sought to live in this
area, as contrasted with Europe's 393 million and North
America's 213 million. Asia's peoples faced famine often,
poverty regularly. Primitive sanitary conditions militated
against good health. The tools they used for agriculture
were thousands of years old. Although the European nations
had brought many achievements, the Asians considered many
of the business men as exploiters, indifferent to the needs
of the natives. Now the period of the great Western empires
in Asia came to an end.

War's Impact on People-- Winner of the Pulitzer
Price in news photography in 1951, this picture
shows the Korean refugees crawling perilously
over girders of Taedong River bridge at Pyongyang
in December, 1950. The photo was taken by Max
Desfor of the Associated Press.

Associated Press Photo

In accord with the agreements worked out, India, Burma, Cambodia, Vietnam, Pakistan, Laos, Ceylon, Indonesia became states. The United States gave the Philippines their freedom in July, 1946.

Chinese Go Communist   China, which had been an ally of the Western powers in World War II, went Communist after the war and drifted into the Red orbit. The Chinese communists supplied by arms from the Kremlin, in 1949 overthrew the regime of Chiang Kai-shek and established the People's Republic. Peiping became the Capital. Chiang withdrew to the island of Formosa. Although he claimed to speak for the people of China, he had only a small army to back him. When the Chinese sought to invade Formosa, the United States saw this as another Soviet imperialistic gesture and raised a protest. China was not recognized as an independent nation by the United States, which feared it would tip the balance of power in the United Nations in favor of the Soviet Union. This became a point of contention between England and the United States.

Korean War   China was not content to remain within its borders. Its aggressive action produced open fighting which many thought might be the beginning of a third World War. In June 1950 the People's Democratic Republic of Korea, organized by the Communists, in the northern section of Korea, moved South, invading the territory of the Republic of Korea, of which Dr. Syngman Rhee was President. The United Nations Security Council, at an emergency meeting, considered this a breach of the world peace. Meanwhile, the United States went into action. President Harry S. Truman ordered General Douglas MacArthur to defend the South Koreans. MacArthur was named commander of all U.N. forces. The North Koreans, aided by the Chinese Communists overwhelmed the South Koreans. The United States troops were aided by armies supplied by other nations who were UN members. An allied counter-offensive began. The fighting wavered back and forth chiefly around the 38th parallel. The General Assembly of the U.N. voted Communist China the aggressor in Korea, in February, 1951 by a 44 to 7 vote, with 9 abstentions.

Continued reports of Communist buildup and airfield construction caused fears in Washington and London of an expanded war. President Truman on April 11, 1951 relieved General MacArthur of commands in the Far East. President Truman and the Joint Chiefs of Staff were convinced that General MacArthur would not stop making public statements critical of military and foreign policies in the Far East. They concluded he had disregarded instructions to clear all statements with Washington. They feared he might precipitate a third World War. The general had frequently criticized the handicaps placed on his troops by orders to limit the war to Korea, stop airplanes from pursuing hostile aircraft and prevent bombardment of the enemy's base over the Manchurian border. He thought Chiang troops in Formosa should be used, and this opinion was made public.

General MacArthur returned to the United States and

became a storm center of great controversy. The U.S. Senate held an investigation in May, 1952 which was reported widely. A majority voted President Truman had been right.

Lt. Gen. Matthew B. Ridgeway replaced MacArthur in Korea. A report was published in November, 1951 which indicated that the Chinese had killed 2,513 prisoners during the previous year. 7,000 South Korean troops and 250,000 civilians were killed, the report declared. Re-enforced with Russian-built planes, the Communists were able to challenge Allied air superiority. Large numbers of Chinese planes appeared in the air. Prolonged peace negotiations were finally completed by the end of 1952. The repatriation of prisoners was one of the chief issues before the United Nations, with Chou En-Lai, foreign minister of Communist China, backing Soviet Russia. Korea was a symbol that the United States and the U.N. would not permit Communist aggression to go unchallenged.

Indo-China
Southeastern Asia proved to be another region where the conflict between the Western allies and the Communists broke into open gunfire. Because of its strategic economic resources, Indo-China was important. It produced 26 per cent of the rice of the world; much rubber. From its mines came 62 per cent of the world's tin, 4 percent of its bauxite to make aluminum. If Indo-China fell all Asia might fall into communist orbit. Siam, Burma, Malaya Peninsula and Indonesia were at stake. A nationalist movement began in Indo-China in 1941, gaining impetus during World War II. France recognized the Vietnam Republic in March, 1946, as a free state within the Indo-Chinese Federation and French Union. Following Communist-inspired guerilla attacks, France withdrew its support of the regime. It recognized a new anti-Communist Provisional government of Vietnam, as a member of the state of the French Union. In March, 1949 Bao Dai was made chief of state of the independent Vietnam. The Communists supported Vietnam forces, seeking to gain control.

When the Korea fighting was over, the Communists had arms which they brought to the Indo-China fight. The colonial war now became a struggle between Communism and the Free world. The United States regarded this event as another step in Communist aggression and called on Great Britain, France, Australia and New Zealand to help. At Dienbienphu in May, 1954 the French forces were given a setback. It was a great defeat for France, and the Western powers saw the danger.

Geneva Conference
Representatives of Britain, France and the United States sat down with the Soviet Russia and Communist China to negotiate on Korea and Indo-China in 1954. The Western Powers were not united on a plan. But the Soviets called for the evacuation of troops from Korea and Indo-China. The Western powers were divided, and the Communists saw this and were

FEBRUARY 11, 1956   **20 Cents**

Editor & Publisher
THE FOURTH ESTATE

The Chicago Daily News digs for the significant when it reports foreign news. Its service is syndicated to many newspapers. The above is an advertisement which appeared on the front page of the trade magazine, Editor & Publisher.

unwilling to compromise. Finally an armistice agreement
brought the fighting to a close. Vietnam was divided into
two parts, equal in population. Vietnam Communists were
given the territory North of the 17th parallel, and the
French-sponsored government of Laos and Cambodia remained
in non-communist hands.

Middle-East Seeths
The age-old conflict between the Jews and the Arabs
continued, with Soviet Russia seeking to use the troubles
as a weapon against the Western bloc.

The extablishment of the Republic of Israel was the
culmination of sustained efforts by the Zionists to build
a homeland for the Jews. Palestine had been a protectorate
of England since World War I. The Zionist movement for a
homeland was led by Dr. Chaim Weitzmann, who was able to
persuade the British Cabinet to support the Balfour Declaration, which promised the dispersed Jews a homeland, in
1917. The open opposition of the Arab world led to indecision in Great Britain. When the Nazis persecuted the Jews
in Germany, many set out for Palestine. After World War II
an attempt was made to close the frontiers, pending settlement of the territorial disputes between the Jews and the
Arabs.

Then the General Assembly of the U.N. voted in November, 1947 to partition Palestine into two independent
states by October, 1948. The Arab state would have 4,500
sq. miles. A separate section, Jerusalem, was to be administered by a British governor appointed by the U.N. British troops were to be withdrawn and separate governments
elected. Attacks on the British officers resulted. Great
Britain gave up its mandate and withdrew its forces May,
1948.

The New Zionist state, the Republic of Israel, was
proclaimed the same month. It occupied the territory designated by the U.N. but also laid claim to Jerusalem. It
took charge of the New City in Jerusalem. Jordan held the
Old City. The U.N. wanted to internationalize the city
Jerusalem, but both states rejected this. Dr. Chaim Weitz-
man was elected president and David Ben-Gurion was chosen
premier of the Republic of Israel by a coalition of four
parties. Israel was elected a member of the U.N. in May,
1949. It planned new schools, industrial support and irri-
gation for the farmers. In 1950 it received 47,000 refugees from Eastern Europe. Israel applied for Point-4 aid,
and floated a $500,000,000 bond issue.

From the start Israel met with opposition from the
Arab League, which established headquarters in Damascus to
enforce an economic boycott. Armed interference or attacks
were also begun by Syria, Egypt, Iraq, Lebanon, Saudi-Arabia,
Jordon. Israel retaliated and there were bombings on both
sides. In May, 1951, further hostilities broke out when
Israel began draining the Huleh swamps and presumably en-
croached on Arab villages.

THE MIDDLE EAST—FOUR CONFLICTS THAT BUILD UP TENSION

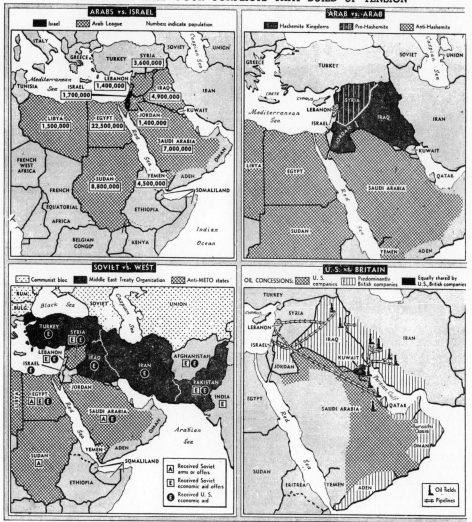

Nations of Mideast are aligned differently on each of the conflicts illustrated by the maps. The intra-Arab dispute is based on enmity to the Hashemite family, rulers of Iraq and Jordan, on the part of other Arab states—and is intensified by rival ambitions of Egypt and Iraq. Commercial rivalry between British and U. S. oil companies is now focused on control of Buraimi Oasis, which is key to access to new oil fields.

THE NEW YORK TIMES,

Gradually the Israelites pushed the Arabs back. In 1949 Egypt and later Jordan, Lebanon and Syria signed UN - sponsored armistices. But the armistices did not bring lasting peace. The Arabs set up diplomatic and economic boycotts against Israel. In the following year the United States, Britain and France issued a declaration that they would keep military balance by limiting arms shipments to both Arabs and Israel and would "take action" to prevent frontier violations.

The U.N. Security Council entered the complex situation, by calling on Egypt to lift its anti-Israel blockage at the Suez canal. Its efforts were rejected, and Arab circles became increasingly resentful of the Western power support of Israel.

Over Syrian protests, the Security Council voted to permit Israel to build a power project on the Jordan River. Russia vetoed the resolution. This was Moscow's first open bid for Arab friendship and the first of a series of vetoes on the Arabs behalf.

In 1954 Lieutenant Col. Gamal Abdel Nasser became premier of Egypt. Then when Britain agreed to quit the Suez Canal zone, it was believed this would induce Egypt to join a mideast defense system. Instead Egypt convened a meeting of the Arab League to block the projected Mideast defense organization. Nasser announced Egypt would obtain heavy arms from the Communist bloc. The Egyptian-Communist block shocked the East and alarmed Israel. Isreal could not obtain heavy arms to match the Communist shipments to Egypt. Now Britain, Iraq, Iran, Turkey and Pakistan formally organized the Middle East Treaty Organization as a deterrent to Soviet expansion. To counterbalance this alliance Premier Nasser organized the anti-Israel bloc of Egypt, Syria and Saudi Arabia.

One of the perplexing problems was the Arab refugee. These were the men, women and children who fled from their homes in Palestine during the war of 1948 and immediately thereafter. They totaled more than 900,000, squatting in various degrees of poverty. The United Nations contributed nearly $27,000,000 to help them in 1956. They lived in camps and packed the disputed Gaza strip. Palestine did not want them because they were all indignant and possibly hostile, nor did the various Arab countries want them because the refugees would have to be supported. The situation became so critical and explosive that U.N. Secretary General Dag Hammarskjold left on a peace mission to try to get both sides to settle the problem in the Spring of 1956.

3. Examples of Backgrounding

Following are some examples of background news-features which give meaning to the world news.

Korean War
In June, 1950, the North Koreans sent their armies into South Korea, and headlines across the United States

THE ARAB THREAT — AS SEEN FROM ISRAEL

To the North Danger from Syria's 45,000 men and Lebanon's 8,000 is increased by Communist arms offer and joint Syrian-Egyptian command.

TURKEY
CYPRUS SYRIA
Med. Sea LEB.
ISRAEL IRAQ
JORDAN
SUEZ
CANAL
EGYPT SAUDI ARABIA
0 Miles 300

LEBANON

Kefar Shemar
Acre Safad
Haifa Sea of Galilee
SYRIA
Nazareth
Givat Oz Afula
Beit Shean

Hadera
Mafraq

Taiyiba Tulkarm
Nablus
TEL AVIV
Jaffa
Ramle Lydda

To the East Jordan's Arab Legion, 25,000 strong, well trained and freed from Britain's restraining influence, would be a threat in any concerted Arab attack.

ISRAEL

Mevo Beitar
Yad Mordekhai Beit Guvrin JERUSALEM
Gaza Mefalsim Hebron
Khan Yunis Tsiqlag Dead Sea
Kisufim
Nir Yitshaq Beersheba

Mediterranean
Sea

El Auja
(Nitsana) Hatseva
Sedom

N E G E V JORDAN

EGYPT

To the South Egypt's armed forces, at 75,000 strong, are rapidly being built into an efficient military machine equipped with modern Communist weapons and jet planes.

Beer Menuha

Yotvata

▲ Fortified villages
■ Arab refugee camps
══ Roads +++ Railroads
0 Miles 40

Elath
Aqaba

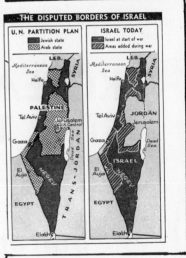

THE DISPUTED BORDERS OF ISRAEL

U.N. PARTITION PLAN
■ Jewish state
▨ Arab state

Mediterranean Sea LEB.
Haifa
PALESTINE
SYRIA
Tel Aviv
Jerusalem
U.N. Control
Gaza
TRANS-JORDAN
El Auja
N E G E V
EGYPT
Elath

ISRAEL TODAY
■ Israel at start of war
▨ Areas added during war

Mediterranean Sea LEB.
Haifa
SYRIA
Tel Aviv
JORDAN
Jerusalem
Gaza Dead Sea
ISRAEL
El Auja
N E G E V
EGYPT
Elath

blared this fact. The residents North of the 38th parallel were called "The Democratic People's Republic of Korea", and the dispatches which were sent out said this government was backed by Russia. The Republic of Korea, to the South of that line, had been promised help by the United States after World War II. Soon American soldiers were in the midst of the war. Headlines and news on page one told the facts about troop movements and the battles, as indicated below.

But most of the American newspaper readers and radio listeners were baffled by the whole situation. How did we come to be involved in the Korean problem? What was the history of our association with this little republic? Why should the United States take sides? James Marlow, a news-feature writer for the Associated Press, was one of those who sought to explain in his regular column how the United States became involved in the Korean issue. This story came over the teletype to newspaper members of the AP.

KOREAN TANKS STAB TO SEOUL

Surrender Demand Broadcast as Reds Reach Outskirts

Prospects of Total Defeat Loom For South Through Bad Morale; American Help Now En Route

Seoul, Korea, (Tuesday) (AP) - Invading north Korean Communists stabbed a tank column to the outskirts of this Southern republic's capital early today and broadcast a demand for southern surrender.

How US Got Mixed Up in Korea

By James Marlow

WASHINGTON, (AP) - How did we come to get mixed up in Korea in the first place? This will explain.

Korea, with its 85,000 square miles, is about the size of Utah. It juts out from the northeast coast of Asia, almost touching Japan.

Korea now is divided into two Koreas: North and South. The dividing line, very important in this story, is the 38th parallel of latitude.

North of the line, where the population is about 10,000,000 Koreans, is the communist-run, Russian-sponsored government called "the Democratic People's republic of Korea"

South of the 38th parallel, and backed by the U.S., is the republic of Korea. Its population is about 20,000,000 Koreans.

South Korea is largely agricultural. Most of the industry is in the North. So both Koreas need each other but haven't been able to get together peacefully.

This is not the first time the United States has had a hand in Korea's fate.

In 1907, after Russia had lost its war with Japan, those two nations signed their treaty of peace at Portsmouth, N.H.

President Theodore Roosevelt assured the Japanese this country would look upon it favorably if the Japanese took control over Korea, which at the time was all one Korea and had its own government.

The Japanese took control, abused and despoiled the Koreans, and in 1910 just made Korea part of Japan. In 1919 some Korean patriots asked the Japanese to let Korea have its independence back.

They were slaughtered. But other Korean patriots outside Korea, set up a temporary government-in-exile. They elected Dr. Syngman Rhee president. He had studied at Princeton university under Woodrow Wilson.

World War II

Then World War II. In 1943 - at a Cairo conference with other leaders of the allies - President Franklin D. Roosevelt agreed that when Japan was licked the Koreans should have their independence again.

In 1945, when the war was coming to an end, there were Japanese troops in Korea but neither Russian nor American troops. Russian troops were on Korea's northern border. American troops were no closer than Okinawa, 600 miles away.

If the war suddenly ended, the Russians could rush down and take over all of Korea. Then, state depart-

70

HOW U.S. GREW TO WORLD POWER IN 50 YEARS

YANKS BLED along the Marne in World War I to make the world safe for Democracy. It was America's trial run in world affairs. This is from a famous drawing.

THE BIG FOUR, left to right, Lloyd George, Orlando, Clemenceau and Woodrow Wilson. They hoped in vain the United States would join the League of Nations.

WORLD WAR II boomed production in American industry in a climax to the developing strength of the nation. This is a view of plastic noses for U.S. bombers.

THE BIG THREE, left to right, Stalin, FDR and Churchill, met at Teheran in World War II with the United States firmly established as a leader of the world.

Background Feature   These photos accompanied an excellent Associated Press

news-feature on the development of the United States as a world power.

ment people explain, this is what happened:

The heads of the U S Army, navy and state department figured out a plan. When the war ended, Russians would come into Korea from the north and accept the surrender of all Japanese forces north of the 38th parallel and occupy the country there; American troops would enter from the south, accept the surrender of Japanese troops south of the 38th parallel, and occupy the country there.

The Japanese offered to surrender Aug. 10, 1945. The Russians entered Korea Aug. 12. The Americans didn't arrive until Sept. 18.

(There have been statements that this splitting of Korea between Americans and Russians at the 38th parallel was agreed to by President Roosevelt at his Yalta conference with Marshal Stalin.)

(State department people say this is untrue, that President Roosevelt, who died four months before the Japanese surrender, had nothing to do with it.)

The Russians threw up a barrier at the 38th parallel between North and South Korea. A commission of Americans and Russians sat down to talk about wiping out this barrier.

This got nowhere. The problem was taken to the United Nations. Meanwhile, Russian troops occupied North Korea, American troops occupied South Korea. The Russians would let neither the Americans nor UN officials into North Korea.

Finally, the UN decided to let the Koreans set up their own government, as promised at Cairo, by holding their own elections. Since the UN people couldn't get into the North, the elections were held in the South.

The southern republic began life on Aug. 15, 1948. On Sept. 9, 1948, the Russians established the northern republic. Finally both Russia and the U S announced they had withdrawn all their occupying troops from Korea. The U S left behind it said 500 officers and men to train the southern Koreans.

The north and south remained apart, with the communist-run north pecking away at the south. Finally, this week it attacked the south. But the U S had promised to help Korea if trouble started. Yesterday President Truman sent help.

This government has spent about $526,000,000 in southern Korea to help get it on its feet: The army spent $380,000,000 and left behind $56,000,000 in equipment. The U S Marshall plan this past year spent $90,000,000 there and proposed spending another $100,000,000 next year.

Tallahassee, Florida
Democrat

72

Information for understanding an international news
event such as this can be discovered in such sources as
these:

Official

Documents of the United Nations
(these documents have been indexed since 1950)

The U.N. Bulletin

Publications of the Council of Europe
(indexed)

Documents of the Organization of European Economic
Co-operation
This is the official agency of the Marshall
plan in which Korea participated.

United States Documents
These would contain information on the Marshall
Plan, Korea and other matters.
Marshall Plan Documents

Reports from Individual European Nations
(indexed)

Yearbooks

Statesman's Yearbook
Yearbook of the United Nations
Yearbook of Encyclopedia Britannica
New International Yearbook
Colliers Yearbook

Almanac Service

World Almanac and Book of Facts

Europa, an almanac service on European countries

Orbis, an almanac service on other countries outside of Europe

Keesling's Contemporary Archives (British) (texts
from speeches)

Information Please Almanac

Political Handbook of the World

Periodical Indexes

Readers' Guide to Periodical Literature
International Index
New York Times Index
Public Affairs Information Service
Facts on File

In addition to Marlow's column, the Associated Press
furnishes two other interpretive columns. J. M. Roberts
Jr., foreign affairs analyst for the service, writes one
called "Interpreting the News". In the following column
Roberts sought to focus attention on Tibet which came up in
the news. Something of Tibet's previous history and its
importance in the international chess game were pointed out
by the writer. Although Tibet was mentioned in news dispatches, it meant little more than a far-off name to most
newspaper readers. Roberts helped to fill in the background for the reader.

An AP News-feature for Thursday AMS Oct. 26.

Interpreting the News

----

by J.M. Roberts, Jr.

    To the western mind, what happens in Tibet would
seem at first to be of little more importance than
what might happen on the moon.
    It's a little place in the far-off Himalayas,
visited only rarely by Westerners, ruled by a strange
theistic government. It never has much contact
with the outside, and in winter ground travel
through the mountain passes is next to impossible.
To most people its existence is almost as imaginary
as the Shangri-La which the story said was located
there.
    But when the Chinese communists move in, as they
will even if the new announcement of an invasion
has not already been implemented, Tibet will take
on a new aspect.
    For it is there that a nervous India will be
brought into direct contact with the powers of Communism which so far have failed to make much impression on her. Prime Minister Nehru doesn't believe,
yet, that the Peiping regime of Mao Tse-Tung is
a puppet of the Kremlin.
    But Chinese Communist armies, willing to drive
through the already-falling snows of the "top of
the world" to carry out a gesture involving little
but face, will present the Indians with something
which they cannot take chances on the mere basis
of opinion. They will have to be prepared for the
possibility that they are wrong.... From AP teletype
                                        machine

    Dewitt MacKenzie, another of the AP's foreign

affairs staff, furnished a column which sought to piece
together the various bits of past news and link it with
the current happenings to discover its meaning. When Pandit Nehru, Prime Minister of India, visited the United
States, this called for an explanatory article regarding
Nehru's history and his importance.

Nehru's Visit To America An Historic Event

by Dewitt MacKenzie
AP Foreign Affairs Analyst

A dozen years from now we are likely to be remind-
ing ourselves that today's arrival of Pandit Jawa-
harlal Nehru on his first trip to this country was
a far-reaching event.

The Prime Minister of India is one of the outstanding leaders of our time. As head of this
great new nation, with its population of more than
300,000,000 Nehru already is demonstrating a leadership which is making itself felt throughout Asia.
His influence on world unity will be vast.

Therefore Nehru's visit to Washington, where he
is to be entertained by our President, becomes a
matter of moment. For upon the impressions which
this brilliant and highly sensitive guest forms may
well depend future relations between the United
States and an India which is going to play a dominant
part in the development of the Orient.

Nehru, who will be 60 on the 14th of next month,
not only was born into a family of great wealth but
he is a Kashmiri Brahmin -- the highest aristocracy
of all India. He was educated in England. He attend-
ed Harrow, one of the country's famous public schools
(really private) and the University of Cambridge.
Later he studied law in London and returned to his
native land as a polished intellectual, who had the
marks of genius.

At the outset he showed little interest in the
Independence movement, but soon he joined and thereafter devoted his whole life to the idea. He became
one of the most devoted disciples of Mohandas K.
Gandhi and followed the saintly little Mahatma faith-
fully in the drive for Indian independence until the
latter's assassination on January 30, 1948.

The disciple, like the master, became a plague to
the British and he was several times in prison, serving all-told some 13 years. Like Gandhi, Nehru tour-
ed the highways and by-ways of India to preach independence to the people until he became an object of
hero worship among the masses.

So it was natural that Gandhi should have designated Nehru as his "political heir" and that the
disciple should become the first prime minister of
the Dominion of India when Britain granted independence....

Nehru is an internationalist and a socialist
and is a bitter opponent of dictatorship. He is,
however, what might be described as a middle-of-the-
road Socialist. He believes in what he calls a
"mixed economy" in which the state assumes management of key industries, but still allows plenty
of chance for private enterprise to operate.. He
has been championing the cause of other Asiatic
countries which are seeking independence from colonial status.   Associated Press Dispatch

Facts about Nehru or other prominent international
figures in the news may be derived from a number of sources.
Among these printed sources would be:
1. World Biography
2. Current Biography
3. Who's Who
4. Webster's Biographical Dictionary
5. Political Handbook of the World
6. Information Please Almanac
7. Collier's Yearbook
8. New International Yearbook
9. Encyclopedia Britannica Yearbook

To find related information about these people in the
news the reporter would check also information about the
individual countries. These sources would include references to encyclopedias and other documentary matter listed
before.

Other Newspaper Services Background World Affairs
Reporters for the Newpaper Enterprise Association also
devote special attention to foreign news background features. "NEA's News Page", issued from New York, carries
interpretative dispatches on international issues, research
and interview pieces that seek to clarify issues, and background articles.

The late Jack Oestreicher, author of The World Is Their
Beat, chosen as the best book written by a newspaperman in
1945-46 by the National Headliners' Club, was the foreign
director of International News Service, a Hearst wire news
service. He wrote an interpretative column which was sent
to the many clients of this service.

Iran Issue Explained, Correlated
When Iran voted to nationalize its oil industry in 1951,
this event produced a news storm which lasted for months in
the American press. The Anglo-Iranian Oil Company, which
had developed the oil in Iran, was controlled by the British.
Negotiations and more negotiations for the settlement of the
dispute were engaged in by both parties. The British government sought to bring the matter before the World Court and
the United Nations Security Council. The Iranians attempted
to involve the United States on their side. The newspaper
reader had a difficult time following the news developments
for they lasted over a long period of time. Edgar Ansel

Mowrer recognized the needs of the bewildered reader and sought to correlate and highlight the previous history at the time the dispute was brought before the UN Security Council.

Here is a brief resume of Mowrer's article, distributed through many papers:

Controversial Points in Anglo-Iranian Oil Dispute Now Before U.N. Are Listed
By Edgar Ansel Mowrer

LAKE SUCCESS - If you don't understand the full details of the Anglo-Iranian oil dispute now raging before the UN Security Council, take heart: Neither does anybody else - including the principals.

I know that I don't. But I have tried to set down a few of the more conspicuous facts as signposts in the debate.

1. The Anglo-Iranian Oil Company developed Iranian oil, contributed considerably to Iran's prosperity, and consistently treated its employes better than other Iranians.

But - it gave Iran a niggardly share of the profits, offended the Iranian's self respect - and only reluctantly and at long last consented to revise the latest 60-year agreement of 1933.

The Iranian Government has as much right to nationalize economic enterprises as do the British or the Chinese, against due compensation.

But - it has gone farther and wants to eliminate the British company altogether from exploitation of Iranian oil in favor of some new company formally directed by the Iranian Government...

Today, Iran's Prime Minister Mossadegh and his followers are ready to bankrupt Iran and give it to Russia rather than yield. The British intend to ruin Iran by trade boycott if forced out. Either event would be a disaster to the free world - including the United States.

On July 5, 1951, the British obtained a decision by the World Court instructing both sides to refrain from anything likely to prejudice a future settlement - that is, not to prevent the normal production and sale of oil. The Iranians have ignored the World Court and expelled the British technicians on the ground that the World Court is not competent. The British have appealed to the UN Security council.

The Iranians deny the competence both of the World Court and of the UN Security Council on the ground that the 1933 agreement, as a private contract between the Iranian Government and a private company, fails under the domestic jurisdiction of Iran...

Most observers agree that if Iran can eliminate
the British, Egypt can denounce the Anglo-Egyptian
Treaty of 1936 (due to expire in 1956) and invite
the British out of the Sudan and the Suez Canal
Zone. Some think that should Egypt succeed in this,
Panama will attempt to throw the Americans out of
the Panama Canal Zone.

On the other hand, if the British keep either
Iran's oil or the Suez Canal and the Sudan by force,
former colonial peoples all over the world would
denounce "white imperialism" and perhaps turn to
the USSR for aid.

The only solution satisfactory, in the long run
to Iran, to Britain and to the United States is
one that will leave the ownership of the wells and
refinery and a large share of the profits with
the Iranian Government and leave the exploitation,
refining and marketing of the oil in the hands of
Britain...

Here you have the facts - as I understand them.
If I had to sum up the case in one sentence, It
would be this:

Ethically, the Iranians are right; economically
both parties are already in agreement; legally, the
situation is too complicated to be adjudicated;
politically, America's interest is predominantly
on the side of Britain.   Jacksonville, Florida
                                    Times-Union

Middle Europe in The Headlines
England's colonial empire again became headline news
when the Egyptians sought to evict the British from
their land. The spot news story covered the riots
which resulted as the following indicates.

Britons Battling Egyptian Rioters

*Troops Fire on Mobs in Two Cities; 17 Persons Dead
and Scores Injured; London and Cairo Announce
Reinforcements on Way to Troubled Area*

CAIRO, EGYPT, Oct. 16 -(AP)- British troops fired
on rioting Egyptians in two cities on the Suez Canal
today. From seven to seventeen persons were reported
killed and scores injured.

The British commander pledged that his troops
will remain in the canal area despite the efforts
of King Farouk's government to oust them. Britain
announced that reinforcements are on the way.

A British army communique said "a small number

of rioters" were killed and a British enlisted man
wounded in clashes at Ismailia and Port Said.

Two Britons Slain

Egyptian officials at Ismailia said seven
Egyptians were killed and 74 injured there and
that four more Egyptians had been killed in rioting at Port Said. A Cairo newspaper put the total
dead at 17, including two Britons, and said at
least 80 had been wounded.

The western half of Ismailia, where all the
British and Europeans in the town have their homes
was grimly guarded tonight by British troops behind barbed wire barricades... Associated Press
                                         Dispatch

At the same time came the shocking news of the assassination of Liaquat Ali Khan, Prime Minister of Pakistan,
a small but critical country in the Middle East.

Pakistan's Premier Victim of Assassin At Punjab Meeting

LEADER SLAIN

AP Wirephoto

Killer Seized And Slain by Angry Crowd

**Liaquat Dies Attempting
to Pacify Groups in
Kashmir Dispute**

KARACHI, Pakistan, Oct. 16
(UP) - Liaquat Ali Khan,
Prime Minister of Pakistan
was assassinated today by
a fanatical member of a
sem-Fascist political or-
ganization which demands
a "holy war" with India.
The 56-year-old Liaquat was cut down by
two bullets fired into his chest at point-

blank range as he arose to address a crowd of
20,000 persons at Rawalpindi, in the Punjab.

As he fell, the Premier murmured: "There
is no God but Allah, and Mohammed is his pro-
phet," an eye witness said.

Mob Slays Assassin

A howling mob seized the assassin and tore
his body to bits as the Prime Minister sank
to the floor. He was identified as Said
Akbar, a member of the radical Khaksar sect.

Liaquat died at a military hospital after
being rushed there for a blood transfusion
which failed to save his life.

The news of the Prime Minister's death
shocked the people of this capital city into
grieving silence and plunged Pakistan into
mourning for the death of its leader for the
second time in its short four-year history.
It was only three years ago that the young
country mourned the death of Mohammed Ali
Jinnah, founder of this Moslem Nation of
80,000,000 people...Associated Press Dispatch

Realizing that the newspaper reader knew very little
about these countries and the reasons behind these page one
events, the AP sent out a background story and map which
tied together the facts relating to these critical spots.

Middle East Is Seething With Unrest

LONDON, Oct. 16 (AP) - Anti-British riots in Egypt
and a fanatical assassination in Pakistan today un-
derscored the dangers to the western world that lurk
in the unrest sweeping the Moslem belt.

Super-heated nationalism feeding on poverty and
distress is turning the Moslem world, from Morocco
along the Mediterranean to Pakistan in Southern
Asia, into a soft underbelly for the Western world
in its front against communism.

Rioting in the Suez area, which already had
caused Britain to order in troop reinforcements,
and the assassination of Pakistan's Premier Liaquat
Ali Khan sprang from different political backgrounds.
But both spotlighted a weakening of the rule of law
and order and a bent toward gun-shot politics.

Since near the end of the war there have been
13 assassinations of kings, presidents, premiers,
cabinet ministers and other prominent political
figures in the Moslem world.

These killings have cut down several of Britain's
staunch friends, particularly King Abdullah of Jordan.
They have played a huge part in the post-war politics
of Egypt.

Restless nationalists in Iraq, which remains a
British ally in the Middle East are demanding a
new deal on oil and an end to British air bases.

The assassination of Liaquat raised fears among
Western diplomats here that, unless cool judgment

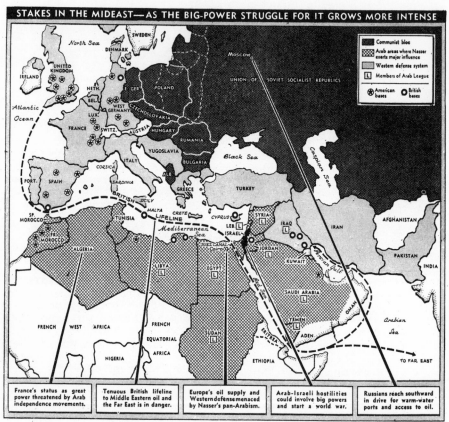

STAKES IN THE MIDEAST—AS THE BIG-POWER STRUGGLE FOR IT GROWS MORE INTENSE

Communist bloc

Arab areas where Nasser
exerts major influence

Western defense system

L Members of Arab League

American bases   British bases

| France's status as great power threatened by Arab independence movements. | Tenuous British lifeline to Middle Eastern oil and the Far East is in danger. | Europe's oil supply and Western defense menaced by Nasser's pan-Arabism. | Arab-Israeli hostilities could involve big powers and start a world war. | Russians reach southward in drive for warm-water ports and access to oil. |

Only overseas bases of the U. S. and Britain are shown. The U. S. has about fifteen major installations in England altogether.

prevails in the Indian subcontinent, the Kashmir
balloon could blow up in war between the two members
of the British Commonwealth. It appeared bound
to unsettle Moslem Pakistanis who have accused
Hindu Indians of never paying more than lip service
to partition.

Foreign offices of the Western world fear that
these developments, if unchecked, can play into
the hands of waiting pro-Communist elements and
an expansionist Russia ready to appeal to the poverty stricken masses.

From the British point of view, the Egyptian
developments were the most alarming immediately.
In the face of nationalistic fervor spilling over
into a number of anti-British incidents, the government ordered reinforcements to the Suez Canal
area and instructed them to hang on with bullets
and bayonets.

Lieut. Gen. Sir George Erskine, commanding
British troops in Egypt, said: "We are not going
to be turned out, forced out or knocked out."

In a broadcast to his troops, Erskine told
British servicemen and their families to stay
away form crowds.

The Associated Press correspondent in Cairo
reported, without confirmation, that the wives
and children of British soldiers would be evacu-
ated from the canal area by air to England. All
military families in Suez and some other bases
were said to have been removed from their homes
to nearby military camps under the guard of British military and Egyptian police.

The British Foreign Office made this announcement:

"As a result of a series of incidents which have
occurred in the canal zone and the action taken
by the Egyptian authorities in denying certain
facilities to British forces there, it has been
decided as a necessary precaution to reinforce
the British troops in the canal zone. This move
is in no way designed to be provocative or to
increase tension there.

Under her 1936 alliance with Egypt Britain
was permitted to station 10,000 troops and 400
pilots in the canal zone, plus supply units.
The best unofficial estimate is that almost
40,000 British troops and air-men there now.

The reinforcing units were not designated. At
Cyprus the British have the Sixteenth Independent
Airborne Brigade - a crack outfit organized for
quick dispatch and deployment. This organization,
believed to number about 4,000, is within easy
flying distance of the canal.

The Suez clash grew out of Egypt's attempt
to scrap the treaty.

The British position is that her troops will
keep their posts in the canal area until some suitable international arrangement to safeguard this

vital military and commercial artery is set up.

The United States, Britain, France and Turkey wish Egypt to join with them in providing an international garrison for the canal. Egypt wants all British troops pulled out before she considers any new arrangement. Egypt also wants the Sudan joined to her under the Egyptian crown. The Sudan now is administered jointly by Britain and Egypt.

The news from Cairo and Pakistan caught the British in the middle of an election campaign. The news was dispatched to Prime Minister Attlee as he prepared to speak to a campaign rally at Trowbridge. He expressed his sympathy for the wife of Liaquat.

King George sent a special message to the Pakistani governor general, saying "I have heard with great sorrow the news of the dastardly crime which has resulted in the death of Mr. Liaquat Ali Khan." He added that Liaquat had performed "distinguished and devoted service" to his fellow countrymen.

Associated Press dispatch

Special Column. The New York World-Telegram and Sun has sought to digest the world news in a special column, heavily interlarded with background information.

As Ray Erwin described it in Editor & Publisher on June 30, 1951 here was the problem facing the Scripps-Howard paper.

Readers want and need more world news and important international information in the atomic age that binds all people into a global community than they ever had before. Yet soaring prices and scarcity of newsprint makes it difficult for newspapers adequately to cover the world beat.

The solution was the development of a column "The World Over", published five days weekly in the left-hand corner of page 2, which has proved very popular with readers. It was given a trial run beginning July 27, 1948. At first it was set in 7-point and contained some feature material. By the process of evolution it was changed to the present 10-point type, set two-column width, with all trivial matter eliminated and only important events recorded. The column had sections labeled, "Europe, Africa and Asia", "Pacific and the Orient" and "Western Hemisphere."

The large type and airy spacing made for easy and quick reading. Emphasis was placed on background information that points up the importance of the story. The column contained important telegraph news which had been eliminated by the telegraph editor or the make-up man and was pushed into the overset.

The Washington D.C. Daily News, another Scripps-Howard paper carried a column with a similar title, "The World Today", but the Washington version dealt with U.S. happenings.

'HEY, MISTER'

THE CLERMONT PRESS AND SOUTH LAKE PRESS, CLERMONT, FLORIDA

Fact and Discussion Questions
on Chapter III, "Global News"

1. Discuss the shifting American attitudes towards world
    news.

2. List some of the fundamental changes since World War II.

3. What was decided at the Teheran Conference?

4. What were the questions decided at Yalta? Do you know
    about the dispute which has arisen since over this
    meeting?

5. What was decided about Germany at the Potsdam confer-
    ence?

6. Describe how Soviet Russia's attitude toward its former
    allies changed after the end of the war.

7. Explain the statement: "The cold war was fought on
    several fronts."

8. What was the Marshall plan?

9. Tell about the provisions of the final treaty with
    Germany.

10. List the various steps leading to the United Nations.

11. Compare the UN with the League of Nations.

12. Describe the various divisions of the UN.

13. What are the strengths and weaknesses of the UN?

14. List some of the weaknesses outlined by Edgar Ansel
    Mowrer in his article.

15. Tell about U.S. after World War II.

16. What happened in Great Britain? France?

17. How was Germany able to recover so rapidly?

18. Explain and illustrate Soviet imperialism?

19. (a) What was the immediate cause of the Korean war?
    (b) What did it symbolize?
    (c) Why was General Douglas MacArthur relieved of com-
        mand?

20. Explain the Indo-Chinese situation.

21. Tell briefly the history of the Israel-Arab problem.

22. Discuss the article, "How the US Got Mixed up in Korea",
    considering style, content, appeal, value to reader.

23. List four periodical indexes for articles backgrounding current events.

24. Discuss Dewitt McKenzie's article on Prime Minister
Nehru's visit to U.S. as to (1) lead, (2) style (3)
content.

25. Where would you get additional information about Nehru?

26. Discuss the article "Middle East is Seething with
Unrest" as to style, content, value to reader.

I. Newsclipping Projects

Select one of the following:

1. Read your favorite newspaper for three days, then select three articles dealing with world affairs.

   (a) Did these carry their own historical background?
       If so, were they informative?
   (b) What events do you think led up to the present
       news? Outline briefly the most important of these
       happenings.
   (c) Do you know of any books or magazine articles
       which would help you build up your background to
       write about these specific events?
   (d) Check the library card catalogue for books bearing
       on these subjects and list the volumes.

2. Get a copy of a current or recent Sunday edition of the
New York Times, or the New York Herald-Tribune.

   (a) Examine the section, "News-of-the-Week-In-Review"
       or "History in the Making". Paste the first and
       second pages on sheets of paper. Clip other ar-
       ticles bearing on international affairs.
   (b) Analyze the first and second pages of the news
       review. Do you think they have a coherent picture
       of the international scene of the preceding week?
       Is any historical material included which you did
       not find in your daily newspaper? Discuss.
   (c) Were any special articles published in the section,
       articles which gave the historical background of
       a current issue in the news, or one likely to em-
       erge from the news? List some. What is your
       opinion of them as to style, content, value to
       reader? How would you improve them? Any other
       angles which might be covered?

3. Get a copy of the St. Louis, Mo. Post-Dispatch (Sunday
issue) or Christian Science Monitor and analyze as in
assignment No. 2.

4. Get a current copy of one of these magazines (1) <u>Time</u>, (2) <u>News-Week</u>, (3) <u>U.S. News & World Report</u>, (4) <u>Reporter</u>, (5) <u>Nation</u>

   (a) Read the foreign news sections or articles carefully.
   (b) Clip the articles and attach them to a sheet.
   (c) Analyze them from standpoint of content, style, value to you.
   (d) Write up your summary and conclusions.
   (e) Class may be broken into groups, each group selecting a different magazine and reporting on their findings.

II. <u>Writing Assignments</u>

   Select one of the following:

1. Write 75o-1000 word news-feature on the history of some world event prominent in the current news.

   (a) Check standard history texts, see the card catalogue in the library for books bearing on the subject, and examine <u>Readers' Guide to Periodical Literature</u> for possible articles. Make a bibliography of the important materials. <u>New York Times</u> or <u>Herald Tribune</u> will prove useful.
   (b) Select out of this material the pertinent reference and develop basic facts for your article.
   (c) What kinds of pictures would you use?

2. Interview the professor of international history or politics for a historical feature on some world news event of interest at the moment. Another group in the class may interview an American history professor for a national event with a bearing on international affairs.

   (a) Ask him to brief you on the highlights of the events which led up to the present situation.
   (b) Get any interpretations he has as to causes and means of prevention or remedying the situation.
   (c) Secure from him a list of pertinent references which might deal with the background of the contemporary news.

3. Write an extended editorial giving more background history than is provided in a current foreign news story in your favorite newspaper.

   (a) Prepare for the editorial by checking reference works, textbooks, magazines and other sources for facts.
   (b) Write your editorial clearly, but graphically, explaining for the reader how the present situation grew out of the past.

4. Write a background feature on the cold war.
    (a) Use information in this text and other sources,
        such as history books, newspapers. See end of
        this chapter.
    (b) Show various moves made by Soviet Union since the
        second World War.

5. Develop a two part series "Spotlight on Asia", on pre-
    sent situation in Far East.

    (a) Show some of the background events in China
    (b) Indicate political, economic causes

6. Write a two-part series on Middle East (Israeli-Arab)

    (a) Tell history of Palestine since World War I
    (b) Give Israelis side of dispute
    (c) Present the Arab side
    (d) Bring in any current news developments on that
        area of the world

7. Develop a series on "Post War Britain" (or some current
    news event.)

    (a) Show political developments
    (b) Indicate economic problems
    (c) Point out current news there

8. Write an article on Post-War France (or some immediate
    current news).

    (a) Bring out the political and economic situations
        and problems France has faced - (De Gaulle, Commu-
        nists)
    (b) Tell about her colonial questions

9. "Divided Germany's Recovery" might be the title of your
    articles on Post-War Germany.

    (a) Bring out the facts about the peace treaty, the
        division of the nation and the industrial improve-
        ment.
    (b) Indicate Germany's acceptance by Western Powers.

10. "Latin-American Relations" can be another subject for
    a series of two articles.

11. "Middle Europe: Key to Peace"

    (a) Develop a 3 part series on Greece, Turkey since
        the Second World War.
    (b) Show relationship to communist expansion

Background References on World History

World History

Raymond Aron	The Century of Total War. Beacon, Boston, 1955.
Frank L. Benns	Europe Since 1914 in its World Setting. 6th ed. New York: Crofts, 1945.
Cyril E. Black and E.C. Helmreich	Twentieth Century Europe. New York: Knopf, 1954.
Geoffrey Brunn	The World in the Twentieth Century. Boston: Heath, 1948. Rev. 1952.
Frank P. Chambers, Christina P. Grant, and Charles C. Bayley	This Age of Conflict, a Contemporary World History, 1914-1943. New York: Harcourt, Brace, 1943.
Walter Langsam	World Since 1914. 4th ed. New York: Macmillan, 1940.
Louis L. Snyder	The World In The Twentieth Century. New York, Van Nostrand,1955.

Some Books on Foreign Affairs by Newsmen

Ray Stannard Baker	Woodrow Wilson and World Settlement. New York: Doubleday, 1922.
William H. Chamberlin	Russian Revolution. New York: Macmillan, 1935.
D. J. Dallin	New Soviet Empire, New Haven, Yale Univ. Press, 1951
Konrad Heidin	Der Feurer: Hitler's Rise to Power. tr. by Ralph Manheim. New York: Houghton Mifflin, 1944.
Hal Lehrman	The Beginning and Tomorrow. New York, Sloane, 1951.
Kenneth Scott Latourette	American Record in Far East. New York, Macmillan, 1953.
Reuben H. Markham	Tito's Imperial Communism. Chapel Hill: Univ. of North Carolina Press, 1947.

William L. Shirer   Berlin Diary: the Journal of a
Foreign Correspondent, 1934-1941.
New York: Knopf, 1941.

Edith Sulkin   Continent in Limbo. New York:
Reynal & Hitchcock, 1947.

Richard L. Walker   China Under Communism. New Haven:
Yale Univ. 1955.

Alexander Werth   Twilight of France, 1933-1940.
New York: Harper, 1942.

Rebecca West   Black Lamb and Gray Falcon: a
Journey Through Yugoslavia. New
York: Viking. 1941.

Theodore White   From The Ashes, Europe at Mid-
Century. New York, Sloane, 1950.

Bertram D. Wolfe   Three Who Made a Revolution. New
York: Dial Press, 1948.

Harold V. Faulkner   American Political and Social
History (6th ed) New York: Apple-
ton, 1952.

Ferdinand Sheville   A History of Europe From Reforma-
tion to Present Day. New York:
Harcourt, 1954.

CYCLE OF POLITICAL NEWS   Members of the Florida State legislature, taking office for the first time, are sworn in by a Justice of the Florida Supreme Court. This is one of the dramatic events which initiate the legislature session.

Student-Reporter Interviews   In order to obtain background on a bill as well as some spot news information about it, Gale Tomlinson, a Florida State University journalism reporter, interviews a representative from the district where she lives.

Editing the News At the horse-shoe copy desk, student copy-editors
process the news, re-writing stories (sometimes) and composing
catchy heads. Mr. Richard Eide sits in the "slot" today.

Printing Monster After the reporting and editing tasks are completed,
the newsmen and newswomen go down to the local printing plant to
see how the wheels go round and to watch the papers roll off the press.
It's always good to see what your copy looks like in type.

Studying the Opposition These reporters are checking on the political
news in various Florida daily newspapers. How much space was given
news of the presidential campaign? where was the news featured? what
size headlines were used?

Chapter 4
News in Its Political Setting

by James Norton
Associate Professor, School of
Public Administration, Florida State University

I. News Has a Political Background

Everything happens in political context. Births,
legitimate or not under the law, are recorded by the government. Lives -- social or criminal -- are lived under protection of governments to which duties are owed. Deaths --
natural or homicidal -- are scrutinized before burial sanc-
tioned by a governmental "burial permit." Whether the news
is economic, sociological or psychological, it has a political aspect, and the political aspect of many events makes
them worthy of the headlines.

2. Newsmen Have a Service to Offer

Today the reporter who seeks to background political
news, using his knowledge of political science, has a real
service to offer his newspaper and the public. His news
stories will be more informative. He will see more opportunities for feature articles for which his editor is looking. The newsman's copy too, will have increased social
value as well as heightened reader interest. If the newsman can spot a needed below-the-surface feature for a political news story, he will prove a more valuable staff member. In addition, the newspaperman who knows the authentic
sources for facts which explain the spot political news and
who can write the article in acceptable style, will be a
more competent reporter.

The newspaper is continually dealing with the activities of government. The editor doesn't call or dignify
this type of news with the title "political science". But
what the city hall reporter covers, what the newsman on the
State House beat reports, what the Washington correspondent
deals with, is municipal, state and national political
science. It is the basic material with which the many col-
umnists and most editorial writers deal.

Leased wires of The Associated Press and United Press

Harry Bridges Sentenced to Five Years Imprisonment For Perjury, Conspiracy

May Compel Witnesses To T... ...r The
Are ...

Union Leader Was Found Guilty of Lying to Hide ...t He Was Communist

By Katherine Pink...
...pril 1

U. S. Will Seek Cut In Tariffs

Is Part of Campaign To Help Other Nations Earn More Dollars

Washington
United ...

Butterworth Dulles Confer Early Jap Treaty

Acheson Seeks Assistan...

preliminary to taking
dus...

Crime Probe Is Ordered By President

Justice Department Ordered to Check Nation-Wide Rac...

Washington, April 13 President Truman said has ordered the Justic ment to get to the bot tionwide crime rackets.

...att... ...me ...ci...

Reckless GOP Backing of McCarthy Charges Said to Be Effort to 'Get' Truman

President 'Afraid' to Release Secret Federal Files, Say Republicans

By Marvin L. Arrowsmith

Washington, April 9 (AP)—A Democrat said tonight ...at Republican leaders are recklessly backing Sen. Mc- ...rthy's charges of communism in the state department ...n e...ort to "get" President Truman.

...cans retorted to this charge h... ...e president is "af ... ...p. Dingell ...
...Vir...

Most events have a political aspect and eventually are funnelled through government channels, a congressional committee, a court or a state department. Hence the importance of understanding the political science backgrounds of the news.

3. Our Big Democracy

In a dynamic and changing world citizens face issues
which individuals or special groups cannot handle. These
are the affairs of the whole community -- perhaps too big
or too costly for individuals. To attack the problems of
the community we use our government. It is an organization
directed by our elected representatives to work with the
problems we have to solve.

These issues may range from the proposal to build a
playground for the children in a town, to a suggestion
that the state construct a highway to a plan to draft an
army. Different ideas are put forward. Interest groups
conflict, and the government seeks the general interest.
Through compromise, give and take, trial and error, the
representatives of citizens in a democracy must weave together solutions to pressing problems.

In 1949, our national government employed more than
2,000,000 persons, and spent more than $40,000,000,000.
Centered in Washington, ten percent of all its employees

96

are there. Another ten percent are outside continental United States; the other employees are spread all over the country. No other organization approaches the national government in size.

On the national, state, and local levels government is concerned with problems of all the people. One man's relations to another man determine issues for a government. Do people work harmoniously, or fight? Does the refuse from one man's business destroy the property of another?

Government is established to meet the needs of the clientele. If it does not satisfy in every particular from broad policy to the minutia of administration, it is liable to criticism. Persistent criticism will result in some change. This liability to constant criticism from every source promotes continuing responsibility of government.

4. Challenge to Reporters

Democracy works best when the public is informed on community issues and problems, and when the public has confidence in its ability to work through the government it maintains. Newspapers fulfill a social obligation when they furnish fair, accurate and complete facts about the issues in the news. Newsmen can contribute to the democracy by presenting not only spot news, but the background to it. Can a reporter write about a public controversial issue so as to provide sound information from which rational citizens can draw conclusions? Can he make this news as interesting and as graphic as a murder story? These are among the challenges of a democracy to a reporter.

5. Local Level

All types of stories are found on all levels of government: national, state, and local. Personalities clash; policies are debated. The legislature debates, and the courts administer justice in varying degrees of quality. Problems are met and solved by administrative departments.

What a city does is immediately important to all the people who live there. If the water supply is cut off, the people's reaction is immediate. If garbage is uncollected for a week, public health is endangered. While a citizen might not think about a service until it happens to be cut off, how these important functions are performed is feature news all the time.

Administration of municipal governments may break into the headlines dramatically. Services may be suspended new policies may be set, or necessary funds become available. News stories and feature articles provide the reader -citizen with information on which he can base his actions. Matters need not be too technical for him to comprehend, nor so difficult to understand that he loses interest. How do we, as a city, protect ourselves against anti-social acts of individuals? How do we maintain order in our trading and professions? What can we do about traffic conges-

97

tion? Must the property tax carry so much of the expense
of government? What will our city look like in 25 years?
How can we hold our administrative servants responsible and
still keep first rate experts where they are needed?

Few newspapers can fail to carry local news. The
reporters who ignore municipal operations as a source of
news and news features miss many important stories. Those
who neglect municipal problems fail to provide the communities in which they operate services which modern democratic societies need.

In 1950 many cities were considering going in debt
for capital improvements they needed. Sometimes the problem was relatively uncomplicated. In Tallahassee, Florida,
the problem could be summed up as water, sewage, drainage
and recreation. But to get them would mean borrowing
$1,175,000. The local daily newspaper reflected the ideas
of most of the city when it supported the bond issue in
news stories and editorials. The features helped to explain, and to pave the way for the election in which the
people ratified the whole policy.

WHY CITY BOND
ISSUE IS NEEDED

By Mike Beaudoin
Democrat Staff Writer

Why does Tallahassee need
$1.750,000 worth of public improve-
ments at this time?
The answer is simply growth.
A phenomenal growth that has happened
so fast since the end of the war that
construction of public, and private
facilities just couldn't keep up with
it.
What will the cost be?
City Auditor George White says
it will be a maximum of 1½ mills, or
less than $1.50 in taxes per each   The problem, where
$1,000 in property valuation. Actu-   it came from how
ally it may be less, depending upon   it can be handled
how much money the state cigaret tax   make up this back-
brings in.   ground story.
How Issue Works
Here are the mechanics of the
bond issue:
The city will borrow $1,750,000,
in whole or part, dependent upon the
vote of the people.
The loan will be paid off in
twenty years or less with the revenue
from the city's share of the cigaret tax.....

Swimming Pools in Bond Issue

By Mike Beaudoin
Democrat Staff Writer

Tallahassee can have two modern, sanitary swimming pools for white and colored citizens which can be operated on at least a break-even basis with no operational burden on the taxpayer's pocketbook.

This conclusion is based on a survey of other Florida cities made by the Democrat.......

(Here the financial soundness of the recreational program is the theme.)

Voters Pass Big City Improvement Plans

Tallahassee's $1,700,000 public improvements project was given overwhelming endorsement by local property owners in the special bond election yesterday when all three projects passed by majorities of 75 to 90 per cent.

The $1,200,000........

(Final Headline
After considering the facts, the people decide)

The value of such newspaper stories would never be underestimated by one who had seen how rapidly a last minute malicious rumor can defeat a proposal for raising money when people are uninformed. For the citizens of Tallahassee the problem was relatively simple when they knew the facts.

Progress or Decay. The need for municipalities to plan systematically and far ahead has been pointed out by political scientists and others many times. Often newspapers will meet the challenge, recognize the need and do a splendid job in helping the citizens understand their present problems and how to meet them. In a notable series of Sunday articles, the St. Louis, Mo. Post-Dispatch presented during March, April and May, 1950, a factual, but highly dramatic account of the critical needs of Greater St. Louis at the mid-century.

99

City Has Central Purchasing Plan

By MIKE BEAUDOIN
Democrat Staff Writer

All purchases for the city of Tallahassee—amounting to about $1,000,000 yearly——are made through a central purchasing agency at an estimated saving of 20 or 25 percent to city taxpayers on many items.

City Manager Malcolm Yancey acts as purchasing agent and all items bought by any city department must first be approved by his office. Yancey is assisted by Ed Britsch, assistant purchasing agent.

bids, thereby insuring the city of getting the best possible price.

The city charter requires all purchases over advertised

Savings on purchases effected by ... quan...

Sanitation Department Has Big Job

By FRANK F O'NEILL
Democrat Staff Writer

The word "government" creates a picture of white buildings such as the new and lovely supreme court in the Capital Center. But government also means the water you drink and the garbage or trash that is taken from your yard.

Collection and disposal of garbage and trash in Tallahassee is the responsibility of Lawrence Stoutamire who has been with the city's sanitary department since 1927. ... by some ... garbage

stay out and the garbage cleanly and odorlessly.

Garbage ditches are block and a half long. them have been filling Spring Hill road dump past years.

Formerly, the cit...

Requests on Zoning Voiced by Landowners North of Florida St

Property Holders From Southern Part of City To Be Heard at 2 P. ...

Almost 25 persons, an...city area north ...paraded before ...sion's micr...audit...

...rest that the tops ... put on securely in ...placed around ...will hold it ...of dogs

ing downtown now put their trash in the receptacles—and Stoutamire hopes they will continue to do so.

During the war Stoutamire says that he was down to 18 men, but the garbage trucks, like the cais-ons, kept rolling.

$300,000 NEEDED TO COMPLETE LAYOUT

First of New City Sewage Plant Completed

Tallahassee's new sewage disposal system is now in operation.

City Manager Malcolm Yancey said the first phase of the plant is complete and will adequately take care of Tallahassee's present sewage disposal problems.

City Engineer Miller Walston said the plant when completed will be able to accommodate a city of 50,000.

Yancey said $400,000 previously earmarked for the project and water system improvement has been spent and he doesn't know where further funds will come from to complete phase two of the plant.

He added the city hoped to get some funds from the new cigaret tax money being returned to the cities as a result of the 1949 state revenue act passed by the 1949 legislature.

The new plant was started nine months ago, when it be-...me evident that the old plant ...handle the city's ...orn facilities of ...only partial

and incompletely treated sewage can infect the ground and streams and lead to many serious diseases.

The disposal process is simply a method of giving nature a helping hand in the elimination of waste material. Principles of sewage disposal are clarification, aeration, digestion and sterilization—all of which nature can accomplish but requiring entirely too long for health safety.

City officials say the new plant will carry out this process with a maximum of efficiency and a minimum danger of spreading disease-bearing bacteria.

Similar plants are envisioned in the future for the north and south city areas, but Yancey said these were a long way off.

...reas of the city are still ...wage lines. These ...art of Betton ...area and 10 ...west, east ...d areas

Features on the operations of local municipal departments make readable ...
copy.

SEWAGE PLANT—First phase of Tallahassee's modern sewage plant is now operating. Final phases of the plant, as shown here, are expected to be completed in the future. The plant is located between Spring Hill road and Gamble st, in the southwestern edge of town.

The series was entitled:

Progress or Decay? -- St. Louis Must Choose

Approaching the area's problems realistically, the series concerned itself with the basic ingredients necessary for building a sounder community for all the people in the more than 2,500 square miles which are on both sides of the Mississippi River in Missouri and Illinois. The articles dealt with a broad variety of fields. The headlines are indicative of the lively manner in which the material was treated:

Traffic's Hardened Arteries

The Sordid Housing Story

The City's Impoverished Schools

Problems of the Negro

Airports and Indecision

Downtown -- The City's Ailing Heart

Public Health -- Pennies for Prevention

Industry's Developing Strait-Jacket

Cultural and Recreation

The County -- Growing Up Isn't Easy

The final article was entitled "Decision Rests with the People."

Richard G. Baumhoff, of the St. Louis Post-Dispatch staff wrote a majority of the articles. Here are a few paragraphs from the first one:

PROGRESS OR DECAY?
ST. LOUIS MUST CHOOSE

Tools are at Hand to Develop a Thriving Area With a Better Life for All Its People -- But Determination, Immediate Action are Mandatory

by Richard G. Baumhoff
of the Post-Dispatch Staff

A monumental choice confronts St. Louis. It can make and keep a date with destiny in the second half of the twentieth century. That way lies a great metropolitan community of health, satisfied people, pleasant homes, thriving industry and attractive landscape. In the other direction -- if St. Louis remains content to

101

PROGRESS OR DECAY ?
ST. LOUIS MUST CHOOSE

Tools Are at Hand to Develop a Thriving Area With a Better Life for All Its People — But Determination, Immediate Action Are Mandatory

By RICHARD G. BAUMHOFF
of the Post-Dispatch Staff.

A MONUMENTAL choice confronts St. Louis. It can make and keep a date with destiny in the second half of the twentieth century. That way lies a great metropolitan community of healthy, satisfied people, pleasant homes, thriving industry and attractive landscape. In the other direction — St. Louis remains content to jog along without aggressive action—there lurks decay, squalor, the threat of steady decline. Ultimately, St. Louis would take a back seat among American cities.

So Utopian dream is involved, if the choice is made for progress. Determination and positive action can turn the trick—just as they did St. Louis of the smoke nuisance. Objectives can be realistic, and tools, fortunately, are at hand for a very large part of the job of building the new St. Louis. They include the recently created Bi-State Development Agency.

Both the low-cost housing and the slum clearance provisions of the 1949 federal Housing Act.

This article is the first in a series defining the critical needs of St. Louis and its metropolitan district — and indicating how these needs may be met. The series will be concerned with physical improvements, expanded social services, industrial development, cultural advancement — all basic ingredients for a better community with a better life for its people. The articles will be published on successive Sundays.

Where's the Money Coming From?

PRINCIPAL sources of money for the making of the new St. Louis include the following:

jog along without aggressive action -- there
lurk decay, squalor, the threat of steady decline. Ultimately St. Louis would take a
back seat among American cities.

No Utopian dream is involved, if the choice
is made for progress. Determination and positive action can turn the trick -- just as they
rid St. Louis of the smoke nuisance. Objectives can be realistic, and tools, fortunately,
are at hand for a very large part of the job
of building the new St. Louis. They are varied some are new, some old. They include:

The recently created Bi-State Development
Agency.

Both the low-rent housing and the slum clearance provisions of the 1949 federal Housing
Act.

The Missouri Urban Redevelopment Corporation
Act.

The City's minimum housing standards ordinances.

Comprehensive official plans for St. Louis and
St. Louis county.

The series was so popular it was later reprinted in
collective form.

Current City Problems

Here are some of the continuing problems of city
government which go beyond the 5 w's. It is true that the
underlying issues emerge in the form of spot news, but the
newsman needs to understand the fundamental aspects. Our
purposes here are to focus attention on these issues and
to point up some of the highlights. Fuller discussion will
be found in references in a later section. Follow-up
assignments, based on reading and interviews with political scientists, should arouse the interest of student-reporters and broaden the base of their understanding.

Metropolitan Government Is Expanding

Cities do not stop growing at the city limits.
People move out into new suburbs. They still center their
lives around the city and want urban services. Sometimes
county governments furnish city services outside the corporate limits. Often new towns are incorporated to provide services and to protect the homes against the tax
burden of the central city.

When cities run into each other, hundreds of problems arise in co-ordinating their activities. Duplicate
offices sap the financial strength of the area and compet-
ing governments frustrate each other. Inter-city agree-

ments, city-county consolidations, and informal conferences
are constantly being tried for solutions to the problem.
The final answer has not been found for any city. Local
governments often over-look the experience of other cities
with the same problem.

Planning Is a Growing Movement

City planning got a start at the Chicago Exposition
in 1889 where the idea was to build "the city beautiful".
Today we seek to redevelop blighted areas and provide adequate services for the "liveable City". Cities in 1955
hired over twice as many planners as they did ten years
earlier. They worked to plan the physical, economic and
social environment. St. Louis just gives ene example of
comprhensive planning.

Zoning Problem is Never-Ending

Zoning is a tool to carry out the city plan. Cities
are divided into special districts and limits are put on
the types of property in them. As cities change, so do the
land uses and zones change. The planners, the boards of
zoning adjustment, and all the city governments are involved in this. The lack of proper zoning and enforcement, the
alteration of the zoning areas for special interests, results in a chaotic, ill-planned city.

Traffic and Parking Problems are Nation-wide and Acute

The mechanical marvels from Detroit have created
problems that stagger our cities. Streets are so congest-
ed they have almost lost their function of providing mobil-
ity. Hundreds of cars pour into downtown areas and cannot
be parked.

Municipal parking lots, metered parking on streets
and special traffic divisions in police departments are
being tried. This, too, is a major problem of the city
planners. Can traffic be moved more quickly over existing
streets? Do new thoroughfares need to be developed? Are
viaducts needed to carry traffic over streets and railroad
tracks, where trains tie up auto and trucks for minutes and
hours? Should the city purchase areas for inexpensive parking? Should these projects be left to private companies?
These are some of the continuous questions planners are
asking.

Police and Fire Protection

Police and fire protection are the basic functions
of a city. How can they be bettered? A major problem is
to get enough of the right kinds of persons and use them
wisely in the police and fire departments. Some cities are
trying a system of combining fire and police divisions. It
offers great promise but many complicated jobs are involved,
and, even if merged, the traditional departments will con-

tinue to have their special problems.

Taxes and Borrowing

The costs of city government are increasing because
the cities are growing and new services and facilities are
needed. How to best meet this problem is one acute question faced by all city officials. Current expenses must be
paid by current revenues, of which taxes are the most important part. Yet the decline of the central core of many
cities causes the tax revenue from real estate there to decrease. At the same time the growth of the suburbs requires additional fire, police, health protection and recreational facilities. For capital improvements borrowing
is wise. In the past the general obligation bond was used
for these improvements, being paid from general taxes. Now
in many cities the revenue bond, which derives its income
from a special project, is replacing the general obligation
bond. There are advantages and disadvantages to each type.

Streamlining City Government

Can our cities be run more efficiently? If so, How?
One answer has been the city manager form of city government, introduced in this country early in the century. It
offers a professional manager appointed and directed by the
elected council. Scores of cities adopt it each year and
leave the traditional mayor-council or commission form of
government. No one form is best everywhere, but the fixed
responsibility and professional qualities of the manager
plan are advantages which recommend it.

6. County Level

County government throughout the nation has been
honey-combed with a fee-paying system left over from the
horse an buggy days. Many have been aware of the system,
but it remained for the Associated Press to conduct a nation-wide survey to show the extent of the problem. The
background survey was not initiated by any particular event
but at the suggestion of the Tampa, Fla., Morning Tribune.
Reporters for various bureaus of the wire service in all
parts of the country were assigned the job of digging into
books and official records to discover what county officials
were being paid on the fee-system basis and how much they
were receiving. The reporters searched libraries for studies which had been made, but found no national study by any
political scientist or research foundation. They did find
and utilize Prof. Clyde F. Snider's American State and Local
Government, which contained material on the justices of the
peace, and George Warren's Traffic Courts, which dealt with
a similar problem.

The following is the first in the series of five
articles on the fee system.

Antiquated Public Office Fee System Still Gouging Nation, AP Survey Shows

Adopting a suggestion by The Tampa Tribune, the Associated Press surveyed the government fee situation through its bureaus in all parts of the country. Indications are that this had never been done before. There is no set pattern, the system varying even within states and counties. It makes an interesting story, however, and one which will be a revelation to most people. This is the first of a series of five stories.

By William J. Conway
Associated Press Staff Writer

The vast structure of modern county government is honeycombed with old-fashioned fee-paying offices.

The men who hold these public offices are paid, in part or in full, on a fee basis.

You may be surprised to learn that there are thousands of them.

Some are richly rewarded. Some fee officials enjoy a larger income than the Governor of their state. A probate judge, in at least one state, can make more than a state supreme court justice. Justices of the peace can - and do - get into the five-figure bracket.

Many sheriffs get fees for serving legal papers. Many coroners get fees for performing autopsies.

Get Fees For Arrests

If a constable arrests you and a justice of the peace convicts you, under the laws of many states each gets a fee taken out of the costs of the case - which you pay.

There is a wide range of other kinds of fees and fee-paid officials. The fee money comes, directly or via tax-fed public treasuries, from the citizens.

The fee system was going strong in the horse-and-buggy era. And, although it has been whittled down or tossed out in some states, it still is going strong in this age of jet planes.

106

Some of the fee-paying offices - those of
sheriff and justice of the peace - originated
centuries back in England. They became established in the colonies and later in the
states.

They grew in number as the nation grew in
size. They grew like hardy weeds in a forest
- little noted by the general public in the
shadows of the huge political trees of the
presidency, the governorship and the mayor-
alty.

Hours of research in general and specialized
libraries fails to show that any nation-wide,
top-to-bottom study of fee offices ever has
been made. Inquiry among sources most likely
to know indicates no general census of fee-
collecting officials ever has been taken.

The Associated Press has explored the subject in a coast-to-coast survey conducted
through its bureaus.

What Survey Reveals

The survey shows:

There are uncounted thousands of fee-paying
jobs.

Fee officers have been under sporadic fire
for decades.

But they still function in most of the states.

One criticism is that some fee officials don't
get enough money, and others get too much. The
result, as the critics see it, is that some
offices don't pay enough to attract able men,
while other officials can become affluent at
the public's expense.

In its report to the 1951 Illinois Legislature, the Schaefer (little Hoover) commission
on efficiency and economy in state government
put it this way:

"The fee system of compensation is today in
most, if not all, cases an anachronism which
results in gross over-compensation for some
public officials and obvious underpayment for
others."

The fee system, by design or chance, is anything
but uniform.

A report from the AP Bureau in Lansing, Mich.,
sets forth:

"Michigan law sets a scale of salaries for
probate judges and their registers according
to county populations, and also sets a scale
of fees which may be charged.

"A recent report of the state's auditor's
office (covering 1950) contained these examples:
in one Northern Michigan county, a judge drew
$1800 in salary and $75.15 in fees. In one
large industrial county, two judges split
$16,849 in salaries and $10,119 in fees."

Frank E. McKinney, the new Democratic
national chairman, was a recipient of fees
for four years.

The Indianapolis AP Bureau reports:

"McKinney was Marion County (Indianapolis)
treasurer for two terms (1936-40). Until
1937 the treasurer retained 3 per cent of
delinquent real property collections and
3 per cent on personal property delinquencies.

"The 1937 legislature raised the fee for
treasurers to 6 per cent on personal property delinquencies, plus a 5o cent fee for
each delinquency retired. The 3 per cent on
real property remained unchanged.

"There is no record of the amount of fees
McKinney collected, but best estimates are
between $30,000 and $40,000 a year - possibly more.

"In addition to the fees, the treasurer
recived a nominal salary -$4400.

"The 1941 legislature put the Marion County
treasurer on a flat $10,000 annual salary.
Since then all fees and delinquent penalities
go into the county general fund."

Fees can be fat elsewhere, as you shall
see tomorrow.

Tampa, Florida, Morning Tribune

COUNTY GOVERNMENT PROBLEMS

The following represents some of the county problems
which newsmen should be aware of today. Background reading
and interviews with county officials and political scientists specializing in this area will broaden the informational base of the newsman.

No Central Authority in County Government

County government exists today as it has for centuries with many elected officials and no central control by
the voters or anyone else. The officials overlap each other
sometimes and run in contrary directions at other times. The
system is as costly as it is confusing. A few counties are
trying the manager plan similar to the cities, but the old
order lingers on in most regions. Serious consideration
should be given to streamlining the county government, with
more authority being given fewer elected officials, including the county commissioners, and holding them responsible.

Too Few Professional Personnel

With every county function under an elected official
there is little opportunity to develop career service. Many

offices have only one term amateurs in technical positions.
The more rural counties are the worst offenders in this, but
getting good personnel is a major problem everywhere.

Fee System Is Obsolete

The fee system of payment, described in the Tampa
Tribune article, is one of the worst aspects of county government. Reformers have made it Number One target.

Taxation

County taxation usually means the property or ad
valoram tax. It has been critized as bad in theory and
worse in administration. Tax assessors can do a professional appraisal job but most of them are not qualified. Further complications are the duplication with the city property tax machinery and the numerous exemptions and exceptions
in it. Overlapping of functions with large metropolitan
cities has been found in tax as well as other functions.

7. State Capitals Offer Stories

Many times the political measures originate in the
state capital. Some states are notorious for the large
number of constitutional amendments upon which they ask the
people to decide.

In 1950 the citizens of Louisiana were constantly
barraged with notice of either a constitutional convention
or two dozen amendments. Toward the end of the year, the
legislature authorized the governor to call off the convention. The people still had twenty-four amendments which
were to be added to the constitution or rejected in the
November general election.

Just how a constitution should be written is a complex question. Certainly most authorities would agree that
the Louisiana constitution is far from good, and that it
will probably never be improved by offering piecemeal amendments for the people to consider a score at a time. How to
get a good constitution is one question, but what to do with
amendments offered is just as real and more pressing.

Many Louisiana newspapers almost ignored the wealth
of stories which these problems offered. One paper, however
followed up the headlines with a few background stories.
After the headline announcing a special session to do away
with the constitutional convention came a feature story on
the procedure to be used. It was a technique that Louisiana
had often used to suspend, but not repeal, a law.

Special Session Set On Tuesday to Cancel Vote on Convention

HEADLINE

Duchein Says Foes Should Be Prepared to Qualify if Move Fails

A special legislative session will convene at 6:30 p. m. Tuesday to consider cancelling provision for a constitutional convention, spokesmen for Gov. Long said yesterday.

Then came this one:

Legislature Session Will Feature Unusual but Not Rare Procedure

BACKGROUND FOR CLARITY

By Edmond Le Breton
(Associated Press Correspondent)

Not only will next Tuesday's session of the Louisiana Legislature be the shortest in history—by a wide margin—but it will highlight a curious legislative procedure based as much on custom as on positive law.

This procedure is unusual, but not rare in Louisiana. Legislatures on a number of occasions in the past have suspended laws or delegated authority to governors to suspend them, by merely adopting resolutions to that effect.

Similar Actions

Such a grant of power was made to the governor at this year's regular session which suspended.

And in a famous instance in 1935, with the late Sen. Huey P. Long calling the signals, the Legislature authorized the governor to suspend four cents of a five-cent a barrel oil refining tax that had stirred up a political tempest in the state.

Yet there is nothing in the state constitution which says affirmatively that a Legislature may suspend laws. All these suspensions have been based.

Opinion Divided

That tribunal in a divided opinion upheld the suspension. The majority incidentally used some

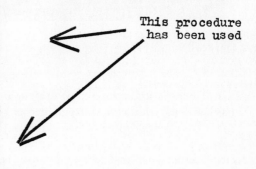

This procedure has been used

The constitutionality was upheld

DEADLINE   *Richard N. Taylor*

Mr. Taylor is an architectural draftsman and renderer who also
has had some training and experience as a cartoonist. That he has
spent considerable time in newspaper offices is evident from the
hard, cold tenseness he has captured in this portrait study of a
city editor with just three minutes between a possible news
break and a deadline that is as firm and as cold as the line and
color the artist has used to portray it.

Calling off the constitutional convention, however, was only part of the big problem of constitutional revision. Twenty-four important constitutional amendments had to be accepted or rejected by the voters.

War of Words Continue on Several Proposed Constitutional Changes

By Edmond Le Breton

(Associated Press Correspondent)
Now that the constitutional convention call apparently is dead as an issue, the Nov. 7 general election inevitably seems like a comparatively tame one.......

To help inform its readers, the editor asked one of his political writers to prepare a series of articles explaining the questions which the voters were to decide. Four front-page stories were the result, explaining what the amendments were, who approved, who disapproved, and why. A voter who read these was much better prepared for his trip to the polls than those who had no such articles to read.

Seven Proposed Amendments Statewide in Application

(Editor's Note: This is the third in a series of stories on proposed amendments to the constitution on which citizens of Louisiana will vote Nov. 7. Other amendments will be discussed in later stories.)

By Margaret Dixon

Seven of the proposed amendments to the constitution on which citizens of Louisiana will vote Nov. 7 are statewide in their application. These are:..........

Several Proposals in Nov. 7 Election Apply to Cities

Editor's Note - This is the fourth and last of a series of stories on the 24 proposed amendments of the constitution on which citizens of Louisiana will vote Nov. 7.

Four of the 24 proposed amendments before the people of Louisiana will directly affect both city governments and residents.
These are:.......

The reporter had several sources open to him. First he could analyze the complete proposal. Ordinary citizens who neither had access to the full texts of amendments nor the time to study them, needed that service. Then, the reporter could use the reports of the legislative committee and the debates on the issue. Then he could turn to interviews with persons who were present at the committee hearings or at legislative sessions when the proposals were discussed. Several citizen research groups, such as the Civic League, the League of Women Voters, Public Affairs Research and others, make studies of these questions. In any case, the newsman could help inform the people on the immediate problem.

The problem of providing an adequate constitution for the state was not solved with the decision on amendments in the election. The old constitution had grown longer, more complicated, and more confusing. The problem of revision was still there.

Many people in the state had never recognized the problem. Others who knew the constitution must be changed did not know how it could be changed or what changes should be made. Very few were aware of a group of highly trained persons who had been studying this problem in that state for four years. The scores of reports they had prepared had scarcely been noticed by the press. These reports would have provided innumerable stories for any newspaper in that state.

Similar problems exist in almost every state. Florida voted on five amendments to her constitution in 1950. None of them satisfied the need for thorough constitutional revision. People in both Florida and Louisiana are more fortunate than in some other states, where the possibility of getting an amendment before the people is almost non-existent.

Current State Problems In The News

Re-Apportionment

An urban legislator in the state capitol often represents 300,000 people while his rural colleagues will have only 3,000 constituents. The state legislature cannot properly represent the people in this manner. Nevertheless most of our states have this type of situation. Reapportionment - or redistricting the legislature - is often hamstrung by power politicians or by a bad constitution. Representatives and senators who have long held power are afraid they will lost that power and their prestige if they vote for proper redistricting which will take into consideration the changes in population.

Constitutions Need Revamping

State constitutions, written and passed in the last century, often need to be streamlined and brought up-to-date. They usually have too much detail. Often the government they provide for is out-of-date. Amending the constitution may be easy, but revising it and modernizing it is a long, hard task.

States' Rights

People often talk about "states' rights" to cover up other issues of economic or social importance. The constitutional system of states is not static. It changes to meet new problems. Today states are bigger than ever. While they may not do the same jobs they once did, they are not useless or about to be trod underfoot.

Administrative Maze

To continue to be important, states must do their jobs well. This may mean reorganizing the administration to avoid overlapping, duplication and confusion.

Other state problems are equally as acute. They involve the improvement of the administration of justice, through a better system of courts; the curtailment and control of the lobbying activities carried on by representatives of various groups with members of the legislature and administrators; and the search for new industries by state industrial and development commissions.

8. National Stories

Dollar Sign in Politics   In Spring, 1950, the necessity for economy in national government expenditures made the headlines every day. The budget submitted by the President was argued pro and con; Congress cut some items and increased others. It was possible for anyone with any political leanings to criticize; and everyone criticized the President, or Congress, or both.

At the same time two experiments in government finance were being carried out: one by the President and one by Congress. Under Public Law No. 216, the Department of Defense -- through the President -- submitted a "performance budget" to Congress. It followed recommendations of the Hoover Commission. The "performance budget" centered attention on the work done -- the aims and activity -- rather than on lists of employees or authorization of purchases. The scope of budgeted activities could be checked immediately.

In Congress, meanwhile, the House Ways and Means Committee prepared to consolidate all appropriation bills into one omnibus bill and report the one bill to the House with estimates of receipts and expenditures for the year. For the first time, congressmen, or laymen, were able to see

at one time the total picture of federal expenditures. The
Associated Press carried this article on the omnibus appropriation bill. The second and third paragraphs bring the
issues to the reader's doorstep.

SINGLE PACKAGE SPENDING PLAN

By James Marlow

Washington, (AP) - For the first time in its
history congress this year will take a crack
at voting a one-package appropriations bill.
    This is an attempt to avoid the kind of
mess congress has made in the past. You have
a stake in the outcome and for this reason.
    It's your tax-money that's being voted.
    Every year in January the President sends
congress his budget message. This is his
estimate made with the help of experts, on
how much it will take to run the government
the next year.
    (The fiscal year starts July 1 and ends
the following June 30, so the budget President
Truman sent congress last January is for the 1951
fiscal year starting next July.)
    All the expenses of the various government
departments and agencies are listed in detail
in the budget.
    In the past congress examined these expense
items, always announced it would certainly cut
them down, and then voted the money it thought
was necessary.

Separate Bills

    But, in doing so, it tackled the agencies one
at a time. This meant that congress, instead
of voting on one bill covering all or most of
the agencies, voted on many separate bills.
    This hodge-podge arrangement often had an
unhappy result because, in voting on single
bills over a period of months, congress could
get lost in the total amount of money it was
voting.
    And therefore it might not know, until the
last bill was out of the way, maybe just before congress quit for the year, just how
much money altogether it had voted.
    This could be embarrassing, particularly
if congress has proclaimed it was going to
cut the president's estimates to shreds and
them discovered it had voted more than he
had asked.
    To get a little order out of this kind of
chaos, congress decided this year it would try
to wrap all the money needs of most of the agen-

115

Readers of the U.S. News & World Report January 20,1950, had this graphic story of the budget President Truman presented.

The President's Budget Billions
(Estimates for year starting July 1, 1950)

WHERE MR. TRUMAN SEES THE MONEY COMING FROM

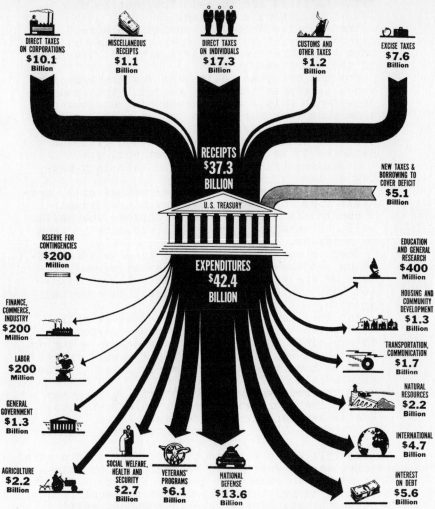

DIRECT TAXES ON CORPORATIONS
$10.1 Billion

MISCELLANEOUS RECEIPTS
$1.1 Billion

DIRECT TAXES ON INDIVIDUALS
$17.3 Billion

CUSTOMS AND OTHER TAXES
$1.2 Billion

EXCISE TAXES
$7.6 Billion

RECEIPTS $37.3 BILLION

NEW TAXES & BORROWING TO COVER DEFICIT
$5.1 Billion

U.S. TREASURY

EXPENDITURES $42.4 BILLION

RESERVE FOR CONTINGENCIES
$200 Million

EDUCATION AND GENERAL RESEARCH
$400 Million

FINANCE, COMMERCE, INDUSTRY
$200 Million

HOUSING AND COMMUNITY DEVELOPMENT
$1.3 Billion

LABOR
$200 Million

TRANSPORTATION, COMMUNICATION
$1.7 Billion

GENERAL GOVERNMENT
$1.3 Billion

NATURAL RESOURCES
$2.2 Billion

INTERNATIONAL
$4.7 Billion

AGRICULTURE
$2.2 Billion

SOCIAL WELFARE, HEALTH AND SECURITY
$2.7 Billion

VETERANS' PROGRAMS
$6.1 Billion

NATIONAL DEFENSE
$13.6 Billion

INTEREST ON DEBT
$5.6 Billion

HOW MR. TRUMAN SEES THE MONEY BEING SPENT

cies in one bill and then vote on that.
That theory as it stands right now may
be all right. And then again maybe it
isn't. For example:
In the past, when it approved a number
of appropriations bills separately, congress
might tack on to a couple of them some ideas
which the president didn't like.

Meant a Problem

That left him free to sign into law the
bills he liked and to veto the ones he didn't.
But - that meant a problem.
The agencies whose appropriations were
approved, could start borrowing on the money voted
them by congress when July 1 arrived, the start
of the new fiscal year.
But the story was different for the agencies
whose appropriations were vetoed. They had no
money when July 1 came unless congress voted
them some temporary funds to use while it did
one of two things:
1-Went back to work on the vetoed bill and
tailored it to please the president, or-
2-Repassed the bill over the veto thus making it law.
But now suppose, in the one-package bill, congress ties on some strings which Mr. Truman
doesn't like. He'll have to approve the whole
bill, or veto the whole bill, sending it back
to congress.
Then if congress delays too long in straight-
ening out the difficulty - say beyond July 1 -
most of the government agencies will be without money unless congress votes them some temporarily.
But that isn't all. The one-package bill
was dumped in the lap of the house yesterday.
It's a cinch that a lot of congressmen - during
the debate and vote on the floor - will try to
whittle down the amount of money listed in the
single bill.
So the one-package bill is still a long way
from being a proven success. Hold your hats.
You'll be hearing more of this.
                              Associated Press Dispatch

     While this was a feature story rather than a straight
news article, Marlow was forced to pack so much into a few
lines that he had to pass over details lightly. The story
could have been turned into a series of explanatory articles.
Or, expanded into space available in a Sunday edition, the
story could have been made more informative and interesting.

     This headline in the U. S. News & World Report on
March 24, 1950, called the readers' attention to a similar article, but dealt with the subject in more detail.

SINGLE KEY FOR FEDERAL PURSE
All Spending Via One Bill Aims at Economy

A single appropriation bill in place of a lot of smaller ones is being tried out to save time and money in U.S. spending.

It won't mean a balanced budget, automatically. Congress may cut Government costs somewhat, but not much.

Idea is that one-shot appropriation gives Congress clearer view of where the money goes. It makes deficits easier to see.

A brand-new device aimed at getting some economy in Government is about to be given a fling in Congress. This device is an omnibus appropriation bill, providing at one whack the money it will take to run a 40-billion-dollar Government during the fiscal year 1951, beginning nex July 1.

This one-package money measure, which probably will be the most voluminous bill ever offered to Congress, is being written by the House Appropriations Committee. It is expected to be ready for House debate beginning late this month.

U.S. News & World Report
Mar. 24, 1950

After he saw the story, the too-busy voter was able to get the gist of the story easily because of the way it was written. Point-by-point writing focused attention on important ideas and changes in the budget process.

One-Shot Appropriating has been adopted as a way of letting members of Congress see the Government's whole spending program, all in a single bill. Theory is that this puts the House and Senate on a spot, and might make them hesitate to vote a spending total that exceeds the Treasury's expected income.

First, Here is what this problem really is..

In past years, Congress has made its regular annual appropriations in 11 or 12 separate bills, one for each of the Government's major programs. Sometimes these bills have been passed without even a record vote. Doing the appropriating job in bits and pieces this way, few members of Congress can keep track of how spending bills are running in relation to Government revenue.

Whether single-shot appropriating actually will save any

money for the taxpayer remains to
be seen. Some authorities, skep-
tical about the whole thing, believe it might lead to confusion,
delay and logrolling. The public,
therefore, needs to understand what
is involved in this latest economy
effort.

    Mechanics of the plan is
simple. As before, appropriations
will originate in the House. There,
the Appropriations Committee has
been divided into subcommittees to
hold hearings on money needs for
the various federal programs. However, instead of reporting separate
bills for each of these programs,
the subcommittees will submit recommendations for inclusion in one
master bill...

You ought to know
something about it....
And here is how it
works...

    On one side, it is argued
that the single-appropriation plan
is the only way open to Congress
to get a firm grip once more on
Government purse strings. This is
the position of Senator Harry F.
Byrd (Dem.), of Virginia, chairman
of a joint committee seeking ways
to cut federal spending...

There is a lot to be
said for this bill by
its proponents.

Appropriation bills
will not come before
Congress one at a time,
giving only a part of
the picture.

    On the other side, there are
those who believe the single appropriation bill may invite trouble...

Opponents of the meas-
ure, too, have their
say.

    A veto by President Truman,
coming after the beginning of the
new fiscal year, might bog down
the whole operation of Government,
since every agency would be affected.

A presidential veto
would bog down the
whole operation of gov-
ernment.

    Logrolling, in the opinion
of some opponents of the scheme,
might be encouraged. Appropriations for the Agriculture Dept.
and the Interior Department....

Another argument: log-
rolling would be en-
couraged, some say.

The points were made forcefully, explained, and evaluated.
Then the U.S. News reporter concluded:

    Thus, the single appropria-
tion bill holds no magic formula
for ending the Governments financial troubles. About the most
anybody expects is that it will
make Congress more conscious of
those troubles.

These stories tell the voters of real efforts of Congressmen to do their job better. They also tell the reader some of the problems that might develop -- that he should not expect too much.

The alert reporter also sees hints of other stories he could write when he thinks over these reports. Just how does the government spend our money? Is this the "best" way? How do other countries get by without our great wealth? What "reforms" have we tried before? Have they worked? Why? Here are leads for front page items, for newscasts, and newspaper feature articles. Here are stories the voter could read profitably.

Information on how the government spends money will always be news in our society. Planning where dollars should go, securing community approval, and spending money -- all part of our fiscal process -- interest taxpayers. Yet very few know anything about how it was decided to spend $40 billion instead of $30 billion, or -- in your city -- $3 million instead of $7 million.

Whether one is reporting national, state, or local news, where the money comes from and how it is spent makes a story. Sometimes these stories strengthen government programs and secure consent to them. Under other circumstances a story may arouse citizens to make new demands for more activities, or more efficiency, or less corruption.

Fact Sources -- Where a dollar comes from and where government spends it can make a fascinating narrative. A reporter who analyzes a budget has a wealth of information at his fingertips. Turning to sources such as the Bureau of the Budget or the Bureau of Census (for state and local records), or compilations such as Facts and Figures on Government Finance, published by the Tax Foundation of New York, a writer has facts to compare his budget with others like it. He can compare his government today with that of previous years. When the reporter helps the reader trace a trend in expenditures or revenue collection, the newsman is giving a worthwhile service. Leonard White's Introduction to Public Administration or a similar text will give the reporter pertinent, useful facts for his story.

People Need to Know -- When the American Institute of Public Opinion (Dr. George Gallup, Director) polled the people of the United States in the period February 6-18, 1950, 48 per cent of the people thought the main problems before the government were taxes and government finances. If all the people had written their congressmen, these subjects would have been mentioned more than any other.

But if newsmen were partly responsible for that, they also had to share the blame for the fact that another Galluppoll about the same time showed that only 39 per cent of the voters had heard about the Hoover Commission for Executive Reorganization, and only 31 per cent of the voters knew its general purpose.

The most widely heralded attack on irresponsibility,
inefficiency in the executive branch of the federal government was recognized by only 31 per cent of the people.

Here are exciting stories people have not read.
Many of them have not been written. The Commission on Organization of the Executive Branch of the Government, under
its chairman, Herbert Hoover, prepared an exhaustive study
of the government. A non-partisan, unofficial Citizens
Committee for the Hoover Report was organized to inform the
public and push legislation to implement suggested reforms.
Here was a deep fund of stories, far from exhausted by the
numerous stories written.

An alert reporter should be wary, here, though, that
his stories do not deal too exclusively with dollars and
cents. American voters seem to show the political discern-
ment that recognizes the real necessity of sound governmental finance and knows, at the same time, that there may be
things more important than the number of dollars spent.
The Hoover Commission expressed this same acumen in listing
its aims. The recommendations
> ...are directed to the achievement of reforms
> which it (the committee) hopes will bring about
> a more responsible and a more reponsive govern-
> ment, a government which will act with dispatch,
> with greater internal coordination and harmony,
> with consistency of administrative policy, and
> economy of operation.

The priority of these aims should never be forgotten
by those who write for a democratic press even when finance
does make the lead.

A story about the Hoover Commission Report on the
postoffice could begin:

> Out-of-date equipment and organization contributed
> to the $500,000,000 deficit of the Post Office
> Department in 1949, according to the report of
> the Hoover Commission.

To make the report fully clear, one might begin a second
story like this:

> Part of last year's $500 million Post Office deficit
> was used to help American commercial air-lines keep
> up in the world race for air supremacy.

This story could drive home the Hoover Commission re-
ommendation that subsidies not be hidden in postoffice costs.
Then an editor could either emphasize the other recommendations of the Commission on Reorganization, or open the per-
ennial question of subsidies to American Business.

The dollar sign in politics calls for skillful research and well backgrounded stories more than for wordy polemics.

Perennial Political Stories

Not only do routine administrative problems continually reappear in the news; highly dramatic political situations appear in similar patterns decade after decade. A political news reporter can copy a lawyer's use of precedent. Here is today's news. A similar situation occurred thirty years ago. Here is what happened then. The situation today differs in these respects. Will the same result come about? Do you want the same result this time?

One of the persistent political patterns is the attempt to crush minority groups. In the 1850's, a nativist reaction to immigrants(particularly Catholics) produced street fights, violent intimidation of voters, and the Know-Nothing Party. Later the I.W.W. provoked charges of alien dangers regardless of its policy at the time. But the big red scare following World War I showed the violence of stresses of modern society.

As Frederick Lewis Allen put it in his highly interesting book Only Yesterday

> Those were the days when column after column of the front pages of the newpapers shouted the news of strikes and anti-Bolshevist riots; when radicals shot down Armistice Day paraders in the streets of Centralia, Washington, and in revenge the patriotic citizenry took out of the jail a member of the I.W.W. -- a white American, be it noted -- and lynched him by tying a rope around his neck and throwing him off a bridge; when properly elected members of the Assembly of New York State were expelled (and their constituents thereby disfranchised) simply because they had been elected as members of the venerable Socialist Party; when a jury in Indiana took two minutes to acquit a man for shooting and killing an alien because he had shouted "To hell with the United States"; and when the Vice-President of the nation cited as a dangerous manisfestation of radicalism in the women's colleges the fact that the girl debaters of Radcliffe had upheld the affirmative in an intercollegiate debate on the subject: "Resolved, that the recognition of Labor unions by employers is essential to successful collective bargaining."
> It was an era of lawless and disorderly defense of law and order, of unconstitutional defense of the Constitution, of suspicion and civil conflict -- in a very literal sense, a reign of terror.

Cut from the same cloth were many headlines following World War II. The Hatch Act of 1939 had already made it unlawful for anyone paid in full or part by the federal government to belong to any organization advocating

overthrow of our constitutional form of government. The
infamous Dies Committee on Un-American Activities (and their
successors) had begun intemperate investigations during the
war. Then in 1946, President Truman established a commission to make a full investigation of the loyalty of government employees. A Canadian spy exposé set the stage; and
proponents and exponents of the Loyalty Review Board joined
Congressmen in arguing about how loyalty should be insured
in our type democracy.

An alert reporter might have regarded all this as
background when in 1950, Senator Joseph McCarthy (Rep. Wisconsin) broke into a headline rash with a series of sensational charges. The first he made in a Lincoln's Day speech
at Wheeling, West Virginia. "I have in my hand 57 cases of
individuals who appear to be either card-carrying members
or certainly loyal to the Communist Party, but who nevertheless are still helping to shape our foreign policy." Later,
he claimed a letter from former Secretary of State Byrnes as
authority for the charge that 205 persons were kept after
the security boards disapproved them. On the Senate floor
these charges began with 81 cases; and with his senatorial
immunity, McCarthy's charges went from bad to worse.

State Department activities were disrupted around the
world as employees returned to Washington to counter Senator McCarthy's charges; U.S. prestige fell abroad. The
President, the F.B.I., the Democratic Party, and some Republicans all were splattered with charges that climaxed as
Owen J. Lattimore, writer and sometime State Department con-
sultant on Far Eastern affairs, was named as the chief Russian agent in the United States.

Lattimore Denies Being Spy for Soviet Union;
Brands Senator McCarthy "Madman"

Sees Lawyers
About Possible
Libel Action
New York, April 1 (AP) - Owen J. Lattimore,
accused by Sen. Joseph McCarthy, R., Wis., of
being a master spy for Russia, today called
McCarthy a "madman" making an "obviously political attack upon the State department."
Lattimore repeated previous denials that
there is any basis for McCarthy's charges, and
said he was consulting his lawyers about possible
libel action.
Lattimore also brought up the question of
whether he ever was a State department employe.
Associated Press Dispatch

Many types of political issues poured through the
headlines. The press was partial to sensation through the
whole affair; but as some of McCarthy's charges were dis-
proved, the stories were handled in a judicious manner.
Such papers as the Milwaukee Journal and the St. Louis
Post-Dispatch saw the possibilities early for backgrounding
McCarthy.

123

One of the most thorough short stories published while
accusations were at their height was contained in the New
Republic, March 20, 1950. First came the news lead of the
current event.

> At a critical moment in world history Senator
> Joseph McCarthy charges that our State Depart-
> ment and our foreign policies are directed by
> our adversary, Soviet Russia...

Then, pointing up the obvious truth that politics is relations among people, the writer inquired into the type of
person McCarthy was reputed to be.

> McCarthy began his political career as a trial
> judge in Wisconsin. He presided over the case
> of a dairy combine and was reprimanded by the
> Wisconsin Supreme Court for his arbitrary and
> arrogant action in suppressing evidence and in
> falsifying the court record. Twice he was ex-
> posed for income tax evasions. When he ran for
> the Senate in 1946, he refused to resign from
> the bench, subjecting those who opposed him to
> the danger of retaliation from his court, if he
> should lose. Again the State Supreme Court re-
> buked him, ruling that his action 'was in viola-
> tion of the terms of the Constitution and laws
> of the State of Wisconsin', and that he 'Violated
> his oath as a circuit judge and as an attorney
> at law' and that he was 'guilty of an infraction
> of the moral code.'

Finally, the action of the Senate investigating subcommittee which had been prompted by McCarthy was reported so that
the action was put into constitutional perspective.

> In clear violation of Constitutional practice
> established over the life of our republic, the
> Senate "Directed" the President to turn over to
> the State Department files...

In this article the writer for the New Republic covered several aspects of this issue, which could be found in
any political story. The news, backgrounded as a political
scientist should, reflected an appreciation of the fact that
the total picture must be presented. Historical perspective
gives the writer an opportunity to see what turned out as
significant in earlier stories of a similar nature. In
Spring, 1954 the AP ran a series on McCarthy; the New York
World-Telegram and Sun also published a thorough series on
the Senator.

Political science, in its real sense, is nothing less
than a systematic knowledge of the political aspects of
society. In a newspaper, personalities and why they are
what they are (psychological background) and the society and
social setting of the news (sociological background) are
focused by political news and its political precedents (political background) into a meaningful story which gives

citizens of a democracy information on which they may act.

The U.S. News & World Report, April 7, 1950, published a story that put all the spy headlines into proper perspective. It was a story of just how the government checked
all federal employees for subversive activity, and what had
been found then in the greatest spy hunt in history.

```
        Sulzberger Advises Make
        Complex News Interesting

    While the trivial and the sensational are
almost always easier to read than the complex
and serious, it nevertheless remains imperative
that we find ways and means of making things as
easy as possible for busy readers.
    It is more urgent for newspapers today to
inform a thousand readers than to entertain a
million.
    The mastery of certain techniques is certain-
ly imperative in the newspaper business, but
those who gather and present news on the intri-
cate questions of today need much more than
technical skill if they are really to understand
what they are handling and convey their under-
standing to the reader.
    Any number of experts can be found who can tidy
up a reporter's sentences, but what we need is
somebody to tidy up our minds.

                      Arthur Hays Sulzberger,
                      New York Times publisher,
                      on receiving the University
                      of Missouri Honor Award,
                      May 5, 1950.  Reported in
                      Editor & Publisher, May 6,
                      1950.
```

9. Grass Root Backgrounding of News

The opportunities for backgrounding national headline
news are not limited to reporters who handle the headlines
originally. A writer for a small town paper can and should
exploit feature stories on national events just as effectively as the reporter in Washington or New York. Giving
a national story a local slant -- telling what a federal
program means to a rural community -- is a real service a
small newspaper can offer, and often attracts more readers
than a generalized feature.

This same idea was expressed by Houston Waring, the
editor of the Littleton Independent, a small town (pop. 3,000)
weekly in Colorado. Writing in the New York Times Magazine
May 15, 1949, Mr. Waring said:

It is possible for the country editor to help
interpret the foreign affairs without abandoning
his role as an expert on local affairs. In fact,
it is the local angle which he should exploit.
For example:
When our community heard that 200,000 displaced
persons were coming to America this did not mean
much to the people of Littleton. How could the
Independent give the story real meaning for local
people? Well, we were able to point out that Littleton's quota or share would be only four displaced
persons. We suggested that our community could
easily double or triple this quota. In editorials
we reminded our readers that America had been built
on immigration. In 1907 the United States admitted
one immigrant for every seventy-five people. Under
the displaced persons bill we should be admitting
only one for every 700 of our population.
Then followed articles and editorials on how
the displaced persons came into their present
distress, the courage they displayed, the skills
they had, the use they would be in Littleton with
their new ideas, opportunities, and outlook. The
result has been that arrangements have been made
for a DP family to come to Littleton this summer...

Here is the complete pattern for backgrounding the
news. Headline-features to make the story real and reduce
it to local size, and more features to get back to all the
problems involved.

What steps did Houston Waring take to develop a local
background news-feature for the national news story? The
first requirement was the spotting of the local angle. The
news about the Displaced Persons Act prompted Waring to
determine the number of displaced persons which would be
Littleton's share. This figure was obtained by simple math-
ematics. A knowledge of the history of the United States,
particularly facts about the flow of immigrants and how they
helped to build the country was useful as background for the
articles in the Colorado paper.

If Waring needed he could have consulted the Statistical Abstract of the United States for figures relating to
the population of other cities and towns. With these figures he could determine what their proportionate share of
the displaced persons would be in comparison with Littleton's. The United Nations Yearbook would have given other
facts about displaced persons for background material.

Waring could have examined also an American government
textbook, such as Ogg & Ray's Introduction to American Government, for political and legal backgrounds for the immigration problem. For further social background of immigration in this country he could have found information in almost any U.S. history book, such as Allen Nevins and Henry
S. Commager's Pocket History of the United States.

126

Where Do We Get the Information?

One does not write all these stories a few minutes before a deadline. Some stories take time to background. The reporter may know his story is there -- and still have to work to get it.

Where can one find the information? One place to go is to the person who knows -- the expert. Sometimes this is the man in the news. But often he is under the pressure of immediate problems, and besides may attempt to bias the reporter. A trained person who can see the problem in perspective will usually have much to offer.

The reporter might interview the political scientist. Well-trained members of civic research bureaus often have information that can help. Trained career administrators in related fields can suggest material. Each professional may share the bias of his employer to a degree, but the insight the professional offers can be used by an apt reporter.

Information on many problems can be gathered by writing to the Public Administration Clearing House in Chicago. This is the co-ordinating agency for the 1313 groups (so-called because they are located at 1313 East 60th Street). The agency includes the Council on State governments, the International City Managers' Association, and others. Their reports are usually available to anyone for reasonable charges. Many state universities provide similar clearing houses for information about their states.

10. Books Useful to Reporters of Political News.

Edwin S. Corwin, The President: Office and Powers. New York: New York University Press, Third Edition, 1948. This book, with a foreward by Arthur Krock, is a thorough study of the presidency, what it is, how it has developed, and the men who have made it. Mr. Corwin is an outstanding authority on his subject.

Robert Eugene Cushman, Leading Constitutional Decisions. New York: T. S. Crofts and Co., Ninth Edition, 1950. Mr. Cushman's book is a handy source on important constitutional matters which have been before the courts.

George B. Galloway, Congress at the Crossroads. New York: Thomas Y. Crowell Company, 1946. Mr. Galloway has had broad experience working with Congress and its problems. This book contains much of his criticism which was considered in passing the Legislative Reorganization Act of 1946, and also analyzes the Act as passed.

Alvin H. Hansen and Harvey S. Perloff, State and Local Finance in the National Economy. New York: W.W. Norton and Co., Inc., 1944. Messers, Hansen and Perloff, out-

127

standing economists, have dealt with general concepttions in government finance as it must be in our federal society. They review socio-political problems, discuss possible solutions, and explain various aspects of current economic theory in this field.

A general textbook on American government: There are many of these, any one of which might be adequate.
For example: Frederic A. Ogg and F. Orman Ray, Introduction to American Government. New York: Appleton-Century co., Inc., Ninth Edition, 1950.
William Anderson; American Government. New York: Henry Holt and Company, Third Edition, 1946.
Albert Saye, Merritt B. Pound, and John F. Alluns, Fundamentals of American Government. New York: Prentice-Hall, Inc., 1950. If only one book were to be purchased, it should be of this general nature.

A general textbook on municipal government. For example: William Anderson and Edward Weidner, American City Government. New York: Henry Holt and Company, Revised Edition, 1950. Arthur Bromage, Introduction to Municipal Government and Administration. New York: Appleton-Century-Crofts, 1950.
Marguerite J. Fisher and Donald G. Bishop, Municipal and Other Local Governments. New York: Prentice-Hall, Inc., 1950.
Ernest B. Schultz, American City Government. New York: Stackpole and Heck, Inc., 1949.

United States Government Organization Manual. Washington: Government Printing Office. Published annually, This Manual is the official organization handbook of the Federal Government. It contains sections descriptive of the agencies in the legislative, judicial, and executive branches. Supplemental information following these sections includes (1) brief descriptions of quasi-official agencies and selected international organizations, (2) charts of the more complex agencies, and (3) appendixes relating to abolished or transferred agencies and to government publications.

B. Periodicals

1. Congressional Record. Published daily while Congress is in session. Washington: Government Printing Office. All debates and proceedings in both houses of Congress are reported, as well as correspondence, documents, speeches, articles, etc. which members wish to include.

2. Congressional Quarterly Almanac, published yearly. Washington: Congressional Quarterly News Features. This is a volumnious facts and figures reference book of all the activities of Congress. It covers bills, amendments, committees, debates, hearings, investigations, lobbies, outside pressures, vote records. It also gives the age, party seniority,

128

congressional activities and professions of each
Congressman.
The Almanac summarizes every public bill including
amendments, acted upon by either house. A synop-
sis of the debate is given on all major bills. The
Almanac summarizes the recent background of the
issue. It is divided into eight broad subjects:
Agriculture, Appropriations, Education and Welfare,
Foreign Policy, Labor, Military and Veterans, Mis-
cellaneous and Administration, Taxes and Economic
Policy. It is more thorough and can be used more
easily than the official Congressional Record.

10. Summary

Politics is news; and events with political significance will continue to take more and more front page space.
In a democratic society, the people have to make decisions.
To make those decisions wisely, they must know the alternatives, and the results of any possible choice. Most of the
people will rely on journalists for the information on which
they will act.

The social responsibility of those who disseminate
the news is constantly increasing. Newsmen who ignore the
multitude of background stories political science furnishes
will not fulfill that function. The reporter's "eye for
news" has to be a penetrating one. A wide variety of news
events on the national, state, county and municipal level
were discussed and the need for going below the surface for
news-features was indicated.

Fact and Discussion
Questions on Chapter III, "News in Its Political Setting."

1. Do you agree with the statement nearly every news story has a political aspect? Illustrate.

2. Why do newsmen need to have a background in political science?

3. Show how the government affects us from the time of birth to death?

4. What do you think is the function of government in the solution of problems of people?

5. (a) Explain the function of a newsman in a democracy,
   (b) Why does the newsman's role present a challenge to him?

6. Is local news important to readers in your community? Defend your answer.

7. How did the Tallahassee, Fla. Democrat aid public opinion in the local vote on the power issue?

8. What kind of articles did the St. Louis Post-Dispatch publish to acquaint the citizens with municipal problems there?

9. (a) What county problem did the Associated Press survey?
   (b) What newspaper localized the story? (c) Comment on it.

10. How did the Louisiana paper handle the issue of constitutional revision?

11. (a) Explain the term "performance budget"; (b) how did the AP handle the story? (c) Compare it with the article in the U.S. News & World Report.

12. What volume could you use to compare governmental costs?

13. What conclusion can you draw from the Gallup poll about the need to be informed?

14. Compare the two leads in the Hoover Commission report about the post office.

15. List some persistent recurring political stories.

16. How did the New Republic background the McCarthy issue?

17. Summarize Publisher Arthur Hays Sulzberger's views on journalism. Do you agree? Disagree? Explain answer.

18. (a) How did Houston Waring localize a national issue?
    (b) What other books could he have used?

19. List some information on political news you would use in

backgrounding a story.

20. Discuss some current city problems facing officials and voters.

21. Outline some key county issues today.

22. What are some state issues in the news today?

23. List some national issues in the headlines today.

PROJECTS

Newsclipping Project

1. Clip a national political story every day for a week.
   A. List possible stories which would background the news.
      (1) If such stories were actually written, clip them and analyze.
      (2) Indicate sources to which you, as a reporter, would go for this immediate background.
   B. What fundamental (continuing) political problems are illustrated by these stories?
      (1) If stories on these problems were written, clip them and analyze.
      (2) Indicate sources to which you would go to prepare news-feature articles on these problems.
         a. Information in periodicals.
            Check periodical indexes such as Reader's Guide to Periodical Literature, International Index, Index to Legal Periodicals, New York Times Index.
         b. Material from a general textbook.
            Read generally on the problem and check chapter bibliographies and footnotes for further references.
         c. Encyclopedias give general information.
            Check Encyclopedia Britannica, Encyclopedia of the Social Sciences, etc., and indicate value of articles found.
         d. Books furnish background.
            Check three books listed in the library card file and indicate value to a reporter. Investigate possible government publications on your problem.
   C. Write a lead for a feature you would write on the fundamental problem illustrated by some of your headlines, and outline how you would develop the article. Check with instructor.

Spot News

Choose an item of political news that continues in a series of daily stories. Write the news story itself for one day using background information to see what pertinent

features should be reported. Compare your story to a story
actually published for that day.

Feature Article Assignments

Select one of the following:

1. Examine a source of background material such as
   those following and outline several possible feat-
   ures.
   A. Choose a subject discussed in a current law
      journal. Write a feature article of 750 words
      for a Sunday paper.
   B. Choose a story prompted by th Hoover Commiss-
      ion Reports. (Go to the Reports themselves as
      well as secondary sources.) Write a news fea-
      ture.
2. Write a feature article backgrounding a current
   Supreme Court decision.
   A. Read a decision in the U.S. Reports, Supreme
      Court Reporter, or other official reports.
      Write a feature explaining the decision and its
      background.
   B. Possible cases for use are:
      Adamson v. California, 332 U.S. 46 (1947)
      Tray v. New York, 332 U.S. 261 (1947)
      United States v. California, 332 U.S. 19 (1947)

3. Interview a city or state official and explain the
   work of his department in a series of two stories.
   A. Check the yearly printed report of the depart-
      ment to the mayor or governor for facts you
      can use.
   B. Make the material you get graphic and lively;
      show the reader the importance of the depart-
      ment.
4. Write two articles on a current municipal problem
   in your town or city.
   A. Interview the head of the city government for
      a list of important problems facing the admin-
      istration or the residents. Select one issue.
   B. Visit an opponent and an advocate of the pro-
      posal to deal with the situation and get the
      varying views.
   C. Inquire of the city department which deals with
      this issue what the background and history of
      the problem is.
   D. Check the library for more information.
   E. Visit the instructor in political science on
      the campus and get his views and further leads
      on the problem.
   F. Write a news-feature about the issue with a
      lively lead and concrete detail.
   G. What pictures, graphs, etc. would you use?
5. Write a two-part series on city planning in your
   community or county.
   A. Check to discover if there is a planning agency.
   B. Study any reports it may have issued.

C. Interview the agency head for your articles. Inquire as to its history, functions, accomplishments, present and future plans.
6. Write a two-part overall series on the acute traffic problem in your community.
   a. Have surveys been made? What did they find?
   b. Interview the offical (police, or traffic department head) responsible.
   c. Check through the city yourself for traffic snarls.
   d. Write a lively article on your findings.
7. Write a three-part series on the "Drift Toward the Suburbs."
   a. Check library for any studies. Check morgue for clips.
   b. Interview city officials for views as to causes, new shopping centers, effects on city's taxes, business, transportation, utilities.
   c. What plans does the city have for further growth of community?
8. "Where Your Tax Dollar Goes" might be the head on a series you can write on city, county taxes, always of interest.
9. "Behind The Zoning Law" can be a series on an important question.
   a. Something of the history of the zoning ordinance should be mentioned.
   b. The various zoning areas?
   c. The value of zoning, the abuses of zoning.
   d. Some present zoning cases and problems.
10. The "Streamling of County Government"
    a. Many students have pointed to the need for improving county government. Some believe closer working relations between city and county governments should be effected, with overlappings eliminated.
    b. Check texts on county administration. Check surveys.
    c. Discuss the local situation with a professor of political science.
    d. Interview county officials on this question.

Book and Magazine Report

Reporters will find in addition to the volumes mentioned before several others which will be useful in writing about political news.

Paul H. Appleby. Big Democracy. New York: Knopf, 1945.
Elmer E. Schattschneider. Party Government. New York: Farrar, 1942.

Further References: Journalism texts with chapters on government reporting.

Chilton R. Bush, Newspaper Reporting of Public Affairs, New York: Appleton-Century, 1940.
(Chapter VIII, "Federal Building"; Chapter IX, "City Hall"; Chapter XI, "County Building"; Chapter XII, "Politics".)

Laurence R. Campbell and Raymond E. Wolseley, Newsmen
    At Work, Houghton, 1949 (Chapter 17, "Focus on
    Collision"; Chapter 18, "Money in the Bank".)
Victor Danilov, Public Affairs Reporting, New York:
    MacMillan, 1955.
Stanley Johnson, The Complete Reporter. New York: Mac-
    millan, 1942. (Chapter 21, "Government and Polit-
    ics.")
John Paul Jones, The Modern Reporter's Handbook. New
    York: Rinehart, 1949. (Chapter 12, "News in Sta-
    tistics"; Chapter 13, "Reporting Local Government.")
Curtis D. MacDougall, Interpretative Reporting. New York
    Macmillan, 1949. (Chapter XXII, "Politics," Chapt-
    er XXIII, "Government".)
Robert M. Neal, News Gathering and News Writing. New
    York: Prentice-Hall, 1949. (Chapter 32, "City Hall
    Reporting"; Chapter 33, "Political News.")
Carl N. Warren, Modern News Reporting. New York: Harper
    1934. (Chapter XXX, "Politics and Elections.")
George Bird and Frederic E. Merwin, Press and Society.
    (Chapter 10, "How The Press Sees Government.")

Magazine Articles

Richard L. Neuberger, "News at the Legislature", Nieman
    Reports, Spring, 1949, 3:2.
James E. Pollard, "Roosevelt and the Press", Journalism
    Quarterly, September, 1945, Vol. 22, no. 3, p. 197-
    2o6.

U. S. Camera

SMOKING STACKS   These smoking stacks-- symbols
of industry-- represent the economic system which
produces a vast amount of news affecting vitally
the lives of readers. Such news requires accurate,
fair, complete and graphic backgrounding.

Chapter 5
Economic News in Focus

1. Significance of Economic News

Pick up any front page today and observe how many stories involve economics. You will find a surprisingly large number deal with economic activities on the international and national, state and local levels. Much of what passes for current political news is basically economic. Many believe that politics constitutes merely the surface ripple on the vast ocean of underlying economic interests.

Headlines such as:

PROPOSED TAX BILL
WINS SENATE APPROVAL
IN RECORD TIME

or this one:

CONGRESS VOTES
FOREIGN AID,
REJECTS CUT

are clearly within the realm of economics. Although apparently a political and military story on the surface, the following has an economic base:

BRITISH FLY PARACHUTE
TROOPS TO SUEZ CANAL;
ACHESON BACKS LONDON

The Suez Canal was an important economic life-line of the British Empire and had not only economic, but military and political significance. Disturbances in Egypt were a threat to economic security of the British to which the United States was closely allied, economically, culturally and militarily.

Economic news is important on a closer-to-home level particularly, because the reader can see how it affects his pocketbook. He wants to know how and why certain news in the nation and in his home community will affect him. He wants to know what the federal price and wage ceilings will do to his way of living -- how they will affect his earnings, his business, his family. The reader is concerned with the inflationary spirals of the prices of eggs and autos, or, if the country is hitting an economic slump, he wants to know what is being done constructively to check this roller-coaster.

He is also concerned about the local utility company's request for an increase in rates because he will feel the

136

effects at the end of next month on his gas and electric bills. He is directly and immediately affected by taxes on national as well as state, county and city levels, and so he reads a story of this kind to discover what dent the taxes will make:

Pay Check Shrinkages Due as T-Day Nears

By James Lee

Washington, Oct. 28 (INS) - Your pay check is going to shrink next month, you will ante up a penny more for a pack of cigarettes, and there will be a boost in the price of a beer.

Next Thursday is T-Day - "T" for taxes.

Along with other Americans, on November 1 you must start giving Uncle Sam $5,691,000,000 in higher taxes each year to pay for the increased cost of running the world's greatest and richest nation.

Very few citizens will escape the pinch. It will be applied to just about every part of everyday life, from driving your car to hoisting a highball.

Most people will get their first jolt when they pick up pay checks issued on or after November 1.

For example, if you are a single man earning $5,000 a year, the Federal withholding tax deduction from your check will amount to $108 more annually than it does now.

The thing to remember is that withholding rates are being increased by at least 11 per cent. For most people, it will be close to 12 per cent.

That, of course, is only part of the tax story. New excise taxes also go into effect November 1.

That means that cigarettes, gasoline, whiskey, beer, new cars, and a lot of other items will cost more.

It's going to cost you a little more to write your Congressman, though. There is a new 15 per cent tax on such gadgets as fountain pens and mechanical pencils. The same applies to cigar and cigarette lighters.

Should you want to survey the new tax picture from the angle of a business firm, rather than an individual, you will notice some sizeable increases.

There will be an additional one cent tax on a pack of smokes. A fifth of whiskey will cost 26 cents more in taxes than it does now. The gasoline tax increase rate is half a cent a gallon. The beer and wine tax will go up 12 and one-half per cent....

International News Service

If he checks through the various measures before congress, the reader notices the majority of them are economic bills or ones which clearly have economic aspects.

Here's Legislation's Status

Washington, Mar. 10. (AP) - The status of major legislation at the end of the week:

Draft law: The senate has passed a bill extending the draft law, lowering the induction age to 18 and providing for universal military training in the future. The house armed services committee has completed hearings on a companion bill.

Rent Control: A bill extending the federal control program 90 days from Mar. 31 comes up in the senate next week. It is pending in the house banking committee.

Aid for India: The administration's bill to give 2,000,000 tons of grain to India is hung up in the house rules committee. It has not been considered by the senate.

Defense Housing: A bill designed to encourage private enterprise to build housing in defense areas is on the house program for next week. It has not been acted on by the senate.

Taxes: The house ways and means committee is holding hearings on a bill to raise $10,000,000,000 in new taxes. There has been no senate action.

Appropriations: The first of a dozen departmental budget bills is due to be sent to the house floor late next week by the appropriations committee. It will finance the treasury and postoffice departments for the fiscal year starting July 1.

Reciprocal trade: Legislation extending the trade agreements program three more years has passed the house and is pending in the senate finance committee.

Troops for Europe: Two resolutions have been approved by the senate armed services and foreign relations committees. They are identical, both calling for approval of both houses before sending troops to Europe under North Atlantic pact agreements...

Defense: A bill authorizing a $2,300,000,000 warship construction and modernization program has been sent to the president. Both branches have passed a bill giving $10,000 free insurance to GIs killed in action: the bill is in a senate-house conference.

Associated Press Dispatch

News editors, city editors, managing editors of newspapers and wire services are aware that much economic news is newsworthy, and the significant economic news is featured.

2. Economic News Subordinated

While today economic news fills our newspapers, and on many days rates top position on page one, this was not always so.

Prior to the depression, which was precipitated by the stock market crash of 1929, the dikes holding back economic news in too many American newspapers were closed. True, the business recession of 1920-21 made newspapers and their readers conscious of the importance of economic news. The Dawes and Young Plans for improving the international economic situation had stirred interest among certain levels of readers. Editors, however, believed the general public was interested solely in a spectacular flash about a violent murder, or news of airplane accidents or municipal corruption. News of the industrial system, of the problems of capital and labor, of the revolution the machine brought to American life, was not newsworthy enough for page one. Such news did get into the larger metropolitan newspapers and many of the smaller ones. But it hardly rated a banner, or three-column spread in the upper right-hand corner as the big news of the day. It was the giddy age of post-World War I, with its fads, crazes, love nests, trans-Atlantic hops. Newspapers reflected this era.

Then came the spectacular stock market crash. Down went the employment curve. The dull thud of 10,000,000 men tramping the streets in search of elusive jobs could be heard by 1932 throughout the land.

3. Economic Depression Release News

The American public was faced with an unprecedented economic situation. Slowly, the news dikes began to open. Editors, responding to the changing interests and needs of their readers, began to push the depression problems onto the front page.

Shortly after President Franklin D. Roosevelt took office in March, 1933, his attempts to prime the stalling economic machine put economic news on page one and kept it there. First, he closed all the banks under a national banking holiday; then he started the National Industrial Recovery Act. His Agricultural Adjustment measure, his continuation of the Reconstruction Finance Corporation, his Civil Works program and finally his official departure from the gold standard -- all made the front pages of the American newspaper.

The news remodeled the front page. To the chromatic news scale of sex, crime, municipal corruption and automobile accidents was added the economic note. Editors discovered that the newspaper reader was potentially interested in economic news because he was faced with a new set of social and economic problems, brought on by the apparently fathomless depression. Newsmen recognized the importance

of the efforts made to keep the economic organization running, and each new industrial, agricultural or labor measure
proposed and discussed meant millions of readers would be
affected and therefore vitally interested. Reporters, col-
umnists, editorial writers and photographers sought to make
economic news understandable. Make-up men and copyreaders
attempted to attract attention to it.

4. What Causes Economic News?

The newsman sees that economic news results from the
dynamic character of our economic organization. If we had
a static society where people would remain the same, where
desires would remain fixed, we would have little or no conflict -- no economic news.

Changing desires of the public create new industries
and this produces economic change. The introduction of new
means of industrial production act as stimuli for altering
and, indeed, remodeling our economic system. The great
impact of the Industrial Revolution more than a century ago
is still being felt throughout the world. The harnessing
of steam, then of electricity, and now atomic power to machines to do man's back-breaking work has or will upset the
economic system. The repercussions extend in many directions and affect all parts of the economic and social organization. The great advances, too, in chemistry, physics and
other physical sciences have changed industrial processess,
and brought into existence new industries.

Economic change causes conflict between groups in the
population, producing news. Capital and labor and farmers
battle for a greater part of the national income and make
news. Maladjustments in our social system may be produced
by an economy which is being rapidly modified. The new in-
ustrial situation, which has not been adequately met, may
cause unemployment, depressions, and may develop a large
poverty class. These we call "economic problems." We seek
to adjust ourselves to the new industrial picture each decade, each generation, and we attempt to solve these problems.

We call them current economic issues, urgent economic
controversies of today. But they are all problems arising
out of the economic system and they become headline news.
The character of economic news also changes, reflecting the
modifications of the underlying organization, its stresses
and strains. The economic news of the period in American
life, 1840 through 1865, was concerned with the fast-growing
northern industrialism vs. the older southern agricultural
system, devoted to cotton.

Today economic news has altered.

Tomorrow it will be different.

But some basic, long-range patterns will remain -- although the details and specific types of economic problems

will change.

The newsman needs to focus his eye on some of these
major issues and develop an understanding of them. He can
learn the sources of information about them and what various authorities have to contribute. Newspaper readers and
radio listeners will not digest raw chunks of economic theory
or chapters from textbooks. Nor will they eagerly eat up
columns of statistics. So the reporter, as he investigates
the real problem of bringing economic news to the reader,
will seek effective techniques for writing and presenting
such material in palatable form.

Here again the meaning of spot economic news must be
made clear and understandable to the reader and must be
placed in its context.

THE ECONOMIST SPECIALIZES

The reporter assigned to an economic story
should remember specialization has developed
within the subject, and by relating his news to
the proper branch of economics, he can locate
the best book or specialist more quickly.

General Economics
>covers the over-all problems of produc-
tion, distributing and consumption.

Economic History
>deals with the economic development of
various countries as well as the growth
of certain industries and business concerns.

Transportation
>deals with the features and problems of
rail; highway, air and inland-waterway
transportation.

Marketing
>is concerned with the problems of the
distribution of raw materials, agricultural products and manufactured goods.

Agricultural Economics
>concerns itself with the problems of
farm production and distribution and
the facts which affect them.

Money, Credit, Banking
>studies the mechanisms of the credit,
monetary and banking systems, the life-
blood of the economic organization.

Labor Economics
>deals with the role of labor in the economy and the problems it has faced in the past, and the current issues.

Public Finance
>considers the economic, administrative and legal aspects of public revenues, debts and expenditures.

Public Utilities
>deals with the questions of ownership, regulation, financing and rate determination.

International Economics
>studies inter-relations of economic systems of various countries, and their resources, and the movement of international capital and goods.

Business Management
>studies methods of efficient management of retail, wholesale and manufacturing establishments.

5. Modern Economic Problems in the News

Here are some of the larger, persistent problems which America faces in the post-World War II period. These issues are constantly changing their character and importance. But no matter what the disguises, they play a significant part in the modern economic drama of our times. They will persist as problems for some time to come, because they represent surface manifestations, reflecting the changes and nature of our economic organization.

Key U.S. Economic Problems
Persistent, Long-Range Issues
Which America Faces

1. "Boom or Bust"
>The control of the economic system to bring stability, employment and higher standard of living.

2. Spiraling Prices
>An important issue faced by every family, every employe. It is tied up with wages and the stability of the economic machine.

3. The Question of Deficit Financing-Taxes
>This is a new concept in American public finance. What job does it do? What are the results? What role does it play as a means of combatting depressions?

How the PRESS can promote SOCIAL PROGRESS

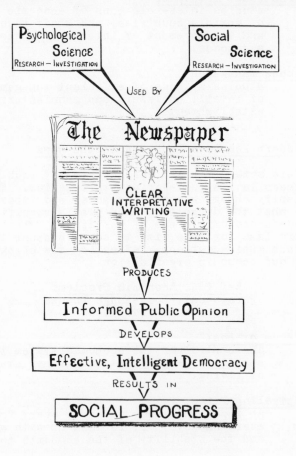

4. **Government and Its Relations with Business**
   How far should government go in its
   control and regulation of business, industry, agriculture? Has the laissez-
   faire system been abandoned? If not,
   to what extent has it been modified?
   Government is also participating in
   business-producing power and low-cost
   housing. Why is this necessary? How
   far will it go?

5. **Co-operation or Strife in American Industry**
   The conflict between labor and management
   seems to be developing more sharply. Is
   there machinery for settling disputes, reducing tensions, building a constructive
   industrial democracy?

6. **Social Security in American Life**
   A broad movement to provide various types
   of employment, old age and even health
   security has been growing. Will it continue? What new fields will it enter?
   What are the costs? What is the fundamental significance of this trend?

7. **The Farm Problem -- What to Do with Surpluses**
   Our farms can produce an abundance of
   food, but they cannot be disposed of in
   the usual channels. Government has entered the picture. How can this problem be
   solved satisfactorily?

8. **Trend towards Larger Industrial Units: but
   Decentralization of Plants.**
   This trend began decades ago, but is moving more rapidly. What is its significance
   as far as the American public is concerned --
   employes, consumers, small competitors?
   How does it affect the establishment of new
   enterprises, the control of prices?

9. **Foreign Aid -- International Economics**
   We will continue to supply money to foreign
   countries for years. What are the reasons
   for this policy? Are we pouring our money
   down a drainhole? Are there other consider-
   ations involved?

   As an example of how economic problems arise in the news
and how they may be backgrounded, one of the foregoing issues will be presented.
   Excessive inflation and mass unemployment are the principal afflictions that threaten the stability of modern
economic society, says economist Henry W. Spiegel in Current
Economic Problems. All too often orderly progress is dis-
turbed and insecurity created by these perils. Since the
Great Depression the American public has sought in vain

that happy balance which avoids both extremes.

The criticalness and importance of the issue are readily noted. The question is tied to the issue of wages, prices and the production capacity of the economic machine. Key to the problem is full but steady employment, with millions of employes earning enough to consume the products of industry and farm.

Here is an example of the issue and a background story which dealt with it. It is a story based on a monthly report of the President's Council of Economic Advisers. Economists were interviewed for an interpretation of the report. You will note the down-to-earth style of writing, a great change from the old-style economic reporting.

US Getting Richer—But Not Fast Enough, Advisors Say

Washington - America is getting richer and richer. But still it isn't getting rich fast enough. If it doesn't get rich faster, serious trouble lies ahead somewhere.

Lead:
Lively,
brief.
Short sentences
with a
snap

That's the substance of the conclusions experts draw from the latest monthly report to Congress by the President's Council of Economic Advisers. Nearly all business indices have been rising in recent months, and business prospects look good. So said the President, and so say his economists.

Yet the nation is affected with creeping unemployment. If unemployment keeps on rising indefinitely, any economist will agree that a day of reckoning must come. About the only healthy way to avoid unemployment is to provide more and more jobs. And that's what industry is doing. But it isn't providing new jobs fast enough.

Leon Keyserling, acting chairman of the Council, told a reporter: "We are not getting the expansion in industry and investment that we need to absorb the steady increase in the labor force. That is a serious problem."

The total number of employed persons has been rising for the past three months. But the monthly average is still lower than the monthly average for either 1947, 1948 or 1949. In March civilian employment stood at 57,551,000 - slightly under the total for March of 1949, which was 57,647,000.

Force Grows

But the labor force keeps growing - the body of persons working or seeking work. It totaled 62,305,000 in March 1949. It was 63,021,000 in March of this year - a gain of 716,000 persons. Unemploy-

ment increased from 3,167,000 in March 1949 to 4,123,-
000 in March of this year - a gain of 956,000. Those
figures worry government economists. They, the President and Congress are committed to the principle
that America's economic hope lies in full employment.
That means creating new jobs fast enough to give
work to the ever-growing mass of persons who need it.
      In order to do this, according to the econ-
omists, the nation's industrial production must increase at the average rate of $2\frac{1}{2}$ to 3 percent each
year. Two percent of this increase would be to give
new jobs to persons who have been displaced in industry because of increased productivity - the ability
of industry to turn out more goods per worker as a
result of new machines and techniques. That means
fewer workers are needed to do a given job.

Tallahassee, Fla., <u>Democrat</u>

The news about full employment, boom and bust recurs
on front pages regularly. George Soule, who attempts to
popularize economics, was asked to write an article for the
<u>New York Times Sunday Magazine</u>, an article which would
background the issue for readers. Mr. Soule, in his news-
feature on May 8, 1949, sought to place the news in its
context and to draw a comparison between 1929 and 1949.
Here is a brief excerpt:

HAVE WE LEARNED THE LESSONS OF 1929?

      Yes, says an economist, because we have
erected defenses against 1929's mistakes.
      The last time a really bad smash occured
was in 1929. Every expert has his favorite theory
about what brought it on, but almost all would
agree on the main disturbances which characterized
it. The most dramatic was the collapse of the stock
market, in which more people lost more millions in
a shorter time than ever before....
      Whatever may have been the chain reaction
leading to the 1929 explosion, the American people
were so stunned by it that they could not get the economy going again for a long time. Unemployment spread,
income shrank, and finally the wheels nearly stopped
altogether when the banks had to be closed.
      Have we learned our lesson? Is it likely
that we shall let the same thing happen to us again?
We do not yet understand how to eliminate all upward
and downward swings of employment. Only a rash pro-
phet would say that there never will be another serious depression .
      But we have made headway; if we diligently
apply what is now known we can somewhat moderate the
vagaries of the business curve. In particular we
have erected defenses of some sort against every one
of the major mistakes which are plainly visible in
the years preceding and following 1929....

Mr. Soule pointed out that in 1929 the nation did not
have unemployment compensation. While unemployment insurance, he said, cannot prevent depression, it can serve as
a cushion to sustain consumer demand when need arises.

"Many believe that when a serious depression is in prospect the government should step in to bolster employment by
increasing its expenditures on public works, reducing taxes,
or both," the economist wrote. "There are many projects
which can be undertaken. Conservation of soil, forests and
minerals, river valley developments, urban redevelopment,
the building of schools and hospitals, repair and improvement of roads."

Perhaps the most important of all the
safeguards against depression is the mental preparation to tackle the problem. In 1929 the
country was victimised by a fatuous optimism; the
prevailing conviction was that we had achieved a
self-balancing economy which never again could suffer
a serious crisis.
Now there is widespread recognition of
the need to think ahead and to be alive to any
possible danger.

Mr. Soule concluded by pointing to the work of the Council of Economic Advisers which puts together and interprets
a vast amount of pertinent economic data about our system.
He declared that "if we had such an agency in 1929, together with the growth of information and analysis which has
taken place since that date, the chances are that we should
not have been overcome by so tragic a series of follies and
misfortunes."

<u>Christian Science Monitor</u>   Noted for its constructive
point of view, the <u>Christian</u> Science Monitor seeks to interpret objectively a variety of economic and other news.
Without the same economic pressures of other dailies, the
<u>Monitor</u> frequently backgrounds business and industrial news
in thorough-going fashion, displaying the explanatory article on the front page. Richard L. Strout, Washington correspondent for this distinguished paper, interviewed a number
of economists for an article which presented the over-all
picture of the economic scene. It follows in part:

U.S. Boom Spiral Seen Periled By Lack of Planning

By Richard L. Strout

Staff Correspondent of The Christian Science Monitor

How prosperous is America?

President Truman in an optimistic press conference here declares things are booming and evidently is keying the 1950 congressional campaign to the traditional and appealing slogan, "a full dinner pail."

Republicans wrathfully reply that the country is prosperous all right - but it's not due to Mr. Truman.

A third point of view is expressed here by quiet economists. They are not directly concerned with politics. They raise a more profound and a potentially disturbing question. By what standard, they ask, is the present so-called "prosperity" measured?

The President's economic council, headed by Leon H. Keyserling and John D. Clark, has expressed apprehension repeatedly over rigid prices and alleged failure of key industries to make appropriate reductions. The council singled out steel as a case in point, explaining that "steel affects the whole economy, and some reduction in steel prices would favorably influence the whole economic situation."

Another field is the automobile industry. Demand for cars, it is argued, is not being supported by expansion of national income but by rapid expansion of consumer credit. Such a situation cannot last. Automobile prices are out of line with declines elsewhere, it is charged. Many are waiting for a forced adjustment, and when this comes it may cause a good deal of unemployment.

Elusive Calculation

Speaking in general terms, the economic view here is that there exists a high level of American prosperity, but its size depends a good deal by what standard it is measured. Assuming that in a dynamic economy like America's "you have to grow to stand still," there is little comfort in finding that present figures slightly surpass previous years.

The standard that should be used, it is argued, is a growth of national productivity of from 2 to 2.5 per cent a year, annually compounded. America's expansion has set a "normal" rate of growth producing a doubling of total output every 20 years.

If the nation falls behind this level and the distribution of income that permits this steadily deepening stream of goods to be absorbed by the public, then it is actually falling behind in the race to maintain full employment.

Failure to absorb goods means there will be unemployment. Unemployment in turn produces declining purchasing power. The process feeds on itself.
Christian Science Monitor

Government is playing a larger and more diversified role than ever before in the economic life of the community and nation, and news about this activity is persistent. It is likely that this news pattern will continue and will produce copy and headlines for decades to come. This issue presents many angles, but in this section we will limit ourselves to placing the question in its context and pointing up some of its phases which produce news repeatedly.

The issue appears frequently in different guises and is related closely to the monopoly issue. In 1950 the issue came up when a subcommittee of the Judiciary Committee of the U.S. House of Representatives conducted an investigation to study the monopoly question and to discover if any of the large companies were violating the anti-monopoly laws.

President Benjamin F. Fairless of the United States Steel Corporation testified before the congressional committee, and the <u>Associated Press</u> sent out the story over its wires.

Steel Firm's Head Assails U.S. Controls

Washington, April 26 (AP) - U. S. Steel President Benjamin F. Fairless today assailed Government "Theorists" who he said are trying to punish success and good service by breaking up big corporations.

"By dismembering business", he declared, "They would turn back the clock to the horseless buggy days of 50 years or more ago, and would try to squeeze a modern, dynamic, efficient America into the puny production patterns of industrial childhood."

Charging that "powerful agencies" are aiming at Federal clamps on steel and other industries, Fairless added:

"By subjecting American productive enterprise to the deadening hand of political regulation, they would borrow from the old world the dismal economic philosophies that have led most of Europe to desolation and despair."

Testifies at Hearing

The U.S. Steel executive gave that testimony to a House Judiciary subcommittee which is
making a special study of the steel industry to
determine whether the Nation's anti-monopoly laws
need changing.

Fairless, whose firm has been a frequent
target of Congressional investigations, told the
committee that the charge U.S. Steel restricts
competition is a "myth."

U.S. Steel, he said, "is successful, it
is profitable, it is efficient and it is a large
enterprise."

"Those are the simple facts and I am
proud of them," Fairless added.

But he asserted that "statistically-mind-
ed theorist" in the Government hold that this is
all wrong.

"They hold that there is something inher-
ently vicious in bigness and growth and success,"
Fairless said and went on:

"Successful service to the Nation now
strangely seems to be the signal for the political
punishment of those who have performed it."

The steel official was questioned closely
by committee members about the corporation's present holdings and comparative size.

On this point Fairless said that when U.S.
Steel was founded in 1901 it produced 66 per cent
of all the steel then made in this country - "Twice
as much as all of its competitors put together," he
said.

But today, he added, it makes only 33 per
cent of the Nation's steel while its rivals turn
out twice as much.

"Now our critics may call this monopoly,"
Fairless said, "but my guess is that our competitors would welcome more of it."

Bigger Than All Others

Committee Counsel Edward H. Levi asked
if it is true that U.S. steel's capacity is bigger than all of the mills of all other countries
combined.

"Yes, and I think that's the reason why we
are the greatest Nation on earth," Fairless replied.

Fairless told the committee U.S. Steel owns
approximately 19 per cent of all the known domestic
iron ore, and about 51 per cent of the Lake Superior
ores.

It has about 84 subsidiary companies, of
which he said only about 14 could be classed as
major subsidiaries. The rest include companies

150

in name only, sales organizations and warehouses.

When committee members inquired about U.S. Steel's post-war purchase of the government-owned Geneva Steel plant in Utah Fairless said the base price was only a small part of the cost of getting it into "full integrated" operation.

Through this integrated operation, Fairless said, U.S. Steel now furnishes the 11 far Western states about 1,500,000 tons of steel a year at prices "relatively cheaper" than had ever been charged on the Pacific Coast before.

Associated Press Dispatch

A background article dealing with this question would show that government policies affect the economic scene in many ways. Direct government participation frequently takes the form of regulation of private economic activity. Railroads submit to considerable regulation by the government. Under the Federal Reserve System the banks of the country are regulated in many ways, say A.E. Burns and D.S. Watson, in Economic Problems in the Modern World, a book edited by Willard L. Thorp.

The reporter could indicate that the government now engages in a great variety of activities designed to stimulate the economy. The research and informational services, for example, of the Departments of Commerce and Agriculture aim at the stimulation of trade, industry and agriculture.

The investigator-writer would show that still another general type of government policy might be termed protective. In this category would be placed the extensive welfare and relief activities and the protection of home owners against foreclosures. Labor legislation is also in this area. This type of governmental activity involves giving income to those whose normal source of income has failed, or providing financial assistance to groups who are unable to obtain credit through existing channels. In the area of labor legislation it aims to protect both of the parties to the labor contract.

The backgrounder would also point out that government engages in many activities which have indirect influences on the economic system. The government, for example, must raise funds and spend them...In the process, the incomes of taxpayers are reduced while those of the recipients of public funds such as those on relief are increased. Government is a positive factor in the life of a nation. No sphere of economic activity is left untouched by the influence of government.

Economic Spirals

The economic system is never static, never operates on an entirely even keel. Prices are a close reflection of economic health. In a period of depression or inflation they become particularly important. In 1950 the US economic system moved into an inflationary era, and headlines such as this appeared on the front page:

FEDERAL LIVING COST INDEX
CLIMBS TO NEW HIGH RECORD

This was followed by headlines like the following:

8 Million Prices Due To Be Frozen

By End of Week

OPA HEADS

SEEM AGREED

ON OBJECTIVES

Here are economic news events which can be backgrounded
in a variety of ways and, because they affect directly the
pocketbook of families everywhere they may be localized.
In order to get behind the headlines and turn the index of
living statistics into a significant human interest article,
the reporters compare the budgets of several housewives for
previous years. Specifically, they ask how much was being
spent in 1939, the base for the index, 1945, 1950, when the
Korean war began, and the prices began to mount, and the
current year. What could $10 worth of food buy in each of
these past years? Today? What could $20 buy in clothes?

Accompanying this might be a news-feature on the increase
in wages in all industries, as indicated by the indexes,
and in the predominant industries in the community. Figures
for prices and wages may be found in the publications of the
U.S. Department of Labor. A reporter may obtain local information from housewives and from the Chamber of Commerce,
and he can get figures on prices by a visit to the local
grocery stores.

A deeper investigation into the factors which in combination produce the current prices may be pursued. Here
again the sources would be similar to those mentioned above.
In addition, economists might be consulted for facts and
information.

The United States has embarked on a price control program several times, once during World War II and the second
time following the beginning of the Korean war in 1950.
Closely tied in with price control was a wage stabilization
program. A study of the newspaper and magazine files for
the period, checked through the New York Times Index and
Readers' Guide to Periodical Literature, would enable the
reporter-investigator to reconstruct these U.S. economic
experiences. Seymour Harris has written Price Control and
might be used to study the first program during World War II.

6. Press Services Interpret

Conscious of the need to make spot news dealing with economic situation intelligible to the readers of its member
papers, the AP has made an effort to supply this lack.

Economics is a ticklish subject, of course, and AP clients
in all parts of the country have a wide range of political
complexions. The AP seeks to present background economic
features while walking a narrow tightrope.

Its special business writer, Sam Dawson, offers "Today's
Business Mirror." Written in an informal, chatty style, the
column is a vast improvement over many heavy financial columns. Dawson tries to explain business and financial terms
whenever they are used and would prove a stumbling block to
understanding.

Here is an example of his work taken from the teletype
machine.

TODAY'S BUSINESS MIRROR

BY SAM DAWSON

NEW YORK, APRIL 11 - (AP) - IF YOU WANT
TO KNOW WHAT'S AHEAD FOR BUSINESS IN GENERAL, WATCH
THE TREND OF INVESTMENT SPENDING. IN THE OPINION
OF AT LEAST ONE BUSINESS LEADER, THAT'S A MUCH SAFER
GUIDE THAN TRYING TO FOLLOW THE OLD-FASHIONED BUSI-
NESS CYCLE METHOD.
          AS ESTIMATE OF FUTURE EXPENDITURES OF AN
INVESTMENT NATURE GIVES THE AVERAGE BUSINESSMAN WITH
LIMITED RESEARCH FACILITIES A SHORT-CUT METHOD OF
TELLING WHETHER TIMES WILL BE GOOD OR BAD. THIS
IS THE VIEW OF FRANK D. NEWBURY, A RETIRED DIRECTOR,
VICE PRESIDENT AND ECONOMIST OF THE WESTINGHOUSE
ELECTRIC CORP...
          "BECAUSE THE SIZE OF GROSS NATIONAL PRODUCT
GIVES A DIRECT MEASURE AND THE MOST INCLUSIVE MEAS-
URE OF BUSINESS ACTIVITY, AN ESTIMATE OF THE FUTURE
SIZE OF GROSS NATIONAL PRODUCT IS A FORECAST OF THE
LEVEL OF BUSINESS," HE SAYS.
          GROSS NATIONAL PRODUCT INCLUDES THE PRODUCTION
OF THE ENTIRE LABOR FORCE, IN FARMING, MANUFACTURING,
AND IN THE SERVICE INDUSTRIES AND OCCUPATIONS. IT
MEASURES THIS IN MONEY, SHOWING THE EFFECTS OF YEAR-
TO-YEAR PRICE CHANGES...

When Iran was in financial difficulties in 1951, she
borrowed $8,750,000 from the International Monetary Fund.
This story might have been passed up with an account of the
event and a few quotes from the officials involved. The
reader would have asked "What is this International Monetary
Fund? How does it operate? How can Iran borrow from it?
Why does Iran need the money now?" The Associated Press
anticipated these questions of the reader and sought the
answers to them. The reporter wove his findings right into
the account of the spot news event.

World Fund To Give Iran Large Credit

**Loan of $8,750,000 Is
Approved for Nation
to Offset Oil Loss**

Washington, Nov. 12 (**AP**) - The
International Monetary Fund has
decided to grant hard-pressed Iran
an $8,750,000 credit to offset the
financial crisis caused by loss of
oil revenues, it was learned tonight.

Spot News Event

Informed fund officials who dis-
closed this said that the money is
urgently needed by Iran to help it
buy food and raw materials.

Economic Reasons
Behind Event

Premier Mohammed Mossadegh's
financial experts negotiated the
loan during the Iranian leader's
current round of talks here with
State Department officials on
the Anglo-Iranian oil crisis.

The $8,750,000 to be granted
Iran represents the maximum that
the Iranian government can withdraw from the fund in any year.
The Iranians have a quota of
$35,000,000 in the fund but like
all members can withdraw only 25
per cent of it yearly.

Background Explana-
tion of Internation-
al Monetary Fund

The fund's action undoubtedly
will give Iran a big financial
assist at a critical time in the
Iranian fight with the British
over nationalization of the bill-
ion-dollar Anglo-Iranian Oil company.

The fund was set up in 1946 as
an international agency to promote
world trade. It extends short-
term credits to member countries
which are temporarily short on
cash. The main task of the fund
is to keep world currencies on an
even keel, thus permitting an expansion of world commerce.

A top fund official in telling
of the fund's action said that it
would be announced formally tomorrow. He said that the decision to

Quotes from
Officials

grant Iran the credit shows the
"truly international character" of
the fund.

It was not known whether Britain's representative on the fund's
board of directors opposed the move.
The British have been counting on
a financial crisis in Iran to persuade Mossadegh to relax his determination to kick the Anglo-Iranian
company out of Iran.

Iran has several applications
before the fund's twin institution,
the World Bank. But an Iranian em-
bassy official said that these applications are not under active consideration at present.

Iran has been getting no money
from its oil for the past four
months. Tankers stopped hauling
oil from the Abadan refinery in   More Background
late July when the Iranian-British
argument brought and Iranian order
expelling British technicians from
the country.
                Jacksonville, Fla. Times-Union

7. Local Economic News Backgrounded

Many local stories are concerned solely with economics
or have economic aspects, and explanatory articles would
contribute to the readers' understanding of them.

In 1951 the city of Tallahassee, Florida, had to decide
in a referendum vote whether or not it should lease and
then sell its newly-built electrical power plant. A statewide power corporation, from whom the city for a number of
years had been purchasing electricity for re-sale to home-
owners, desired to buy the plant. After long negotiations
between the corporation and the city, the City Commission
in a 3 to 2 vote decided to dispose of the generating plant,
but a referendum by the voters was required by law. The
issue was hotly debated by various groups. Important to
the understanding of the current controversy was the economic history of the power issue in the community and the previous relations between the company and the city. The editor of the local newspaper, The Democrat, assigned a reporter, Mike Beaudoin, to the significant story, which went
back 50 years.

The reporter went about the job methodically.

1. He interviewed the city comptroller for facts he
    knew about.
2. He talked to the city attorney regarding previous
    legal negotiations.
3. He discussed prior episodes with the city manager.

COAL

OWI photo by Collier

OIL

FSA photo by Rothstein

Local Industry Can Be Made Interesting with photos such as these

4. He obtained the company's view from officials.
5. He checked old city records and contracts.

The reporter then sat down and pieced together the various bits of factual threads, weaving them together into a Sunday feature. It illuminated the issue for many voters, giving them an historical, factual basis upon which to make a judgment and cast their ballots.

Reporters investigating this kind of news identify it as falling within the field of public utility economics. They obtain information from volumes such as these:

Eli W. Clemens, Economics and Public Utilities
Emery Troxel, Economics of Public Utilities
Herman H. Trachsel, Public Utility Regulation

The reporter is this instance could have secured a comparison of electric rates in various cities from the Federal Power Commission. He could have secured additional facts and leads for further investigation from university economists specializing in the utility field.

Utility news is recurrent in many communities, but so is the tax issue. This is a county or municipal problem at this level and falls into the lap of the reporter covering the county building or city hall. The problem is presented in the chapter on political science, but it is clear that the story is basically an economic one, and the political reporter can do a better job if he is familiar with economic matters and has a grounding in municipal finance and economics.

Often reporters are called upon to write articles, surveying the economic growth of the city or county and outlining future prospects. These articles are occasioned by anniversaries of the newspaper or of the community. Many editors have year-end surveys of growth and change in the area. Then the reporter is assigned the job of writing an economic background story. When the Tallahassee, Fla., Democrat, moved into its new plant a special issue carried several articles of this kind. One which stressed the employment changes was topped with this head:

FACTORS CITED IN CITY'S GROWTH

A few paragraphs follow:

> Tremendous strides have been made by Tallahassee in the span of the past dozen years. Its income and wealth have grown by leaps. More and better houses, streets and public buildings evidence its wealth...
> Employment played a very important part in this gain. It might well be the most important factor in thecommunity's growth. A community has two sources of wealth -- its natural resources and its human resources. To a large degree natural

resources do not change, although they may be
often fully developed or utilized. Human resources are changing.

   The city's change from an agricultural to
an urban community parallels a change in its labor
force. These changes are apparent through a comparison of Bureau of Census data for 1940 and 1950.

   During this period of time employment increased to a point where 1 out of every 3 persons
gainfully employed received his pay from the Federal,
State. County or City government. In Tallahassee,
of course, the majority are state employes. This
includes the public schools and universities.

   Leon County's labor force increased from
13,000 in 1940 to nearly 20,000 in 1950, an increase of 50 per cent. Since 1950 the labor force
has probably increased another 10 per cent.

   That Leon County's population growth is
largely the result of expanding government and
educational agencies is reflected in the shift of
employment during the past 10 years...In 1940 approximately 16 per cent of the labor force was employed by the Federal, State, County and City governments. In 1950 this figure had increased to 32 per
cent. Private employment meanwhile had decreased.

   Between 1940 and 1950 several new state
office buildings were erected and administrative
offices of various agencies were moved from other
parts of the state to Tallahassee. Florida State
University and Florida A&M experienced tremendous
growth.

   Retail trade expanded in proportion to
state employment and emerged as the top local industry. Agriculture and manufacturing dropped...
The five leading industries were:

Retail trade	3148
Education service	2759
Public Admin- istration	2339
Construction	1902
Private households	1672

   During the past ten years Tallahassee had definitely emerged as a "white collar" town. The 1940
census figures show 32 per cent of employed workers
in professional, technical, managerial, clerical and
sales occupations. In 1950 this had increased to
45 per cent...

   Information for the article was derived from the United
States Census for 1940 and for 1950, available in the public
or university library, and in the files of the Florida State
Employment Service, located in Tallahassee.

Often economic change takes place within a city so
slowly it is not noticed by the public. Industrial change
alters the character of the city. Likewise the direction
of the movement of retail business occurs and alters the
face of the community. The movement since the first World
War of retail trade has been towards the suburbs. How fast
is the change? What is the future of the old down-town
heart of retail business? The reporter can investigate
this kind of economic development and produce an article
which may have unusual appeal. Business Week reporters
came up with this article.

THERE ARE LOTS OF PEOPLE DOWNTOWN

People are customers. Where there are
customers, there are stores. It's as simple as
that.

It's true that, when the war ended, city
dwellers started rushing to the suburbs in vast
herds. Department store operators, with their
pockets full of money ran right after them. Suburban branches - trim, uncongested, irresistible
to madame - sprang up in all directions.

The decentralization of retailing became
a well-established merchandizing phenomenon. On
top of everything else, branch stores tend to
show a better profit per sales dollar than the
mother store. Success of the branches thus poses
a question: Have the merchants given up on their
downtown stores?

More Investment - The answer is a flat no.
Investment in the downtown stores is too heavy to
let go by the board. And such stores are still
drawing plenty of customers. As a result, many
retailers are actually pouring a lot of money into the parent stores. A spot check of some key
cities from coast to coast turns up figures like
these:

In Boston, Jordan Marsh is in the midst
of an $11-million program to rebuild its main
store. Filene's has just announced plans for
modernization of an entire city block.

In Cleveland, Halle Bros. is putting $7.8
million into intown modernization and expansion.

In the heart of Atlanta, Rich's just opened a new $2-million Store for Men.

In Chicago, State St. Stores have spent
some $50-million in the past five years to update
and expand operations.

In Dallas, Neiman-Marcus is putting $5-
million into downtown expansion, $1.5-million into
suburban.

In Manhattan, Gimbel's is undergoing a
$7-million refurbishing.

Pittsburgh, which calls itself "the department store town," has seen $10-million worth of
improvements on its intown stores since the close
of World War II.

These are only a handful of the bigger
examples. Renovations, new parking lots, new
buildings, added space are reported from city
to city.
It's true that many retailers are putting up new branches at the same time. But
plainly they are still putting heavy stakes on
the mother store.
Crowds - Primarily, the big market accounts
for all this. Half a glance at any downtown district during the noon hour tells the story.
                                    Business Week   Oct. 6, 1951

Many other stories on local economic events may be
written. The Baltimore, Md. Evening Sun has demonstrated
that local industrial background features can have a wide
appeal. Neil H. Swanson, then managing editor, sought not
only to make such articles interesting, but to produce financial pages which would made an appeal to a larger number
of readers than those who poured over the stock and bond
quotations and analyses of market trends. Mr. Swanson believed that the financial pages of the newspaper should
share the quality which marked the rest of the paper.
They should be interesting. Everybody should read them,
wrote Harry S. Sherwood, Sun staffer, in describing the
program for the July 19, 1941 issue of Editor & Publisher.

The Evening Sun editors found that a complete stock and
bond quotations and the routine of finance could be com-
pressed into 16 columns. That gave a whole page for stories
which would appeal to everybody. The Federal Reserve System and the way it worked were described. Little known and
curious facts of freight handling and industry in Baltimore
were made the subjects of other articles. Romance was not
neglected. There were tales about ships from all over the
world that sailed into the Baltimore harbor. Here was an
opportunity for the use of facts and imagination by the reporters. Evidence of the increased interest of the reader
in the pages was immediate.

One of the first to manifest interest was Dr. Joseph L.
Wheeler, then librarian of the Enoch Pratt Free Library.
These industrial pages filled a need which his library had
been doing its best to supply for years. All kinds of
people, and especially school children, had been digging in
the library shelves on the hunt for just such information
as was given here. The articles were written in the common
speech.

Men at the head of business and industrial houses began
telling their employes to read the pages. Women began to
read the pages. Housewives and mothers read them for the
light they threw on the family budget. The stories were
often started on the first or the last pages of the paper
and continued on the financial page. Rodney Crowther,
business editor, did the articles on hidden taxes and the
Federal reserve system. John E. Conley did a series on the
histories of Baltimore business and financial corporations.

BALTIMORE'S LIFE LINE

The Baltimore Evening Sun's articles dramatized the
news behind the routine shipping news and made the events
very readable.

Joseph Jean Shaner did a series on the port of Baltimore.

Pictures were used generously to add appeal to the articles. At times full page lay-outs were used and full advantage was taken of the picturesque possibilities of the subject.

Care was taken to make the articles easy to read. Mr. Crowther took dry government and financial reports and worked them into easy running stories which showed the purpose behind government activities and how the government agencies functioned. Mr. Conley and others in writing the histories of local financial institutions worked in the changing history of the times, and the development of new business functions.

Howard Carswell, financial writer on the New York World Telegram has pointed out that editors believed business and financial news was essentially dry and listless and could not be made to attract the reading public.

He referred the reader to Time's section on business and finance for proof that this was incorrect. In an article in the Journalism Quarterly for June, 1938, Mr. Carswell, presenting ideas which are still applicable, said: "The reader cannot but be impressed by the contrast if he reads Time's business section and then the daily newspapers." He cited many examples to show that business news did not carry much interest for the average reader.

"The fact is that business news could possess the most general human interest of any presented to men readers. Business affects everybody; everybody talks about it.

"It would be possible to present business news in such a manner that everybody would read it, understand it and enjoy it."

Yet he pointed out the daily newspaper missed the mark by just about 90 per cent. The metropolitan daily offered its page upon page of statistics, tables, regular formula news and other dull routine; the small daily presented skeletal tables on commondities, livestock and securities with local business news carried in the main news section and getting somewhat legitimate and effective play.

Carswell argued that both were failing to do their job. Dr. George Gallup's investigation of 100,000 newspaper readers over a period of years showed that 19 per cent of men readers read the New York stock tables, while 5 per cent of the women read this material. Compare these to the familiar figures for reader interest of both sexes in weather, comics, page one banner stories, pictures, general news, and even editorial page and want ads. Business news suffered by this examination.

The writer urged editors to apply to business news the same imagination and the same techniques they used on their front pages. The editors have an unplumbed and almost un-guessed wealth of material.

There are trends and developments in management and merchandise policies; in technology and research; in adver-tising and promotion. He pointed out there are timely as-pects of retail, wholesale and foreign trade.

The photographic microfilm for the recording and stor-age of knowledge and the printed word is so significant that enthusiasts call it the greatest discovery since Gut-enberg invented movable type for the printing press 500 years ago. Its potential market for replacing paper files and records of business firms, banks, libraries by minified photos is immense.

Copper and gold mines are now air-conditioned to permit penetrating far deeper than would otherwise be endurable to human workers. Flash-drying printing inks, industrial chemicals derived from coal hulls, soapless soaps are with us.

There is a lush field for features, and especially for edited pictures, or visual news. Much is reported in trade and technical press which the newspapers could re-write for public reading.

The financial writer answered the objections to such news. Is such news free advertising? Mr. Carswell argued that the newspapers give the New York Stock Exchange more free advertising than any institution in the world in pub-lishing stock exchange quotations. Commercialized sports are business enterprises, and so are the movies, stage, book publishing, women's fashions.

The objection that such business news has a subject matter which is technical, Carswell answered by saying that stories on industrial research and new manufacturing pro-cess are no more technical than those on excess banking re-serves or statements of the bank of France.

He concluded if business news is to be popularized and a public readership attracted, it seems apparent that sev-eral things must be done. The editorial point-of-view must be re-oriented to the average business person; editing must be done for the reader and not the investor; the obsession in stocks and bonds must be shaken; and the human interest must be handled as on the front page.

Business Week has developed a number of reporters who not only gather facts about industry and commerce but write them into lively, readable articles as Carswell advocated. The Business Week staff makes a specialty of translating what might otherwise be dull material into snappy leads and appealing text. Here's a bright example of an article on some new developments in the baking business. Notice the catchy lead. Watch the easy, informal style. Examine the brief, but pointed sentences.

For Fluffy Bread, Try Fungus

Bakers are men of many woes. Their product is temperamental. Sometimes it won't fluff right; the dough sticks to the machinery; it gets stale too fast; it doesn't get white enough.

To beat all these raps, or at least to control them, the baker has been using various chemical and natural additives. And in time that got him in trouble with the Food & Drug Administration. A year ago FDA proposed new bread standards that did not permit the use in anything that called itself bread of synthetic chemical emulsifiers and softeners such as polyoxyethylenes and monostearates. FDA suspected these of being toxic. Tests are still going on, but the chances are that the standards will be adopted by the Federal Security Agency, parent of FDA.

On the Market - But the bakers are already wiping away their apprehensive tears. For a new additive has just come on the market, comfortably inside the FDA rule and said to pass multiple miracles in the making of bread. The newcomer is a first cousin of penicillin; it's the first fungal enzyme supplement for bread to become commercially available, The name: Magna-Zyme, put out by Sche-Rose Corp., of Dallas. Here are some of the things it can do.

The fungal enzyme cuts down the chances of making a bad loaf of bread. The why of it: Millers add malt to flour to improve edibility and speed fermentation. But no two mills add the same amount, so the baker has to add some more. It's guesswork, and he can guess wrong. Fungal enzymes eliminate malting at the bakers; they automatically compensate for variations in the mill malting.

Like the chemical softeners, fungal enzymes slow the staling process. That's because they retard the crystallization of starch.

Bread made with fungal enzyme looks whiter and fluffier - hence larger in volume. By doing an improved job of breaking down large starch molecules into smaller sugar components, the enzyme causes the little holes in the bread to be smaller, more uniform, and better reflectors of light. At the same time, the dough's resistance to swell (called gel strength) is reduced. The fluffier the loaf, the larger it gets...

Business Week

Newspapers Publishing Effective Articles

The New York Times during the weekdays, but especially on Sundays, publishes newsy articles on a great variety of businesses. The articles are effectively written and are informative.

In a similar category is the New York Herald Tribune, whose general lively news policy is reflected in its business and financial pages.

8. SOURCES FOR ECONOMIC FACTS

Here are a number of sources for economic facts.

1. U.S. Council of Economic Advisors. Annual Report to the President.
   Gives a resumé of the year's work and recommendations to the President. Also, each report includes a treatise on our economic system.
2. U.S. President. Budget of the United States.
   This includes the President's budget message, summary and supporting tables of the budget, and detailed supporting statements and schedules.
3. U.S. Bureau of the Census. Statistical Abstract of the United States.
   An annual statistical presentation of figures pertaining to most fields. This work serves as excellent source material for background articles.
4. U.S. Federal Reserve Board. Federal Reserve Bulletin.
   This reviews the financial conditions in the country -- credit, sales, profits, etc.
5. U.S. Labor Department. Monthly Labor Review.
   This is the medium through which the Bureau publishes its yearly reports and studies on such subjects as salaries, hours, industrial conditions etc.
6. U.S. Department of Commerce. Survey of Current Business.
   Contains articles and statistics of current interest to the economist and business man; supplemented by weekly and annual publications.

9. Getting Your Story Across

What has been the technique and appeal of the popularizers and synthesizers of data published in economic books which give the background of the news? Can these methods be employed by newspapermen?

The techniques have been many and varied, ranging all the way from the graphic Stuart Chase, who uses familiar objects in everyday life to illustrate the processes of mass production and distribution, to W.E. Woodward, who chats about economic issues with the informality and tang of the late Will Rogers, and presents his ideas with great clarity. All of these writers utilize picture-words, dramatic illustration, and frequently the technique of the fiction-writer to bring home the significance and relevance of their ideas.

Throughout his entire book, W. E. Woodward writes
in the informal fashion with which he opens his
"Money for Tomorrow."

> I hope to God nobody will enjoy reading
> this book. If you tell me that you enjoy-
> ed it, I shall be as depressed as if you
> had told me that you had a grand uncle at
> the sinking of the Titanic... I don't want
> to be clever or amusing or brilliant. All
> I want to do in these pages is to present
> a handful of facts and four or five ideas.
> I want to make them so hard and gritty that
> you are not likely to forget them.

He lures the reader on from page to page. Even
when he discusses statistics he remarks:

> I don't like statistics any more than you
> do, but one cannot make head or tail of an
> economic discussion unless they are brought
> by the handful. I am doing all I can to re-
> duce them to a minimum in this book. With
> that apology will you bear with me while I do
> a little figuring?

Economics, as Woodward shows, does not have to be
a dismal science. He presents his ideas in effective form with illustrations, and makes even his
necessary statistics palatable.

As any newspaperman or advertising man knows, materials and facts in themselves do not glow with
drama, excitement, romance, humor, picturesqueness.
People participating in an event rarely see these
elements. Unskilled writers whose eyes are not
trained to see and whose hands are not trained to
present them, fumble the "stories." They have to
be dramatized and electrified into life for the
reader. Economics, a neglected field, has received
such treatment from popularizers,who use every art
of the story-teller or dramatist or descriptive
writer to make the subject live.

William T. Foster and Waddill Catchings, for example, in their"Road to Plenty" have written an entire
book on economics in conversational form, in which
various characters project the ideas and discuss
them. The first chapter was called: "In which the
Gray Man and the Three Wise Men Show What It is All
About." The volume began:

> A stout and florid manufacturer in a pink
> silk shirt, sitting next to the window in
> the smoking room of a west-bound train out
> of Boston, pointed with a jerk of his thumb
> to a group of men in overalls, just outside
> a railroad repair shop...

The authors then drew various personalities into
a discussion of business. Soon economic abstract-
tions acquired concrete meaning in the conversations.
Foster and Catchings also have written on economic
news for the McClure syndicate.

Sources: Tips for news about local industry may come
from the executive secretary of the local Chamber of Commerce. Literature is usually available at its offices, and
an overall picture of the manufacturing, wholesale and retail pattern will be supplied by officials if requested.
Frequently the bankers in a town have an accurate and detailed knowledge of the economic situation in the community,
or they know the sources for such information.

The city directory and the telephone book have list-
ings of various businesses and this helps to fill out the
picture. The manager of the credit agency, Dun and Brad-
street, in the larger cities is an unusually good source
of facts about trends and often supplies articles of value.
Progressive libraries will be of aid and some have source
files for previous articles, tips and suggestions for news-
features.

The alert reporter will discover there is no substitute for an auto tour, followed by a walking tour of the
industrial section of the city. He can gain suggestions
for features as well as a knowledge of the plants, their
physical layout and location. These impressions can be
followed up and verified later. The booming industrial
heart of the community may be explored, with particular
attention being paid to source of raw materials and processes. The reporter, too, should investigate the transportation arteries, the railroads, trucks and airlines, to
discover how they supply the factories, wholesale houses
and retail shops with materials. He should learn too,
where the finished products go.

We have pointed out the catchy leads and simple style
of Business Week reporters who write on economic subjects.
An analysis of the methods which these writers use would be
profitable for the student-reporter. The Business Week
staff uses a variety of writing devices, including stimulating questions, allusions to other familiar fields and
explosive statements, to gain and hold attention.

The lead and first few paragraphs of one article about
Wall street are given in this reprint:

New Life for Wall Street
        The question most frequently asked in Wall
Street these days is: "How long will it last?"
        Against the predictions of Wall street pro-
fessionals, the market this week was moving upward again. The Dow-Jones industrial showed a
spurt. They had been drifting downward after
peaking above 276 in mid-September.

Soothsayers of the Street are a bit rueful
about this turn. But most of them are sticking
to their prophecy of recent weeks that the market is due for a spill...   <u>Business Week</u>

Here's another article which illustrates the methods
used by the magazine's staff to lift the story up.

<u>Blend in Citrus</u>
    In the frozen concentrate industry the citrus
growers are climbing into the driver's seat.
    The California growers made the first bid for
power a few months ago when the California Fruit
Growers Exchange which controls about 70% of that
state's orange crop, put out a concentrate under
the famous Sunkist label.
    Now the Florida Citrus Exchange which controls
about 25% of the Florida crop, is making its bid
through a deal with Clinton Foods... <u>Business Week</u>

In a review of a book on the white collar class, the
reporter used this approach:

<u>Portrait of Mr. Nobody</u>
    The white-collar people just happened. They
slipped into the modern world with a history that
was blank of events. They face a future entirely
of someone else's making. They are here, familiar,
taken for granted, unnoticed.
    Yet they have changed the whole concept of
American society.
    Or so Mr. C. Wright Mills would have you be-
lieve in "White Collar."   <u>Business Week</u>

10. <u>Economic Problems Individuals Face</u>

    Although we have mentioned that the science of econom-
ics is used to understand national problems, individuals
are also faced with their own set of economic problems.
Here are some of the important economic issues with which
individuals and families are concerned. Feature articles
or special columns which throw light on these questions will
generate interest among readers.

    1. How much education should be "purchased" for the
        individual or his children?
        How should the family provide for such needs?
    2. How many children can the family afford?
        How much does it cost to educate a child?
        What does it require financially to meet his other
        needs?
    3. How should the family be housed economically?
        Should the family rent? If so, how much should it
        pay, according to the best economic information?
        Should a house be purchased? What are the relative
        merits of purchasing or renting? What is the best
        manner of purchasing?

168

4. How can the family save and invest?
   What is the best method for saving a nest egg?
   Where should the family put its money--into banks,
   or savings and loan associations, or real estate?
5. How much life insurance should members of the family carry?
   What is the best plan to fit the needs of this
   particular family? How much is needed for protection of the wage earner and the family?

Sylvia Porter does an informative column of this type
for the Hall-Post Syndicate. She is a writer who got a good
background in economics and specialized in financial and
business writings. She tries to background the economic
news and apply it to life and interests of the general reader.

Your Money

**A City Girl Tries To Explain For Us
Just What Is Parity, And How It Works**   *Sylvia Porter*

In this newspaper nearly every day, you are
reading headlines to the effect "Democrats Push
90% Parity Supports" or "Ike Will Veto (or maybe
"Will Not Veto") Rigid Parity Prices."
At nearly every press conference with every
key political figure these days, the farm problem comes up and some question about "parity" is
asked. Even at the press conference during which
President Eisenhower announced he would run for a
second term, a reporter delayed the rush to the
phones when he asked whether the President would
veto 90 per cent price supports. (The President
wouldn't say).
Now I have a deep suspicion that millions of
thinking city folks who want to follow stories
about farm legislation wish somebody would try
to explain in ordinary bread-and-butter words
this jargon about parity, price support loans,
surpluses, etc.
Because it is so vital a question, because I'm
city-raised too and because I detest bafflegab of
any kind, I'm going to try.
If you know all the answers, skip this one. If
not - well, here's my valiant attempt...
QUESTION: Just what is parity?
ANSWER: Parity is the price a farmer has to
receive for his crop to provide him with sufficient
income to buy the same amount of goods he could
have bought in a specified base period. The base
period usually mentioned is 1910-14, the years just
before World War I.
Let's say a farmer produces and takes to market
a wagon-load of wheat. If he receives enough money
for this wheat to buy the same amount of food, cloth-

ing, machinery, fertilizer, etc,, that he could
have bought after selling a wagon-load of wheat in
1910-14, he's getting parity price for his crop.
QUESTION: What is 90 percent of parity? And
what are the flexible price supports
the administration defends?

ANSWER: In 1949, Congress passed and President
Truman signed a bill authorizing the government to
take steps to prevent prices of specified commodities from falling below 90 per cent of that theor-
etical price level explained above. In short, while
the farmer producing these crops wasn't guaranteed
precisely the same buying power as in 1910-14, he
was guaranteed 90 per cent of it.

In 1954, Congress passed and President Eisenhower signed a bill replacing these rigid price
supports with flexible price supports - and the
government now supports the prices on several
basic crops at between 75 and 90 per cent of parity.

The Democrats are urging a return to 90 per cent
parity support to help the farmers. The administration insists on the flexible program.
QUESTION: Do parity prices change?
ANSWER: Yes, frequently. If the prices the
farmer has to pay for essential goods and services
go up, parity prices go up. If the prices the
farmer has to pay go down, parity prices go down.
One of the major issues now is that while the prices
farmers receive are way down, the prices farmers
must pay are still at or near their peaks - putting
the so-called parity ratio at a 15-year low.
QUESTION: Who determines parity prices?
ANSWER: The Department of Agriculture.
QUESTION: How does the government support farm
prices?
ANSWER: It can and does buy a crop directly.
It did this with surplus butter - bought
and stored mountans of the stuff.

It also can and does extend price-support loans
to farmers who put up their crops as collateral.
If prices later are favorable to the farmer, he sells
his crop in the market, pays off his loan. If prices
are not favorable, he just lets the government take
over the crop.
QUESTION: This is how today's surpluses developed?
ANSWER: And how! Uncle Sam's investment in
price-supported farm surpluses today
is at a record $8.9 billion and the
government actually owns almost $6
billion of commodities!
QUESTION: Will this Congress find a real solution?
ANSWER: Not the way it is playing politics with
this explosive issue. Until our legis-
lators recognize the depth and duration
of the economic-social challenge involved
here, our smaller farmers particularly

170

Sylvia Porter, whose informed column on financial matters is a best-read feature of the new DAILY NEWS, chats with Keith Funston, president of the New York Stock Exchange.

will continue in trouble and the whole foundation
of our economic prosperity will be in danger.

Summary

Economic news is of front-page importance because it
bears so directly on the lives of all newspaper readers.
Economic news however was considered too dismal, dreary and
serious during the dizzy 1920's. The stock market crash
and the depression brought economics into the news pattern.
The virtual stopping of the production and distribution
machine and the large scale unemployment all made the public conscious of the importance of economics. The editors
responded to this change of interest. The measures to
bring relief and reform to industry, agriculture and labor,
advanced by the Roosevelt Administration, kept economic
news on the front page.

But explanatory material was needed by the bewildered
reader to understand what was happening to the economic system and what the various laws and projects sought to accomplish.

It was pointed out that student-reporters who expect
to be competent interpreters of current news should obtain
an understanding of economics.

It was emphasized that, since the world is constantly
changing, with new inventions being introduced and physical
scientists exploring new areas which bear on industry, our
economy is not fixed. It is the dynamic character of the
economic world that produces much economic news. Some key
economic problems which remain in the news were referred to.
The need for backgrounding these was shown and some examples
of explanatory articles were presented.

The local economic stories should not be overlooked.
Several types of economic stories were shown, and mention
was made of some editors who have sought to make material
of this kind readable. The individual faces many economic
problems daily, and the possibilities of a column devoted
to these were shown.

Fact and Discussion Questions
on Chapter V, "Economic News in Focus"

1. (a) How important is economic news?
   (b) Illustrate by checking and referring to the front
        pages of your local or favorite newspaper for ex-
        amples.

2. Comment on the article, "Paycheck Shrinkages Due to
   T-Day" by James Lee. Consider how he achieved his
   effects.

3. Describe the attitude of editors towards economic news
   in the 1920's and tell how you account for this.

4. What effects did the depression and New Deal have on
   news slection. Explain.

5. What causes economic news?

6. What causes economic change?

7. (a) Discuss what you think is the basic function of the
   newsman in reporting economic news.
   (b) Tell what you think should be his professional
   standards.

8. Have economists developed specializations? Illustrate
   and explain the importance to newsmen.

9. Mention five recurrent economic problems and discuss
   their importance and meaning briefly.

10. Discuss the news, "U.S. Getting Richer--But not Fast
    Enough Observers Say," considering (a) central facts
    (b) style of writing.

11. What did George Soule, economist, believe we have learn-
    ed about methods of heading off depressions? Explain.

12. Tell what Richard Strout of the Christian Science Moni-
    tor found out about the lack   of planning.

13. (a) What did the Judiciary Committee of the U.S. House
    of Representatives investigate in 1950? (b) summarize
    President Benjamin Fairless' remarks.

14. Outline an article which would show how governmental
    policies and activities have and are affecting the
    economy, management and labor.

15. How can you humanize and background a story on spir-
    alling prices?

16. Identify Sam Dawson and tell about his work.

17. Analyze the methods used for explaining the news in the
    article, "World Fund To Give Iran Large Credit."

18. What local economic news is on the front or inside pages of your favorite or local newspaper today?

19. Explain how the Democrat reporter went about getting information for the power issue story.

20. Comment on the style of the Business Week article on decentralizing trends in retail business.

21. What articles did the Baltimore, Md., Evening Sun publish on local industry? What were the results?

22. What were Howard Carswell's principal points about business news?

23. What New York newspapers have interesting business sections?

24. List some basic sources for economic facts issued by the United States government agencies.

25. (a) Discuss effective methods for "getting your economic story across," (b) discuss some methods for writing leads on such stories.

26. What kinds of economic news can be written for the consumer?

27. Write a two-paragraph summary statement of this chapter.

Projects and Assignments

News Clipping Projects

Select one:

1. Select the economic news in two issues of a current newspaper.
   a. Do you think the "average reader" grasps the meaning of the news, features or editorials?
   b. What are the underlying causes which produced the news?
   c. What were the sources of the news?
   d. How would you find more facts about the issues indicated by the news? More about the background and history of the events?
   e. If they represent controversial issues, can you state the arguments you have read or heard for and against them? Trace objectively the sources of your information and ideas.
   f. Write your conclusions in a paper.

2. Pick two issues of a recent or current Sunday newspaper, focussing on the important economic news. Paste up.

a. Make a list of the general economic subjects, such as "inflation," "monopoly" which
   the news suggests.
b. What would be your technique of gathering additional facts on these subjects if you were
   assigned to write features on them?
c. Select one of the topics and investigate it in
   such reference tools as:
   (1) Reader's Guide to Periodical Literature
   (2) Card index of the library
   (3) Encyclopedia of the Social Sciences
   (4) Index to the New York Times
   (5) Newspaper morgue.
   (6) Public Affairs Information Service
d. Select several references from each of these
   sources which you would use if you were pre-
   paring to write an informative article on the
   topic. List these references in your paper.

II. Feature Assignment

Select One

1. Write a feature about an industry in your community.
   a. Visit your Chamber of Commerce and talk to the
      executive secretary about the important local
      industries. Get whatever literature the com-
      merce organization has.
   b. Then concentrate on one industry. Read the
      best accounts of it you can find.
   c. Go to a factory, typical of that particular
      industry. Explain your assignments to the
      person in charge, and ask to be taken through
      the plant. Observe processes and machines.
      Learn how the product is transformed from raw
      materials to finished goods.
   d. Ask many questions without antagonizing.
   e. Fit what you have learned in your economics
      course about planning, depressions into the
      article.
   f. Write your material into a dramatic Sunday
      feature, weaving together your collected print-
      ed material, your interviews and visits, and
      the pertinent information gained from your
      economics course...about 1000 words.

2. Write a striking effective feature on "The New
   Deal: Background Causes."
   a. Make use of whatever devices you have discov-
      ered about popularization of economic data.
   b. The following references will be helpful.
      Louis M. Hacker and Benjamin B. Kendrick, U.S.
      Since 1865; George Soule, Coming American Rev-
      olution; Gilbert Seldes, Years of the Locusts;
      Frederick L. Allen, Only Yesterday.

3. "Gold, Silver and Rubber Dollars: Inflation and Its Control" could be the title for this one.
   a. Some helpful sources would be Donald B. Woodward and Marc A. Rose, Inflation; Earl Sparling, Primer of Inflation.
4. Write a 1000 word feature on "Planning vs Regimentation."
   a. Planning: Use George Soule, A Planned Society, Stuart Chase, Men and Machines, Rexford G. Tugwell, Industrial Discipline and the Government Arts.
   b. Regimentation: David Lawrence, Beyond the New Deal, Ralph W. Roby, Roosevelt vs Recovery.

5. "Concentration in American Industry," a 1000-word article.
   a. See 1949 report by U.S. Secretary of Commerce Charles Sawyer.
   b. Read also reply by David Lawrence in his syndicated column, shortly after release of the report.
   c. See U.S. News & World Report, Dec. 16, 1949 for summary.
   d. Original documents may be obtained at the library.
6. "Trends in Local Employment" might be the title of this feature.
   a. From the library or Chamber of Commerce find out where most of the people of your town work.
   b. Make simple, comparison charts which will illustrate your findings.
   c. Can you interpret the meaning of your figures?
   d. What photos would you use to illustrate your article?
   e. Write your information into a daily or Sunday feature, describing pouring of people into various industries and stores each morning. Make it vivid, graphic.. about 1000 words.

7. Learn the methods of the popularizers of economics.
   a. Read one of the following and examine carefully, analytically the techniques which the author used.
      Stuart Chase, Men and Machines; the New Deal
      George D. H. Cole, Guide Through World Chaos
      William T. Foster and Waddill Catchings, Road to Plenty
      William E. Woodward, Money for Tomorrow
      Harry Overstreet, Influencing Human Behavior
      F. Fraser Bond, Breaking Into Print
      Rudolph Flesch, Art of Readable Writing
      Walter B. Pitkin, The Useful Art of Writing
   b. What techniques does the author employ to gain attention? to hold interest? to keep the text informal? to simplify material? Which methods are suitable for writing about economic problems?
   c. Write your conclusions in a 1000-word report.

8. Write a feature on "Social Security Act in Operation."
   a. This is a far reaching measure and will bob up in the news for the next decade. What are its features? Its present shortcomings?
   b. Read the background and the events leading up to it.
      Use Seymour Harris, The Economics of Social Security. Notice his method of presenting economic and social material, ordinarily dull.
      Read chapters in Eveline Burns, Towards Social Security, or Abraham Epstein, Insecurity, A Challenge to America.
      For further information on pictorial statistics see Rudolph Modley's How to Use Pictorial Statistics.
   c. Write immediately to Federal Security Board, Information Service, Washington, D.C., for latest amendments to the social security law and other literature on the subject.
   d. Check with local Social Security office for localization of article. Get number of persons covered in various categories, amount paid monthly, other problems.
   e. Organize your materials. Study them. Make a well-integrated outline. Then write a series of three articles on the background of the act itself. Finally give various shortcomings.
   f. Indicate the photographs and pictographs you would use.

9. Write two special columns, "Bread and Butter News", dealing with a current economic problem on page one or featured elsewhere in the news.
   a. Check Readers' Guide to Periodical Literature, the card index of the library, and the New York Times Index for source materials.
   b. Explain and round-out the spot news with a strong background story, giving details and facts not found in the routine story.

10. Write a 1000-word article on "The Aims of the Welfare State."
   a. Seek conservative and liberal definitions of word "welfare."
   b. Point up objectively the basic arguments of both sides in this controversy.
   c. As informative sources read:
      "Are We Headed Toward Collectivism?", New York Times Magazine, Dec. 18, 1949, p.7. This was a lively debate between Senator Harry F. Byrd (D.-Va.) and Senator Paul H. Douglas, (D.-Ill.) Check other references in Readers' Guide to Periodical Literature.
      Newspapers and Magazines of Value
      U.S. News & World Report
      Business Week
      Wall Street Journal
      Fortune

Survey of Current Business
London Economist
Commercial and Financial Chronicle
New York Times (Sunday edition)
Trade Magazines
      examples: Iron Age
                  Automotive Age

III. Magazine and Book Report

    1. Read selected chapters in one of the following
        for a reportorial review.

        Walter Adams, The Structure of American Industry. New York: Macmillan, 1950.
        William H. Beveridge, Full Employment in a Free Society. New York: Norton, 1945.
        Stuart Chase, Men and Machines. New York: Macmillan, 1929.
        Peter F. Drucker, The Future of Industrial Man. John Day, 1942.
        Alvin H. Hansen, America's Role in World Economy. New York: Norton, 1945.
        Henry Hazlitt, Economics in One Lesson. New York: Harper, 1946.
        Albert T. Lauterback, Economic Security and Individual Freedom: Can We Have Both? Ithaca: Cornell, 1948.
        Purdy, Lindahl, Carter, Corporate Concentration and Public Policy, 2nd edition, New York: Prentice-Hall, 1950.
        Louis L. Lorwin, Economic Consequence of Second World War, Temporary National Economic Committee, Corporation and Monopoly In American Industry, Government Printing Office, 1940.
        Paul Samuelson, Economics, An Introductory Analysis. New York: McGraw-Hill, 1948.
        Caroline F. Ware and Gardiner C. Means, Modern Economy in Action. New York: Harcourt, 1936.
        Broadus Mitchell and others, Economics: Experience & Analysis. New York: Sloane, 1950.

    2. Select one article from one of the following
        magazines and newspapers and re-write it as a
        news-feature:
        Survey of Current Business
        Federal Reserve Bulletin
        Fortune
        Economist
        Wall St. Journal
        Commercial and Financial Chronicle
        Business Week

Further References: Journalism texts containing chapters
on economics and business reporting.

Chilton R. Bush, Newspaper Reporting of Public Affairs. New York: Appleton, 1940. (Chapter XIII, "Business News"; Chapter XIV, "Corporate Finance"). (See also 1951 revised edition.)

Laurence R. Campbell and Roland E. Wolseley, Newsmen at Work: New York: Houghton Mifflin, 1949. (Chapter 25, "Business As Usual").

Victor S. Danilov, Public Affairs Reporting, N.Y. Macmillan, 1955.

Stanley Johnson, The Complete Reporter. New York: Macmillan, 1942. (Chapter 21, "Government and Politics").

Curtis D. MacDougall, Interpretative Reporting. New York: Macmillan, Rev. 1949. (Chapter XXVI, "Business, Finance, Labor").

Robert M. Neal, News Gathering and News Writing. New York: Prentice-Hall, 1949. (Chapter 35, "Business News").

C. Norman Stabler, How to Read the Financial News. New York: Harper, 1951.

Carl Warren, Modern News Reporting. New York: Harper 1934. (Chapter XXIV, "Keeping Abreast of Business"). See 1951 revised edition. (Chapter XXVI, "News About Business".)

Joseph C. Carter, "A Challenge to Financial Page Writer", Quill, Feb., 1954.

WORK AND WAGES

Consolidated Aircraft Corporation

OUTGOING SHIFT AT AIR PLANT

News about labor is vitally important, because what labor

does affects the entire nation's economy.

Chapter 6
Behind The Strike Headlines

1. Labor is Front Page News

What action the coal miners take, the negotiations being fought across the desk between the auto workers and the representatives of General Motors, and the pensions being requested by the electrical workers--all of this labor activity arouses a keen interest in every town and city. The entire economic system is so closely interwoven that the actions of the miners in West Virginia, the steelworkers in Pennsylvania, and the auto workers in Michigan have an impact upon industry and the public from Maine to California.

The wage patterns set by these big industries become the models for local bargaining. The work stoppages in coal cut the supply of the community's electric power plant and close the schools. When the production of steel slows down, eventually the purchasers of Chryslers in New York and of Fords in Florida are delayed in buying their new sedans and coupes.

Strikes by labor have always made the biggest headlines. Pickets marched in front of the factory gates... heads were cracked...police hauled the pickets to jail... a judge fined each of the union members $25 and costs for disturbing the peace. These were the surface actions which could easily be reported. Like the fire or murder, they were spectacular, easily recognized, easily understood, easily seized upon for page one copy.

But many editors are beginning to realize that the public wants more adequate background coverage of the union problem than spectacular strikes, although more explanatory material about the cause of the particular strikes is also desired. Readers want to know about the inside operations of unions, the reaction of labor to various national problems. The public is becoming interested in negotiations for contracts long before they are signed or the conflict situation develops into a lockout or strike. This is especially true in industrialized sections. For unions are important public institutions, with a total of more than 16 million members and millions of dollars in their treasuries. The United Auto Workers, the largest, has 800,000 enrolled. What labor leaders say and what their members do have a bearing on public welfare.

2. History of Labor Reporting

During the long and bitter history of the American labor movement, often characterized by great violence, by mass murder, and by dynamiting, newspapers were primarily interested in the conflicts between capital and labor. The struggles frequently resulted in strikes and often in bloodshed. America itself has a violent tradition, and, in the struggle, both sides resorted to violent methods to obtain their goals. The Haymarket affair, the railway strikes, the Homestead steel battle, the big steel war of 1919, are but a few vivid examples from this history. Unions had not become accepted, stabilized institutions in American life.

Because of the coverage of these outstanding national stories and many local ones, union representatives developed a resentment against reporters, editors and newspapers. They believed they could not get their side of the controversy published, or if they did, the account would be biased against them. Investigations of the steel strike of 1919 by the Interchurch World group indicated the extent to which newspapers went in twisting the news. The resentment of union leaders naturally caused them to antagonize reporters who didn't cover their news adequately, or did a poor job of the assignment. A newspaper tradition was established, a habit-groove was cut.

3. Labor Is Growing

Labor today has become important news. Workers through hard struggles and sacrifices have won the right to organize and have secured greater legal and congressional recognition. Instead of having, relatively, a handfull of workers in the crafts, as in the nineteenth century, the A.F.L. reached a high water mark of 4,500,000 by 1921. Then its membership dropped to 2,900,000. The Congress of Industrial Organizations, as a committee, began to organize in the basic industries in 1935, and all membership swelled. The unions today represent 15,000,000 men and women. This is nearly double the number organized in 1937. The A F L and the C.I.O. combined forces in 1956.[1] Thus, millions are interested in labor news because they are union members. Unions, too, are playing a greater role in public affairs and are influencing the trend of federal and state legislation.

Unions have become definitely established as part of the American economy. Organized workers have now been given greater recognition by the federal government. Labor laws were passed by the states prior to the 1930's, but they were largely restrictive. In the 1830's it was considered a criminal conspiracy if employes organized into a union. In the period of an expanding economic system in the nineteenth century, the attitude changed to tolerance toward the formation of unions, but opposition continued to activities of unions. Management could go to court and easily secure an injunction from a judge to restrain union

(1) See American Federationist, January 1956

182

members from various actions. Once the injunction was issued, persons found guilty were punished for contempt of court. Unions considered picketing, the holding of strike meetings, the peaceful persuasion of employes not to substitute for other employes on strike, as legitimate union activities. Courts did not so hold. Historians tell us that troops, police and private dectectives were called out frequently to enforce the injunctions or quell "the riots".

The struggle over the use of the injunction provided many of the page one headlines from the post-Civil War period until long after World War I. Agitation against injunctions continued, and finally a number of states passed laws intended to restrain the issuance of injunctions in labor cases.

Meanwhile, Congress, during the Hoover Administration in 1932, passed the Norris-LaGuardia Act, designed to prevent the issuance of injunctions by federal courts against the peaceful activities of trade unions. Anti-union contracts entered into by the management with certain employes to head off unionization were made illegal.

4. New Laws In Roosevelt Administration

Then a number of far-reaching measures favorable to labor were placed on the books during the Roosevelt Administration. The National Industrial Recovery Act was passed in 1933, containing the famous section 7a, which recognized labor's right to organize. When this law was finally declared unconstitutional, the National Labor Relations Act, already being considered, was passed in 1935. Covering only industries in interstate commerce, the new measure protected labor's right to organize and compelled employers to bargain with a chosen representative of their employes. It prohibited certain unfair labor practices by employers. They could not discharge employes for attempting to form a union, or fire them if they chose to belong. Employers could not dominate or support "company unions."

Attacks were made on the labor act, and the United States Supreme Court finally had to pass on its constitutionality in 1937. The court decided the act was constitutional. The National Labor Relations Act, and its administrative agency, the National Labor Relations Board, nevertheless, were centers of violent controversy since their beginnings. They have been in the forefront of the news since 1937. The reaction among senators and congressmen to the Act became so intense that the law was transformed into the Labor Management Relations Act in 1947.

The battle is still raging over this measure, known as the Taft-Hartley Act. The late Senator Robert A. Taft (R-Ohio), who introduced and advocated the measure in the senate, said its purpose was to even up the labor-management picture. Labor, on the other hand, bitterly opposed the Act, claiming it was an attempt to shackle employes and cripple unions.

In the Taft-Hartley Act some of the old provisions of
the National Labor Relations measure were kept. The employes' right to bargain was guaranteed and unfair labor
practices by the employer were still forbidden. New provisions, however, were added. The Act barred a closed shop
by which only persons who belonged to the union with bargaining powers in the plant could be hired. It likewise
prohibited the union shop, except when approved by the employes working for the company. Under this union-shop type
of contract, a new employe had to join the union after a
certain period of employment at the shop. After several
years of experience, it was found that in nearly every case
the employes voted for a union shop arrangement, and so
this provision was eliminated by Congress. But the Act
permitted states to pass measures banning union shops.

With respect to the workers, the Taft-Hartley measure
prohibited union members and representatives from coercing
employes to join their organization, and it also barred
secondary boycotts and the unionization of foremen. It
loosened up the strict provisions of the earlier act regarding the rights of the employer to discuss with employes
such matters as joining a union. The labor-management law
required unions to file financial reports and file non-communist oaths. An important provision gave the President
of the United States power to get out an injunction to prevent a strike if one threatened to interfere with the national economy during a war or other emergency.

Meanwhile, labor was protected by other federal measures. The Fair Labor Standards Act was enacted in 1938,
prohibiting child labor and setting a ceiling of maximum
hours and a basement of minimum wages for employes in interstate commerce. Sharp controversy burst out over this
measure. The minimum wage was raised to $1 an hour in 1955,
but millions of employes were excluded, and labor protested.

All of this conflict indicated that labor news was
important. News about workers in the mines, the factories
and the shipyards was not to be confined to strikes, although this type of news produced the larger banner headlines. The conflict between capital and labor was now
transferred for the most part to the negotiating table, the
hearing room, the congressional halls and the courts. Here
were the sources of news.

Thus, because of the expansion of union membership,
the increasing protection given employes by the Federal
government, and the vital effects organized labor had on
the nation's economy, labor news became newsworthy. It is
important that editors and reporters seek in accordance with
newspaper traditions to present fairly, accurately and com-
pletely such news.

Reporting such news requires more background and understanding than it does to cover a spectacular fire. To do
an adequate job of telling the labor news, some knowledge
of labor and labor laws would be helpful.

<u>MERGER OF THE AFL AND CIO</u> The merger of the American Federa-
tion of Labor and the Congress of Industrial Organizations was
big news to the American public. After many years of strife and
competition, a consolidation was effected. AFL George Meany
clasps the hand of CIO's head, Walter Reuther, in a gesture of
harmony in the above picture. The convention at which the merger took place was covered by many newsmen who pounded out thousands of words on this event.

Help of the AFL-CIO in covering the big story drew praise
from the press. At the microphone is reporter A. H. Raskin, of
the New York Times.

Photos from the American Federationist

Some publishers have seen the need, and so they have hired or developed labor reporters to do the job. Louis Stark became well known as a result of his work on the New York Times. His pioneering days as a labor reporter were told in the Nieman Reports for January, 1952.

LOUIS STARK, labor reporter, winner in 1942 for his distinguished reporting of important labor stories.

Victor Riesel gained a reputation on the New York Post and his articles were syndicated. He is now writing for the Daily Mirror and other papers. In 1956 he was blinded following his attack on labor rackets but continued to produce his column. In its annual yearbook, Editor & Publisher lists many labor reporters on other newspapers. An extensive article on labor reporters with the title, "Labor Reporting: How Good is It Now?", appeared in Business Week, October 20, 1951. About 200 reporters covered the CIO convention in Cleveland in 1949 and sent out 1,000,000 words to newspapers and press associations.

5. Current Labor Problems

Here are some of the current labor problems which appear in the headlines and news in various forms and which newsmen ought to be familiar with. These issues represent the points of conflict between management and labor unions. They involve, in a sense, the goals of organized labor. They indicate that labor leaders have extended their horizons beyond the immediate issues of wages and working conditions, although these will continue to be fundamental. National union heads are concerned with other federal and local projects, laws, conditions which affect the white-collar and the factory worker. Some of the viewpoints of management and labor on these issues will be presented in the following pages. Fuller explanations and discussion and opinion may be obtained from the references at the end of the chapter, from the publications of the organizations representing management and from those speaking for labor.

Labor-Management Relations - The Taft-Hartley Act

The relations between management and labor is of key importance. If these relations are harmonious, industrial progress results. If they are in conflict, retardation of the economy occurs. Involved always are the rights of labor to organize. Attention centers now around the Taft-Hartley Labor Management Relations Act. This law has provided a source of conflict between management and unions since it was first enacted in 1947. The National Labor Relations Act of 1935 was considered, as already indicated, the Magna Carta of Labor. Unions believed that it established for all time the right of working people to join unions of their own choosing without interference or restraint and to require employers to recognize and bargain in good faith with the unions selected. It was expected that the National Labor Relations Board would have broad jurisdiction over all companies engaged in interstate commerce and that it would check any employer interference with the right to organize.

Then in 1947 the Taft-Hartley Labor Management Relations Act was passed and the scrap over the new measure began. At first unions aimed at eliminating the Act altogether, but the climate of opinion in the U.S. House and Senate seemed to be opposed to this drastic step. Union leaders have since sought to have the various provisions of the law modified.

Management has upheld the Act, insisting that its provisions are necessary to provide the balance which the old National Labor Relations Act did not have. Unions need to be held accountable for their actions as does management, it has been pointed out. Employes should not be coerced into joining unions. Employers should have the right to discuss unions with workers. In national emergencies the government should have the power to stop disputes and keep industry moving.

Organized labor, on the other hand, has found various objections to the Taft-Hartley Act and its administration. Labor spokesmen pointed out shortcomings in the Economic Outlook for February, 1955, September, 1952, and January, 1950 and in American Federationist, June, 1956. They pointed out that the law was substantially re-written through the process of making new interpretations, as a result of the appointment of new members to the board. The Act provides that employers are prohibited from interference or coercion with workers' selection of their bargaining representatives. The board, under new rulings, allowed employers to assemble their workers and talk against supporting the union, they say. Under the old rules a threat by an employer to move his plant if the union won an election was viewed to be coercive and therefore an unfair labor practice. In recent decisions the new board majority views this threat as merely within the realm of "prophesy" and therefore not coercive.

The union advocates also pointed out that by redefining its "jurisdiction" the board has taken from hundreds of thousands of workers even the diminishing safeguards. The Act covers all employers whose operations affect interstate commerce. In the past the Board exercised the jurisdiction broadly. Now the dollar volume of interstate business an employer must do is set before the Board takes jurisdiction. No workers in retailing except in very large department stores are protected under the law. Many other industries are exempt. They cite the study by Professor W. Willard Wirtz, of Northwestern University and former chairman of the National Wage Stabilization Board, in his article in the Northwestern University Law Review, November-December,

1954. He concluded from a study that the duty to bargain
has been substantially cut back and there has been a marked
reduction in the kinds of employe activities protected
against discharge.

Unions have objected seriously to the provision of the
act calling for certain procedures in case of a national
emergency, which call for an 80-day cooling off period.
Management pointed out the severe results from an important
strike and the need to protect the public. The unions cite
a statement by Cyrus Ching, ex-Director of the Federal
Mediation and Conciliation Service, that in national emergency dispute cases employers have too often not engaged in
collective bargaining because of their confidence that the
processes of the Taft-Hartley Act will be employed and the
union enjoined for an 80-day period. The unions assert
that if genuine collective bargaining does take place, and
if employers know that the government will not intervene on
their side by the use of an anti-labor injunction, national
emergency disputes can be settled easily. They point out
national emergency has been too often abused and they doubt
that any of the so-called emergency strikes in recent years
really created a national emergency. Responsibility must
be placed on the parties themselves to settle their dispute, they argue. This does not leave the nation remedi-
less since, in the final analysis, according to them,
Congress is always available and possesses the authority to
act with a remedy tailor - made to the equities of the
particular situation.

A statement of the CIO Executive Board on February 12,
1953 in a pamphlet called, "...Sugar-Coating Won't do" indicated that labor believes that union and management should
be left free to negotiate the terms of collective bargaining agreements without government restrictions. They
should be free to negotiate whatever type of union security
arrangements they deem appropriate and suited to the particular situation. The executive board asserted that the
Taft-Hartley law should be rid of the provisions designed
to harass and weaken unions and that the measure should be
simplified and clarified to reduce the present inordinate
delays in procedure and enforcement. The present law, the
board asserted, is so intricate that it can hardly be understood by the workers to whom it applies, or by employers
either. The board urged that the law protect both unions
and employers in industries organized on an industrial
union basis from disruption of established and orderly collective bargaining by artificially carving out of craft
units. It advocated the banning of employer coercion and
intimidation of employees under the guise of protecting free
speech.

Union Security Right-to-Work Laws

Since 1944 eighteen states, most of them in the South
have adopted "right-to-work" laws. The Taft-Hartley Act
declared the closed shop to be illegal. The Act also permitted states to bar the enforcement of all other types of
union security. The state laws vary but generally ban

various forms of union security-such as the closed shop,
the union shop and maintenance of membership. The proponents of the laws declared that employes have a right to
work where they please and they do not have to join a union
unless they want to. The advocates argued that unorgan-
ized states would attract industry and commerce. States
without industries need a chance to grow, it was said. The
cost of living in various states was less, therefore, high
union wages were not necessary. To fortify their cause
some of the advocates of these laws organized the national
right to work committee, headed by Fred A. Hartley - former
Republican representative from New Jersey and co-author of
the Taft-Hartley law, according to New York Times of April
8, 1956.

Labor union leaders have continued to oppose these
right-to-work laws and this will be an issue for some years
to come. Some believe it is more emotionally loaded than
the Taft-Hartley Act. They point out in the Economic Outlook for January, 1955 and the Economic Review for January,
1956, their views. The right to work is not absolute and
purely personal, they say. The right to work is condition-
al and a social right. It is honeycombed with conditions.
A worker must be qualified for a job and must be accepted
by the employer. No American tradition demands that Joe,
the hod carrier, has a right to a carpenter's job. And
once Joe is on a job he is well aware of many other restrictions. He must report at a specific time, work so
many hours, according to rules and regulations, accept certain deductions from wages for Social Security. No one
claims that these restrictions are un-American and destructive of a workingman's freedom.

The individual worker on his own is at a distinct dis-
advantage in trying to influence the employer's decision
regarding his wages, hours and working conditions. The
union leaders feel that without the strength of the union
to assist him, the individual worker is compelled to
accept wages and working conditions that are established by
the employer.

In answer to the questions what about the employe who
doesn't want to join a union, why should he have to? and
why should he be compelled to pay dues if he doesn't believe in the organization?--the writer in the Economic Review for January, 1956, pointed out that union representation leads to benefits for all workers in the union--for
both union members and free riders. The non-paying non-
member who enjoys the benefits of trade unionism is like a
member of a community who refuses to pay taxes for the
support of the schools, parks, police and fire departments.

Rackeeting in Unions

Rackets and racketeers have plagued legitimate unions
for many years. The extent to which hoodlums have worked
their way into positions of influence is impossible to measure in across-the-board terms, according to A.J. Raskin,
labor reporter for the New York Times, in the April 20, 1956

issue. George Meany, president of the American Federation
of Labor - and Congress of Industrial Organizations, insists
that all the harm is being done by a corrupt 1 per cent in
labor's ranks. Law enforcement agencies, says Raskin, are
inclined to put the figure at 5 to 10 per cent.

The problem is not so much the percentage as it is the
uneven distribution of the crooked elements. They tend to
be concentrated in a relatively small number of unions.
These are honeycombed with racketeers.

Men with criminal backgrounds and no reform record
find it easy to get local union charters from organizations
of this stripe. Unlike most charters, these put no jurisdictional bounds on the new locals. They amount to "hun-
ting licenses" that give their owners freedom to pick up
members in almost any branch of industry.

Armed with such characters, hoodlums are able to use
picket lines and tieups with unions truckers to shake-
down small employers and to victimize their workers. The
wage scales of bona fide unions are undermined by the in-
roads of the marauders. The mobster plays both employer
and employe. New York Attorney General Jacob K. Javits
estimates that in New York alone the take comes to at least
$50,000,000 a year. For the country it may be ten times
that.

Mobsters are especially active in the trucking, construction and garment trades. They are also busy in the
light manufacturing, night clubs, vending machines and
other fields in which operation units are small. The
ability of the employer to hold out against the union
pressure is limited.

Breaking up such practices through criminal prosecu-
tion is far from simple. First, there is the difficulty of
getting anyone to talk. Employers are fearful of being
shot. Within unions there is a traditional reluctance to
"call cops."

With regular welfare funds still in the embryo stage
the money paid into pension and health trusts for the benefit of union members represents another fruitful source of
extra income for the unscrupulous unionist.

Millions of dollars are being built up in funds contributed by the employer to the trust funds. Union officials and insurance agents arrange to split commissions and
service fees, or they set up special benefit arrangements.
These devices siphon off a quarter or a third of the money
intended to protect the workers. Louis B. Saperstein, New-
ark, N.J. insurance broker, got four bullets in his head
and neck for talking about welfare kickbacks in March, 1956.

With the merger of the AFL and CIO, such anti-racketeer
union leaders as George Meany turned their attention to the
rackets within the labor movement. The merged unions

wrote into their constitution an anti-corruption program.
Meany declared he would carry on an active warfare against
racketeering in any of the affiliated unions.

Workmen's Compensation Laws

Workmen's compensation is never far away from every
one of the 64 million members of the American labor force.
Most workers do not expect to be injured, but everyone is
exposed to some occupational hazard. Every 16 seconds
around the clock, an American is injured on the job; every
4 minutes a worker is killed or maimed; every year 2 million workers suffer injury or disease in the process of
turning out the goods and services America needs.

When injury strikes, workers have to rely on workmen's
compensation laws to provide medical care and to replace
lost wages. Not many workers know in advance how adequate
or inadequate the compensation will be. But when injured,
union representatives believe, employes soon learn that
workers' compensation does not offer enough protection to
maintain their families, and sometimes, not enough even to
regain health.

In the January, 1952 issue of the Economic Outlook
the shortcoming in workmen's compensation laws were pointed to. Almost the entire burden of work injuries and disease fell on the injured and their families, or on private
charity and public relief, the writer said. It required
37 years, from 1911 to 1948 for all the states to get
around to passing workmen's compensation laws. But long
before all 48 passed laws, most of them became seriously
out-of-date. Arthur H. Reede, in his "Adequacy of Workmen's
Compensation," pointed out in 1940 that workers were ab-
sorbing half the wage loss. In Illinois in 1952 a study
showed that only 13 per cent of the wage loss was compen-
sated in 1951.

The maximum benefit is most often $28 or $39 per week.
Only in a few states are maximum benefits for a family of
four $40 or more. The average production worker in the
United States earns about $72 week. But a $40 maximum
means that he receives at most only 42 per cent of his
wages when injured. The injured worker has at times become
dependent upon private charity or public relief.

These benefits apply to workers with minor and temporary injuries. Compensation has been made even less adequate for severe and permanent disabilities where the need
is far greater. If you were to become totally disabled for
life, you might lose more than $100,000 in wages alone.
But under most workmen's compensation laws, you could not
possibly receive more than one-tenth of this loss. As many
as 32 states do not provide life-time benefits because of
arbitrary dollar or duration maximums. In thousands of
American communities, therefore, workers hurt on their jobs
are existing only because of the charity of relatives and
of private and public relief agencies, the writer pointed
out.
191

The _Economic Outlook_ said that 22 states have decided
that employers shall pay $10,000 or less for death. The
maximum in Vermont is $6,500; in Maine, $8,000. The prices
set for the loss of specific parts of the body by the various state legislatures are small, it was said. Extreme
variation among the states was noted. Compensation for
occupational disease was not covered in all five states.
A number of the states have limited the cost or duration
of medical care. The only real advance in the idea of workman's compensation has been the introduction of rehabilitation -- new and progressive methods for overcoming dis-
ability. More than 30 states, however, have failed to make
rehabilitation part of workmen's compensation. Poor and
perfunctory administration of compensation laws was found
in many states. State agencies were supposed to review
agreements on settlement of claims, but actually they checked only superficially on them.

Unions have advocated (1) Maximum benefits of from
65 to 85% of state or national wage, whichever is higher
(2) Increase in number of weeks for which benefits are
paid (3) Elimination of unreasonable disqualifications
and extended waiting periods and other penalties to reduce
rates.

Guaranteed Annual Wages

As early as 1953 the United Auto Workers approved the
proposal of the officers that the next forward step in
stabilizing employment and reducing the insecurity of workers would be the guaranteed annual wage. Other unions,
such as the electrical workers and steel workers, joined in
the proposals. Although there are variations in various
plans, they have a number of common provisions.

Under the plan all workers in a plant would be guaranteed employment or payments from the time they acquired
seniority. For each employe with one year's seniority, the
company would guarantee not less than 48 to 52 weeks of 40
hours each at his regular work rate. Employes with at
least three months service would get small guarantees
which would increase with the length of service.

The payments to fulfill the guarantee would be finan-
ced from a fund equal from 4 to 5 per cent of the payroll,
a trust fund which the employer would build up. A laid-off
worker would be required to register with the public employment office and accept suitable work. Since he would receive unemployment compensation, this amount would be de-
ducted from the money he would receive from the company's
trust fund. The fund would be administered jointly by
union and management, with an impartial chairman to decide
disputed questions.

When the company's fund reached an amount equal to 10
week's pay for each employe, the contributions by the employer would be reduced so as to maintain the fund at that
level.

The purpose of the guaranteed annual wage would be to provide security, but also to stimulate management to provide steady full-time employment, week by week, year by year. Management would be encouraged to stabilize production schedules and employment. The plan, the labor leaders assert, would help to improve unemployment compensation, which is too low, about $25, and its duration too short. It would encourage employers to support national economic policies designed to maintain full employment. Insurance plans could be developed to spread the risks of abnormal employment over the widest possible area of economy.

It was believed that the acceptance of the program for an annual wage in the giant auto, steel and electrical manufacturing companies would have a widespread effect throughout the nation in the direction of regularized employment and governmental policies favorable to it.

It was pointed out that the savings resulting from stabilized employment might actually outweigh the costs of the guarantee. Labor turnover would be reduced, so the expenses of hiring and training new workers would be cut down. Morale would be improved. Equipment would be used more efficiently.

The guaranteed wage plans, it was contended, would assure purchasing power for those directly covered and indirectly for millions more. The butcher, baker, the farmer, and others would gain from the constant flow of paychecks.

Management has objected on the grounds that most employers can't forsee into the future and can't predict or control sales or demand for their products. The trust fund burden, they say, would just be another cost of doing business.

Assistance for Distressed Areas

Chronic unemployment exists in many communities. This is a special and exceedingly difficult problem which tends to be concealed by overall statistics on national unemployment. There are communities where involuntary idleness is continuous and often acute even when most other parts of the country may be enjoying peak prosperity. Programs, both public and private in nature - must be developed to help these communities eradicate the idleness and economic decay which have infected them. While about 3.7 per cent of the labor force was unemployed in July, 1955, substantial unemployment, at least 6 per cent, was reported idle in 31 of the 149 major labor-market areas. In 12 the jobless rate exceeded 9 per cent; in 7 it was over 12 per cent.

Full Employment and Production Program to Meet Possible Depressions

Labor leaders have set forth the need for full employment, which they call the key to abundance, progress and peace. Science and technology, they say, have given us the tools with which to conquer poverty, hunger, ignorance and disease. Yet despite the fact that we have the tools, the resources, and tremendous unfilled needs, often there is dangerous and reckless talk of depression. American labor, they point out must demonstrate that there shall be no peace-time depression for we have the technical know-how and economic resources to provide full and continuous employment for every citizen able and willing to work.

We have repeatedly demonstrated the capacity to create full employment and full production, making the weapons of war. We must now demonstrate the good sense to create full employment and full production making the good things for people in peacetime. What we need to do is to provide the American people - workers, farmers, white-collar and professional groups - with sufficient purchasing power to balance our productive power.

If fully mobilized, the American economy is capable of producing enough to meet our defense needs while at the same time devoting billions a year to the carrying out of a possible offensive in the struggle against man's ancient enemies -- poverty, hunger, ignorance and disease.

Our economy is growing rapidly. More people come of working age each year. With improved machinery and equipment, the average workman produces more goods and services each year.

By 1960 - provided we maintain full employment between now and then -- we can have a total national product of $510 billion worth of goods and services compared to about $370 billions in 1955 and $348 billion in 1952.

With that much available we could:

>   wipe out poverty
>   meet our housing needs
>   provide decent schools for our children
>   meet our hospital needs
>   improve and expand our highway system
>   develop and conserve our natural resources
>   control floods
>   provide for national defense and foreign aid
>   maintain the pace of economic progress

The union urged the enactment of Fair Practices legislation at the national, state and local levels. They advocated the increase and extension of unemployment compensation benefits, raising minimum wages and extending coverage. The leaders advocated the increase of the minimum wage to $1.25 per hour and the extension of its protection to workers not presently covered.

Decrease of Tax Burden on Workers

The unions urge the passage of an equitable tax program based upon the principle of ability to pay. This would mean increasing the personal exemption to $1,000, plugging the loopholes in the law that enable many to escape or reduce their tax share.

The Threat of Automation

The installation of automatic machinery may constitute a real threat to workers, substituting machines for human beings, throwing them out of work permanently. Plans should be made for these possibilities. The leaders raise the question, if automation is introduced and productivity of the worker is increased, will the employe share in this? Will the new machinery lower the costs of production and will savings be passed on to the consumer in lower-cost products?

Extension of Social Security Benefits, Raising Pensions

While much progress has been made in social security, the coverage ought to be extended and the retirement benefits raised, thereby expanding the purchasing power of millions of old people who depend on social security as a means of sustenance. The benefits should be raised to $200 per month.

More Extensive Low-Cost Housing Projects

Slums, say the union spokesmen, are social cesspools which breed juvenile delinquency, crime and other social diseases. To permit them to continue is costly and socially irresponsible. Every American family, every American child has a right to a decent home in a decent neighborhood. We must take steps, they say, to increase construction of at least 2,000,000 homes in healthy neighborhoods each year for years to come. Mass production of low-cost housing should be encouraged.

Adequate Federal Aid to Education

The United States must overcome the tragic deficit in the school and educational system. Every American child is entitled to an educational opportunity which will enable him to grow intellectually, culturally and spiritually. In 1953 the U.S. Dept. of Health, Education and Welfare stated there is a need for 300,000 classrooms to take care of shortages. By 1960 six million more children will be going to school in America. 600,000 new classrooms will be required. Also the increased enrollment will call for 250,000 more elementary and secondary school teachers.

The unions advocate a school construction bill to provide federal aid for a comprehensive nationwide school construction program. A bill to provide adequate budgets for school lunch programs and another to raise the salaries of teachers above the present level of $3,400.

<u>Improved National Health Insurance Act</u>

The labor spokesmen say that despite the tremendous progress which medical science has made during the past, millions of American citizens do not have access to hospital facilities and medical services necessary to insure good health. The United States needs to build thousands of new hospitals to remove economic barriers to good health. The country needs to enact a health insurance program just as it has a social security measure and unemployment compensation laws as a supplement to the present private insurance plans.

5. <u>Background Story Needed</u>

Newspapers, as indicated, need to do more than present the spectacular aspects of a strike story. An example of the surface type of news coverage is seen in the rayon worker article following. It became the number one story on the front page of the <u>Miami</u>, Fla., <u>Daily News</u>, June 22, 1950, although the event happened in Morristown, Tenn.

The newsman seeking to give a complete picture of the Morristown situation would have described the events leading up to the tragedy. This particular outburst no doubt was the result of a long-festering labor-management relationship. The reporter would have described the part the company played in the situation, and he would have told the various actions of the CIO textile workers union and also of the AFL textile workers organization which came into the picture. The reporter would have asked what part did the National Guard and the Tennessee Highway Patrol play? Did it help or hinder the settlement of the labor dispute? The Senate Labor Sub-Committee on Labor Management Relations in 1950 held a hearing on the entire strike case and the subsequent violence. What did the testimony show? The answer to these questions would have given the reader a better understanding of the causes of the strike and placed the event in its proper perspective.

RAYON WORKER SLAIN
BY GUNFIRE IN STRIKE

Morristown, Tenn., June 22 - (UP) - A non-striking workman was shot to death and four others were wounded today in a bloody outbreak of violence at the strike-torn American Enka Rayon plant.

The shooting started as the day shift left the plant. It was the second straight day that workers were fired upon, but no one was hurt in yesterday's shooting.

The state highway patrol identified the dead man as "McDaniels." Condition of the wounded was not immediately determined.

196

Sgt. Carl Gilbert said state police reinforcements had been called to the scene.

***

Violence has marked the 12-week-old strike of CIO Textile Workers but the shooting stage was not reached until yesterday.

It began the morning after a union official instructed the strikers to refrain from violence.

At one time, the national guard was called to keep down disturbances at the picket line. A Senate labor subcommittee investigated the matter last week end.

** * *

Workers had previously been stoned and attacked from ambush. Dynamiting of property also had been reported.

The patrol sergeant said he was told by a plant official that the shots were fired from the direction where pickets were standing. Other workers were reported still in the plant, afraid to come out. Doctors also were reported afraid to go into the strife-torn area, Gilbert said.

The wounded, however, were said to be hospitalized.

"We have to get reinforcements and get in there before we will know all the details of the shooting", said Gilbert. He did not know how many troopers are being sent here to bolster the patrol forces.

** * *

An Enka spokesman charged yesterday that three carloads of workers were fired on from ambush as they left the plant, and that the husband of one of them returned the fire with a pistol. No one was injured.

The union denied knowledge of the incident, and said the only shooting it knew of came when the picket line was fired on the previous day.

** * *

The strike had previously taken on an international aspect. Union headquarters in New York reported yesterday that the International Confederation of Free Trade Unions was giving its support. The confederation called on Dutch workers to bring pressure against the owners of Enka in that country.

The CIO, in a brief filed with national labor relations board, charged the company with refusal to bargain, coercion and intimidation of union members, and helping the AFL textile union in its efforts to win a bargaining election during the strike period.

197

In yesterday's shooting, Jack Quinton fired
back at "about five" men who shot at his automobile
as he drove Mrs. Quinton home from the plant. He
said he could not recognize any of them because of
the rain.

Another car loaded with workers was punctured
with bullet holes, and the company spokesman said
the windows of a bus were shattered by stones.

6. Weaving in Background Facts

Reporters have the opportunity frequently to weave
into a spot news labor story background information which
helps the reader get a broader picture. The newsman in
the following Associated Press story tied up to the current
news previous bits of information which placed the happening in its proper setting. The immediate event was the
coming meeting of the CIO United Steelworkers in Pittsburgh.
Notations on the side of the clipping indicate the background facts. In addition to the spot news in the lead, a
second current news event, the Pittsburgh steelworkers resolutions, will be found halfway down the story. This, too,
needed further explanation.

Steelworkers Prepare to Demand Boost in Wages

Pittsburgh, Sept. 19 (AP) - Top
strategists of the CIO United
Steelworkers meet here Thursday
and Friday for sessions that
may bring a demand to boost wages
of nearly 1,000,000 unionists.

1. Spot News Event:
   Meeting of Steelworkers

President Philip Murray of
both the CIO and the Steelworkers called the USW's executive
board into session amid widespread speculation that a wage
increase demand is in the works.

Murray has left no doubt
that he considers steel industry
profits "fabulous."

Wage gains won by the CIO
United Auto Workers in recent
weeks added pressure to demands
from the USW rank and file for
fatter pay envelopes to meet
higher living costs.

2. Immediate Background
   Facts: Pressure from
   Auto Workers' Increase

   Facts: Where decision
   Will Come From

Steelworkers now earn a
national average of $1.70 an
hour compared to about $1.75
for auto workers. Before recent pay gains, the average
auto worker earned $1.65.

   Facts: Average Wage
   Told

Any decision to seek a pay
boost in steel will originate
with the union's executive board.
It is the big union's chief policy
making group. The board is composed of Murray, other international officers and 33 union dis-
trictdirectors.

The board will have before
it a resolution from a group of
28,000 steelworkers in the Pittsburgh area which asks that a wage
hike be sought. The resolution
cites "the tremendous increase
in the cost of living" and the
"huge profits of the steel industry."

3. More Spot News:
Pittsburgh Resolu-
tion

Declaring "the cost of living
has spiraled upward at an amazing
speed," the resolution urges
"strenuous efforts to be made to
regain lost ground."

The reference to lost ground
apparently concerns the futile
fight the union made last year for
fourth round pay increases. The
USW gave up its wage demands then
on the recommendation of a presidential fact finding board. It
settled a 42-day strike by accept-
ing a pension and insurance program.

4. Background Facts:
Previous Fight for
Increase

Under the industry wide contracts signed at the end of that
national strike, the union may
re-open wage provisions next November 1. If no agreement is reached with industry by December 31,
the union is free to strike
January 1.

Facts: What
contracts say

The possibility of a wage-
price freeze by Government is a
big factor. Union leaders want
to win their objectives before
the lid is slapped on - if it
comes. President Truman has said
he doesn't want mandatory controls
now.

Facts: Government
policy in back-
ground

Associated Press Dispatch

As in other tense news-situations, charges are often
hurled by management and unions. False impressions, as a
result, may be created. The reporter working on such stories should bring in the full background to which the reader
is entitled. An aggressive effort should be made to secure
the complete facts and statements from both management and
unions. Unions themselves make strong statements about

REPORTERS DOG HEELS OF JOHN L.   John L. Lewis,
chief of the United Mine Workers, is always news and
his opinions make news. Reporters followed John L.
through a line of independent union's pickets as he
reported for a labor-management conference in
Washington.

each other, and these, too, must be placed in proper perspective by linking up previous events and facts. In the following dispatch serious charges were made by the United Electrical Workers (Ind.) against the United States government and the CIO Electrical Workers. The accusations were reported, then in the final paragraph the previous history of the conflict was summarized.

CIO-U. S. Scheme
For Strike of GE's
Employes Charged

New York, Sept. 19 (AP) An independent union official charged today the CIO schemed with the Government to strike General Electric Co. and then bring Federal mediators to the rescue of the strikers.

Spot News
The Union Makes Charges

The strike came off early this month and since has been settled with the mediators' aid.

"Phil Murray set himself up with Cy Ching," Organizational Director James J. Matles told the fifteenth annual convention of the United Electrical Workers (Ind.).

Murray is president of the CIO and Cyrus Ching is the Nation's Federal mediation director.

Matles did not outline what the purpose of such a plan might be. Presumably, it would allow the CIO union to put pressure on General Electric without subjecting its members to a long, costly strike.

Neither Murray nor Ching could be reached for comment.

The CIO International Union of Electrical Workers was set up after the UE was ousted from the CIO for alleged Communist tendencies. The two unions have engaged in a bitter fight for control of more than 100, 000 workers in General Electric's vast plant system.

Associated Press Dispatch

Background Facts
Previous History
of Conflict

7. Constructive Features

Articles which picture the constructive aspects of unions rather than the destructive aspects of the spot news also need to be written. These would give the third dimension of labor news which is muffed in the usual routine labor story.

The reporter needs to re-examine the stereotypes about employes, the pictures built up by cartoonists of a man wearing a square paper hat and overalls. The reporter must seek to get a more accurate portrait of the worker. While the repetition of strike news hammers away at the conflict and the pathological side of labor-management relations, the background features can stress the positive side of the labor story. The reporter should describe the normal day-by-day relationships in a factory and he should tell how many employers promote goodwill within their organizations.

Here is an example of a story dealing with a health plan for hotel workers. It was given a large prominent head in the Miami Herald.

HOTELS START EMPLOYES' HEALTH PLAN

By Marshal Rothe
Herald Staff Writer

Miami Beach's hotel industry has become one of the first in the United States to inaugurate an employer-financed insurance program for its workers.

Between 12,000 and 14,000 employes, ranging from Managers to housecleaners, will benefit under the setup, approved officially by directors of the Miami Beach Hotel Association after two months discussion and study.

According to the organization's executive secretary, Sam Kaplan, the Beach plan is the first in the South for hotel workers. A few eastern cities, notably Washington, D.C., have similar programs, he explained.

Basically, the group insurance coverage gives personnel $1,000 worth of life insurance $20 weekly accident and health benefits, $7-per-day in hospital costs, and about $350 in miscellaneous hospital benefits.

Designed to better employer-employe relations, the plan was tailor-made for Miami Beach's partly transient hotel workers.

The insured employe can hold onto his policy by paying low-rate premiums during the months he works in another part of the country, Kaplan pointed out. When he returns his premium payments will be resumed by the hotel organization.

202

"It's a kind of Christmas present the
association has been readying," Kaplan explained. The general blueprint of the plan
was taken from the American Hotel Association
which reviewed employe benefits at its national
convention in San Francisco last summer, he
said.

Concluded as one huge policy, the coverage
was written, Kaplan said, with the Continental
Assurance Company of Indiana.

Harry Cohen, of the New Yorker Hotel, is
chairman of the MBHA committee which devised
the local setup. Individual hotels are signing up with the plan now and employe response
has been "surprisingly good," Cohen said Satur-
day.

A few workers already have asked for additional coverage, he said. They will be permitted to buy in excess of the $1,000 policy,
paid for by the hotel operators, at less-than-
standard rates.

A team of four representatives of the insurance company, headed by the chief of its group
service department, will tackle the job this
week of signing up the industry's thousands of
workers.

Miami, Fla. Herald

Many industrialists are becoming aware of the value of
a vacation for their employes, and the National Industrial
Conference Board made a study of what business was doing on
this issue. The Board's report was made the basis of an
article by George Erwin, business editor of the Atlanta, Ga.
Journal.

Employe Vacation Plans
Win Industry Attention

Executives Gaining Awareness of
Personnel's Increased Efficiency

By GEORGE ERWIN

Vacations for employes are getting more attention
from business executives than ever before.

Once these time-off periods each year were considered necessary summer disruptions to business,
which were to be gotten before settling down to
business as usual in the fall.

Now, however, executives are gaining a greater
awareness of the increased efficiency of personnel
when vacations are granted.

Paid vacation practices in the business world
are changing, too. Previously, salaried workers

203

got most of the "breaks" in time-off-with-pay.
In the last several years this has carried over
to hourly employes, so that on the average they
are about equal to their salaried brothers and
sisters in industry.

A report by the National Industrial Conference Board, Inc., as a result of its study of
vacation practices of 303 companies, shows some
interesting trends.

Taking the average of salaried employes of this
group, the Conference Board found the 47.8 per
cent got two weeks vacation with pay. Another
42.9 per cent got three weeks time off each year,
and 7 per cent were given a four-week vacation.
Only 1 per cent received just one week, while
1.3 per cent were granted paid time off of more
than four weeks.

This varies only slightly in vacations for
hourly employes, except that findings were made
in only 273 companies, instead of 301. This
showed time limits in percentages as follows:
Two weeks, 46.9 per cent; three weeks, 44.7 per
cent; four weeks, 4.4 per cent; one week, 3.3
per cent, and over four weeks, 0.7 per cent.

It was pointed out that few companies give
the same vacation time treatment to short-service
as to long-service employes. In most companies,
according to the survey, the longer the employe
is with the company the more vacation he rates...
                    Atlanta, Ga., Journal

The following are examples of constructive news-features about labor-management relations. Although published
on inside pages, they were given top position and strong
two-column headlines.

Labor Relations in Phosphate
Plants Called Best in Years

Bartow, April 7 - (Special) - Labor-management
relations in the Florida phosphate field are the
best in several years at contract-renewing time,
a survey by the Polk County Democrat showed today, with two contracts already renewed, others
in amicable negotiations stages, and the rest not
due for renewal.

There were no indications of impending strikes
such as have disrupted operations in the Polk and
Hillsborough County mines in years past.

Davison Chemical Corp.'s management and union
committees got a jump on the rest of the field in
February, when it was announced that a new labor
contract had been signed "without the necessity
of further negotiations."

A new contract was signed at American Agricultural Chemical Co. last week, providing for a raise

of three cents an hour, two additional holidays
and an extra week's vacation. Expiring
April 5, 1951, the new agreement was reached
in a series of friendly negotiations and without interruption of operations.

"Partial agreement" was reported between management and union negotiators at Virginia-
Carolina Chemical Corp., with the prospect that
the new contract will be signed within the next
few days.

There have been only one meeting each for
negotiations at Coronet, only mine in the
Hillsborough County field, and at Swift & Co.
Coronet's old contract expired April 1.
Swift's contract runs till April 5, 1951, but
is reopenable this month on the question of
wages. Relations were described as friendly
at both plants.

Later expiration dates are in effect at the
other three firms in the field - International
Mineral & Chemical Corp., American Cyanamid Co.
and Armour Fertilizer Works - and no negotiations
have been called at any of them.

IMCC's two-year contract runs until next
year, but is reopenable on the question of
wages May 15. ACC's contract runs until June
1, and Armour's until this Fall.

Tampa, Fla, <u>Tribune</u>

Workers' Needs Cited
For Increasing Output

Ann Arbor, Mich.,
April 1 - If you boss
people and you want to
get production, don't
just harp on more work
in less time - be gen-
uinely interested in the
people who are working
for you.

That is one of the
lessons that psycholo-
gists learned at the
University of Michigan's
Survey Research Center
here in an investigation
directed by Dr. Rensis
Likert.

The supervisor whose
employes turned out the
greatest amount of work,
the scientists found, is
himself concerned primar-
ily with the people work-
ing under him.

Needs Some Leeway
Pressuring for pro-
duction may work to some
degree. But the best re-
sults are achieved when
a worker's internal mot-
ivations are tapped - his
self-expression, self-de-
termination, and sense of
personal worth. A person
works better when he is
treated as a personality,
given some degree of freedom in the way he does
his work, and allowed to
make his own decisions.

The facts discovered
may aid in emotional un-
derstanding.

"The capacity of a
nation or a society to
survive," Dr. Likert
explained, "depends in
small part upon its skill

205

in organizing industry,
governmental and military
activity.... Baltimore, Md. Evening Sun

Harmony Instead of Strikes -- The Jamestown, N.Y. Sun
featured as the number one story on the front page the
signing of a union agreement and emphasized the harmony
between the parties. The paper at this time was owned by
International Typographical Union.

PLOMB TOOL, UNION AGREE ON CONTRACT; PACT HAILED AS FINE LABOR RELATIONS

By James W. Michaels
Sun Staff Reporter

Jamestown's troubled labor picture brightened
yesterday with the reaching of an agreement between
the Plomb Tool Company and two local unions representing some 250 employees.

The settlement immediately was hailed by Federal Conciliator John J. Clark, Buffalo, as "an
excellent example of harmonious relations between
management and labor."

Six paid holidays, a more liberal vacation
plan, 10 cents an hour wage premium for night
shift work, continuation of the union shop and two
hours reporting pay are provided for in the new contract, a joint company-union announcement said.

Members Ratify Terms

Members of Lodge 1791, International Association of Machinists, (Ind.) and Local 38, of the
Metal Polishers' International (AFL) ratified the
terms early in the evening. Ratification followed
a tentative settlement between company and union
committees in the afternoon.

Wage questions can be reopened after Sept. 1,
1949. The agreement runs for 15 months from
May 1, 1949.

Speaking for both unions, IAM Business Representative John G. Jackson told the Sun: "the union
went along on the wage issue because the company
gave us a wage reopening clause for Sept. 1."

"We are satisfied that a good agreement was
reached," he said.

Company "Happy"

Plomb Vice-President Carl W. Coslow said the
Company felt "the unions apparently have been very
smart in their appraisal of the economic situation
and displayed a sound knowledge of conditions in

8. Exploring Further the Labor Scene

The strike reveals what the immediate objectives of the employers are in a certain plant or industry. But what are the general aims of the larger union? What are their long-range programs? Here is the type of explanatory feature which would fill out the picture for the public and would enable the spot news to take on more significance and meaning.

National labor legislation will be in the news for decades to come for the various reasons we have mentioned. Yesterday it was the National Industrial Recovery Act, section 7a. Then came the National Labor Relations Act. Today the focus of attention is on the Taft-Hartley law. Tomorrow it may be a different piece of legislation relating to this vital labor problem. The public gets the completest discussion when congressional hearings are held. But these are neither complete nor coherent. These labor measures must be localized in a fuller objective explanatory article, with all parties to the controversial measure being given an opportunity to present their views and facts.
Some of the critical and important labor problems today should be explored objectively. Charges which are aired in the news may be explored to greater depth than the press association news wire will allow. The issue now is "democracy in labor unions." The locals as well as the national organizations are charged with being little dictatorships, ruled over by fuehrers, who milk the members and operate a racket. It is up to the responsible reporter to investigate the facts about these charges thoroughly. He must study the accusations carefully, visit the union, get its side of the controversy. To this investigation must be added the study of the magazine articles and authoritative books on this subject.

Growing out of this phase are the personality features on the leaders of the unions. Many of the issues can be seen clearly, in the study of careers, personalities and views of the late Philip Murray, of the CIO, the late William Green, of the AFL. Newsworthy personalities also include Walter Reuther, now president of CIO, George Meany, head of AFL, and John L. Lewis, leader of the mine workers. But portraits, too, may be written about the local presidents and business agents.

Many papers have presented interesting series on individual workers in the community. The reporters have avoided the stereotypes, and, instead, have presented the human side of the steelworker, the stevedore, the mechanic. They have written about him as a family man, interested in a hobby, a lover of sports, of be-bop. The reporters have described the goals, ambitions of the truck driver and the oil refinery worker. These are the readers of the paper who never make the news until they murder a neighbor, rob a gas station, or win a huge fortune for naming a mystery tune on the radio.

withdrawing their wage demands at this time.

Coslow added: "the wage reopening clause, which was part of the contract, is for the purpose of allowing them to evaluate business conditions later on.

"I am very happy with the contract. The Plomb Company never has had a strike."

Coslow came here from the concern's office in Los Angeles to take part in the negotiations.

The J.P. Danielson Company here is a division of the Plomb Tool Company of Los Angeles. The firm has plants in three other cities.

Personnel Involved

Representing the International Association of Machinists in the talks were Business Representative Jackson, president of Lodge 1791, and William McCullum, Jabez Carlein, James Palermo, Kenneth Moore, Vern Swanson and William Constantine.

Local 38 of the Metal Polishers, Buffers, Platers and Helpers International Union was represented by International Vice-President Dennis Oakes, Local 38 President Walter R. Anderson, Ellwerd Lawson and George Bryant.

For the company Coslow was assisted in the talks by local plant manager J.P. Danielson and local plant superintendent Claude L. Boring.

LABOR WRITERS STRESS
PEACEFUL REPORTING

Suggestions for various types of peaceful labor reporting were made at the Second Annual Conference of Labor News Writers sponsored by the New York State School of Industrial and Labor Relations. The meeting was held at Cornell University.

The recommendations urged newspapers to present:

1. Successful instances of collective bargaining.
2. Articles which anticipate potential labor difficulty.
3. Features which stress amicable relations under conditions which in other circumstances have produced trouble.
4. News-features about "social action" taken by Union and union-management groups on persistent community problems.
5. News about profit-sharing plans.
6. Articles telling of the achievements resulting from suggestions-box programs.

Adapted from Editor & Publisher
Dec. 12, 1953

Another significant problem bobs up in the news when
jurisdictional strikes are called or when the CIO and the
AFL struggle to become the bargaining agent in a plant.
The first-day's news merely gives the highlights, and end-
result of a series of conflicts. Often this story has its
roots in the craft unit vs industrial unit dispute which
has broken out many times in the history of the labor
movement in this country. The reporter can give an effective and enlightening presentation of this current issue,
which affects industry, the employes and the public. With
the merger of the AFL and CIO it was believed this intra-
union strike would be reduced, if not eliminated.

In some industries workers and employers maintain
jointly camps and hospitals and conduct summer cruises.
The explanation for the growth of this movement might be
investigated and presented along with articles about these
activities.

A number of unions, as indicated, have established
educational departments, presenting speakers, radio programs, conducting workshops in labor-management relations,
and carrying on other community-wide activities. This
phase of organizational work may furnish leads and articles.

The need for charts, graphs, cartoons, pictures and
other visual aids has been shown in other chapters. The
reporter who deals with labor should not overlook them in
presenting complex, intricate ideas to the reader.

Here's a background story on how one union, the United
Packinghouse Workers of America, sought to eliminate discrimination in its ranks. Note the systematic methods it
used and its employment of John Hope II, a specialist in
industrial race relations, to conduct its study.

Union Fights Discrimination

Two years ago, Ralph Helstein, attorney-
president of CIO's United Packinghouse Workers
of America, decided that the union's antidiscrimination policy wasn't working. There was still a
lot of race bias in the industry.
At the union's 1950 convention, he named Russell R. Lasley - a Negro vice-president and top-
flight UPWA organizer - to organize an educational
campaign to fight discrimination in the union...
Of course, racial friction isn't limited to the
packinghouse union, but UPWA has been most active
in trying to stamp it out. Of its 150,000 members,
50,000 are Negroes and 10,000 Mexicans. UPWA is
attacking the problem from the inside out: It's
getting rid of bias within the union, then attacking it where it exists outside the union...
Higher Guidance - Lasley went to one of the
country's top race-relations study centers for
guidance. Last Fall he asked help from Fisk

University, a Negro university in Nashville, Tenn.
John Hope II, a specialist in industrial race relations at Fisk, agree to help UPWA in its fight
against bias.

Questionnaires - First step was to find out how
much bias persisted in the union - where and in what
form. Hope and his UPWA aides sent questionnaires
to officers of 350 locals throughout the country;
searching questions dealt with race relations in
the union, in contract plants, and in the community.

The questionnaires were returned "blind" to
Hope, and the Social Studies Institute at Fisk;
officers didn't sign their names, and neither
national union officials nor local members saw
the returned questionnaires. Fisk analyzed the
answers.

Double Check - As a follow-up, Hope and crews
of volunteer aides are making house-to-house spot
checks in each community surveyed through the
questionnaires. Investigators come generally from
church and civic groups, social-service agencies,
or local colleges. So far, the spot checks have
pretty well tallied with answers given to questionnaires.

Basic Information - When the results are in for
a local or community, UPWA gets a report. It shows:
What discrimination exists in the local.
Whether any plants under contract with the
    local discriminate in hiring, in upgrading
    and promotion or through separate locker
    room and eating facilities.
Community discriminatory practices - in hotels
    restaurants, theaters and business places.
What the local is doing to cut down prejudices.

Tailored Program - With all this information,
UPWA can tailor an educational program to fit the
need.

In the Kansas City report, for instance, the
union says it discovered "structural weaknesses of
our executive boards, steward bodies, and committees" where the antibias program was concerned.
The "structural weaknesses" stymied the union's
efforts to put across its antidiscrimination program. When the organizational structure was
strengthened, results began to show up quickly.

Mainly, locals began cracking down on discriminatory practices in plants and in the community
-practices tolerated before because, local officials
said, "they had always been that way, and everybody wanted them that way." The doorbell check
showed that "everybody" didn't...

Business Week, Oct. 6, 1951

9. Sources for Labor News

Many of the larger cities are the headquarters for the
regional directors or presidents of labor unions. The CIO

210

and the AFL and the independents have offices where the
reporter can get his news. Ordinarily, the unions don't
have publicity men and don't volunteer information, but if
a halfway friendly attitude is shown, they will furnish the
facts about numbers of members, plants organized, contracts
held or being negotiated. The structure of the unions
differs, but generally there is a state organization, and a
local council or federation of unions, such as the City
Building Trades Council, the City Federation of Labor, or
the State CIO Council of Unions.

Although no national labor dailies are issued, a
printed source of information on current labor happenings
and the viewpoint of this group may be found in the many
weeklies. On the national level, the AFL-CIO News, published in Washington, is an effective, well-edited tabloid
filled with news, columns, editorials, and pictures. The
American Federation of Labor issues the magazine, The Federationist, a slick-cover publication, and the United Mine
Workers has the United Mine Workers Journal. Almost all of
the other unions have their organs. Both the CIO and the
AFL publish more specialized monthly "economic outlooks"
from labor's viewpoint. The CIO's publication is called
the Economic Outlook, the AFL's is the Labor Monthly Survey.
These are issued by the research and educational departments
and the articles are carefully documented by the union's
economists and statisticians. They give broad general
pictures of the labor movement and present specialized studies of the economic scene. State federations and city
labor councils publish weeklies and monthlies, the address-
es for which may be checked in the library or the telephone
directory. Many of the editors who have a day-by-day ac-
quaintance with various union activities have a wide understanding of the labor picture. They are frequently artic-
ulate sources for facts about the subject. Reporters seek
them for information about a new or puzzling labor event.

The Federated Press and Labor Press Associates are
national newspaper services which supply labor news, special articles, and mat service to the labor press, the
daily newspapers and other organizations which desire the
service.

The U.S. Department of Labor is also a source of news.
Its officials administer the important wage and hour law
as well as the child labor provisions of the Fair Labor
Standards Act of 1938. The Department of Labor has a Bureau of Employment Security which operated through the U.S.
Employment Service, a nationwide system of public employment offices, and assists the states in carrying out their
unemployment insurance program. A branch office may be
located in your community.

The U.S. Bureau of Labor Statistics supplies information on wages, employment, costs of living and work stoppages. The bureau issues the Monthly Labor Review which
gives a national picture of conditions. The women's bureau
furnishes information for background articles on women's
economic status, their wages, working conditions and employ-

ment opportunities. _Fortune_ also carries extensive, up-to-date articles on labor.

The National Labor Relations Board which administers the Taft-Hartley Act has established, in addition to its headquarters in Washington, regional offices. These offices deal with the cases arising in one large state or in a group of adjoining states. Releases on important national cases as well as information on local disputes are furnished by the Washington headquarters and the local regional directors. The board deals with two types of cases, those arising in connection with disputes about representation of employes and those developing from unfair labor practices. When a representation petition or an unfair practice charge is filed, an informal investigation is usually made by a field examiner. Many of these cases are settled informally. But when the parties to the dispute cannot resolve their difficulties, a formal hearing before a trial examiner must be held. The reporter may cover this hearing as it is generally held in the community in which the factory or store is located. Final decision is made by the Board in Washington. But appeal may be made in the U.S. courts. A number of the papers and documents may be seen. The Information Division of the NLRB provides a variety of leaflets and pamphlets about the Act and the work of the Board, which also issues monthly and annual reports.

State News Sources -- State Departments of Labor, or State Industrial Commissions, are also sources for impartial news in the area. These agencies administer the state laws relating to labor, including such measures as work conditions, safety, and child labor. Consider for example the Florida Industrial Commission. In addition to having divisions which administer workmen's compensation, the commission also regulates private employment agencies, elevator inspections, child labor, industrial safety and the apprenticeship program, according to Mae Campbell, formerly assistant to the director of information for the commission.

News of interest which may be derived from agencies such as this include the number of unemployed persons in the state and the amount of unemployment insurance being paid them. Other news would include the number of industrial accidents and fatalities for which workmen's compensation was paid and the number of minors employed.

As does the Florida Industrial Commission, many state groups of this type have informational or public relations offices. These offices send news releases to the state newspapers, publish monthly bulletins, write magazine articles and carry on many other means of publicity to inform the public of their activities.

These agencies are often not bound by state lines in all respects. Employment information is exchanged among the state employment groups. Where there are great numbers of migratory workers who come to the states often a migratory worker information bulletin is issued by the employment service offices to facilitate the rapid placement and direction of these workers.

"Seasonally during the year, different phases of the commission's program are often pushed. For instance, during the period when high schools and colleges are graduating large numbers of students, special publicity is used to facilitate the placement of these students in jobs," explained Ralph Hager, of the information staff of the commission. During the first week of October a similar campaigning is used to place physically handicapped workers in suitable jobs. Known as National Employ the Physically Handicapped Week, this special program affords one of the major publicity activities of the agency during the year.

The following news feature came through the Florida State Employment Service and was published in many newspapers.

National Week Launched To Gain More Employment. For Physically Handicapped

State, Federal and Veterans' Organization Unit in Drive to Acquaint Public with Value of Hiring Disabled Folk

National "Employ the Physically Handicapped Week," beginning today, will be observed here with an intensive campaign to find employment for disabled persons.

According to Henry C. Tiffany, veterans employment representative of the Florida State Employment Service, who is chairman of local NEPH Week activities, local employers will be requested to survey their present job requirements and disabled persons asked to register with the local office of the State employment agency. A special evaluation of both job opportunities and the qualifications of disabled persons will be made during the week.

Proclamations calling for a general observance of the week have been issued by President Truman, Gov. Fuller Warren and Mayor Haydon Burns.

Emphasizing that "this is not a charity drive," Tiffany pointed out that when properly placed a disabled person is an enthusiastic, hard-working and satisfactory employe. Any such person sent to a prospective employer, Tiffany added, will be just as well qualified for the job as an unimpaired worker.

W.D. Kennedy, local manager of the Florida Employment Service, 40 East Bay Street, added that there are 290 handicapped persons registered there for work, including 139 war veterans.

"There is no question," David M. Brown
of Akron, Ohio, national commander of the
Disabled American Veterans, said in a message delivered last week in Cincinnati, "but
the disabled veteran is an excellent employe
from the standpoint of loyalty, efficiency
and attendance. For every Federal dollar
that has been spent in the rehabilitation of
our handicapped, he has returned $10 in in-
come taxes alone."

Jacksonville, <u>Florida Times Union</u>

EVERY REPORTER COVERS LABOR

If you get a daily newspaper job, you will
have to be a labor reporter sooner or later.

When a strike breaks, every local man becomes, in some measure, a labor reporter. A
new lead may pop up from any direction. Beat
men have to watch developments on their runs.
General assignment men may go to picket lines,
union or employer officers, mass meetings, conference room doors. They may hunt angles by
telephone or take stories on rewrite.

For the moment they are all working on labor.

And frequently, they're pathetically -- yes,
even dangerously -- unfamiliar with the ground
they're supposed to tread.

From "Labor is News -
A Reporter's View."
Arnold Aslakson,
<u>Journalism Quarterly</u>,
Vol. XVII, June, 1940

Summary

In the past labor news meant news of strikes and violence. Today editors are beginning to realize the public
wants more adequate background coverage of the entire union
problem. Organized labor itself has grown and has become
a definite, established part of the American economy and an
influential factor in the trend of public affairs. A number of newspapers recognize the need to cover labor news
systematically and objectively.

On some papers general assignment men have been given
this task, on others, labor reporters devote their full
time to this job. A reporter specializing in this area
should know the structure and operations of state and local
unions and be acquainted with the printed sources of labor
news -- the government publications and the union press.
He should also learn the procedures of the federal and
state agencies dealing with labor and furnishing news.

The labor reporter should understand how to cover
the spot news of labor unions and how to write features
about labor activities and union-management relations,
with the stress on accuracy, completeness and objectivity.

Fact and Discussion
Questions on Chapter V "Behind the Strike Headlines."

1. Why is labor news important today?

2. (a) What kinds of labor news made the headlines in the past?
    (b) What do editors believe the public wants in labor news now?

3. How do you account for the antagonism of union representatives towards reporters.

4. Tell about the growing significance of labor.

5. Give an account of the history of the legal recognition of unions.

6. What protective measures for labor were passed by the New Deal Administration?

7. Outline some of the principal provisions of the Taft-Hartley Act.

8. What knowledge does a reporter need to report labor adequately?

9. Explain why labor is becoming newsworthy.

10. (a) Discuss the rayon worker story from the spot news standpoint.
    (b) What kind of background article could have been written?

11. Comment on the story, "Steelworkers Prepare to Demand Boost in Wages", giving the methods used by the newsman to background the story.

12. Discuss the statement "reporters should revise the stereotype about employes."

13. Tell about some "constructive features" which might be written about unions and labor management relations. Cite examples from the chapter and devise some yourself.

14. What recommendations about reporting labor were made by the Conference of Labor News Writers at Cornell University.

15. Discuss management's defense and union objections to Taft-Hartley Act.

16. What are the pros and cons of the right-to-work laws?

17. What are some of the recent developments in labor racketeering?

18. List some of the shortcomings of workmen's compensation laws.

19. How does the guaranteed annual wage plan operate? What are labor's aims, management's objections?

20. What are distressed areas?

21. What is the basic idea behind full employment program?

22. Describe labor's tax program.

23. What is automation? What are the dangers? Advantages?

24. Describe labor's proposals in housing, health, education.

News Clipping Projects

1. Select from your favorite or local newspaper a current news or feature about labor.

   a. Paste them on news clipping pages.
   b. Analyze them for objectivity, completness.
   c. Is there any more information you would like to have?
   d. Outline briefly the kind of background story you would write on the situation.
   e. Where would you go for information?
   f. Write the news-feature.

Feature Article Assignments

Select one from these:

1. "Local Labor Round-up" is the title for this feature.

   a. Visit the headquarters of the local American Federation of Labor Trades Union Council. Discuss with the officials types of locals, the approximate members in each, and the companies where contracts are held.
   b. Go down to the local headquarters of the Congress of Industrial Organization Council, representing various locals in the community. Ask the president about the CIO picture in town. Find out when the meetings of the council and of the locals are held. Ask whether you might attend a meeting. Get your instructor's consent before attending such a meeting.
   c. Write you findings into a 750-word feature.

2. "The Varied Activities of the State Department of Labor."

    a. Some states might call the agencies dealing with this problem an Industrial Commission. Don't be misled by titles.

    b. The headquarters of this agency would be found in the state capital, but branches may be located in various towns. If possible, pay a visit to the agency, or send a letter to the headquarters for information.

    c. Much literature is produced by this agency in a number of states.

    d. Investigate the work of this department, and write a feature based on your findings.

    e. Make the story readable, with concrete details, actual situations.

3. "Backstop For Depression

    a. Go to the State Industrial Commission for a story on unemployment insurance.

    b. Talk to the head of the agency and to the director of information.

    c. Dig for facts about the agency's program; ask for pertinent literature.

    d. List the number of workers who receive benefits, the amount paid, the qualifications for receiving the payments, the reasons for a worker's losing the privilege of receiving unemployment insurance.

    e. Get some concrete examples.

    f. Write a news-feature, giving the results of your investigation.

4. "Labor Board's Decisions Are Far-Reaching".

    a. Read the summary of the development of collective bargaining in John R. Commons and John B. Andrews, Principles of Labor Legislation, rev. edition.

    b. Write to the National Labor Relations Board, Washington, D.C., for latest literature about the Labor Management Act (Taft-Hartley), or the latest version of this law.

    c. The NLRB has regional boards in various states. If there is one in your town or nearby, visit the headquarters. Discuss your assignment with the regional director. Ask him about his work and the operation of the regional office, the legal division, the field examiners, and the trial examiners. Tell him to let you see the board's forms and permit you to talk to a Field Examiner and a Board lawyer about their work.

    d. Write to the U.S. Chamber of Commerce, Washington, D. C., or the National Association of Manufacturers for literature about the Labor-Management Act.

e. For the other side of the story, write the
Publicity Department, Congress of Industrial
Organizations, and the American Federation of
Labor, Washington, D.C., (Check for complete
address in library.)

f. Write two features of 750 words each on your
investigation. Describe the purpose and work
of the NLRB, the criticism of the Taft-Hartley
Act and the defense. Be fair. Be objective.

5. "Is there Democracy in Labor Unions?"

a. Discover what the facts are by investigating
both sides and all sides.

b. Visit a union headquarters and get the president or business agent to talk about this question.

c. Study the structure of the union and seek to
understand if there is a democracy in operation.

d. Check library card catalogue for books on this
question.

e. Write a news-feature on this controversial issue. About 750 words.

6. "Union Leader: A Portrait".

a. Select a national figure, such as Walter Reuther, John L. Lewis; or a local's president or
business agent in this community.

b. If you pick a national leader of labor, you
will have to use library sources. Biographies
and magazine articles have been written about
most of the controversial figures.

c. You may be able to interview a local president
or business agent.

d. Write a fair, objective personality sketch,
presenting the career, views and dominant
characteristics of your subject.

7. "Portrait of a Worker".

a. Select a local worker in steel, auto, shipyards, a painter or mechanic.

b. Names will be supplied by the local union
through the instructor.

c. Write about the worker as a family man, giving
his outside interests, hobbies, goals, ambitions.

d. Tell about him as a member of the union.

e. Get behind the current stereotypes to the real
person.

8. "Sitting Around the Bargaining Table".

a. Interview the instructor teaching labor or
labor economics on the campus. Ask him to tell
you how contracts are negotiated. Inquire what

219

are some principles of good labor-management
relations.
b. Investigate to see if there are any local companies which have union contracts and which
get along particularly well with their employes and their representatives.
c. Get the history of the company and the history
of the bargaining relations at the plant.
d. The union agent may give you some leads and
names for this assignment.
e. Try to interview both the agent and the company representative.
f. Discover the basis for the underlying harmony
in that plant. What are the features of the
plant policy and the union attitude?

9. "How to Make Workers Happy"

a. Check with instructor in labor on the campus.
Inquire as to what he believes are the long-
range and the short-term goals of labor today.
b. Visit a union headquarters and tell the representative your assignment. Ask him to state
what the immediate objectives are in contracts
he has negotiated during the past year. Ask
what are the long-range goals of his organization.
c. Write a news-feature with the above title.

10. "Recent Trends in the Labor World".

a. New problems are always arising in labor:
Craft vs. industrial unions, unity between
big organizations, and others.
b. Investigate through the usual sources, economics department, union headquarters, library,
one of these issues, or other current issues,
for a news-feature.

11. "Labor and the UN"

a. Investigate this for a feature article, as
labor has an international aspect.
b. The United Nations Organization seeks to raise
the standards of labor throughout the world.
How does it do this? Any concrete achievements?
c. The Information Bureau of the UN in New York
City will supply information. Also write to
the International Labor Office, headquarters,
Washington, D.C., for facts. Check local library for possible sources in books and current
magazines.

12. "The Guaranteed Annual Wage".

a. Check Readers' Guide, New York Times Index,
CIO Economic Outlook.

13. Effects of CIO-AFL merger.

    a. Check New York Times Index.
    b. Discuss this with local labor representatives.

14. "What Labor Seeks In National Legislation."

    a. Check CIO News, AFL-CIO News, for past two years.
    b. Interview local labor.
    c. Write two-part series.

15. "How the Spread of Automation Will Affect Labor."

    a. See Readers' Guide, New York Times Index.
    b. Interview workers and their representatives.

16. Pros and Cons of "Right To Work Laws".

    a. Check CIO's Economic Outlook, Jan. 1955, Vol. XVI, No. 1.
    b. Interview head of local Chamber of Commerce, State Industrial Council for opposite view.

17. "The Mounting Welfare Funds in Union Treasuries."

    a. What is extent of the funds?
    b. How are they administered?
    c. What abuses have developed.
    d. Check Facts on File, New York Times Index, Readers' Guide to Periodical Literature.

18. The Full Employment Program of Walter Reuther.

    a. Check CIO Economic Outlook and other publications of the union.

Reportorial Book Report

Some books on labor of value to the Newsman.

1. Foster Rhea Dulles, Labor In America, New York: Crowell, 1949.

2. Clinton Golden and Harold J. Ruttenberg, Dynamics of Industrial Democracy. New York: Harper, 1942.

3. Herbert Harris, American Labor. New Haven: Yale University Press, 1939.

4. Herbert L. Marx, Jr., comp., American Labor Unions. New York: H. W. Wilson, 1950.

5. Harry Millis and Royal E. Montgomery, The Economics of Labor. New York: McGraw-Hill, 1938-45.

6. Florence Peterson, Handbook of Labor Unions. Washington, D. C.: American Council on Public Affairs, 1944.

7. Lloyd Reynolds, Labor Economics and Labor Relations. New York: Prentice-Hall, 1949.

8. Sumner H. Slichter, The American Economy. New York: Knopf, 1948.

9. Colston E. Warne, and others, Labor In Post-War America, Brooklyn, Remsen, 1949.

Magazine Report

1. "Enterprise for Everyman", Fortune, January, 1950. Vol. XLI, No. 1.

2. John Chamberlain, "Everyman a Capitalist." Life, December 23, 1946, Vol. 21, page 93.

Further References: Textbooks and magazine articles dealing with labor reporting.

Books on Labor Reporting Chapters in Journalism

Chilton R. Bush, Newspaper Reporting of Pubic Affairs. New York: Appleton-Century, Crofts, 1940. Chapter XVI, "Labor News."

Laurence R. Campbell and Roland E. Wolseley, Newsmen at Work. New York: Houghton Mifflin, 1949. Chapter 26, "Labor is Big News."

Leon Flint, The Conscience of the Newspaper. New York: Appleton, 1930.

Robert M. Neal, News Gathering and News Writing. New York: Prentice-Hall, 1949. Chapter 34, "Labor News."

Curtis D. MacDougall, Interpretative Reporting. New York: Macmillan, Rev. 1949. Chapter XXVI, "Business, Finance, Labor."

George Fox Mott, ed. New Survey of Journalism. New York: Barnes & Noble, Rev. 1950. Chapter XVIII, "Covering the Labor Run".

George L. Bird, Press and Society, Chapter 14, "The Frederic E. Merwin "The Press and Specialized Fields"

Magazine Articles

Arnold Aslakson, "Labor Is News: A Reporter's View,"
Journalism Quarterly, June, 1940. Vol. 17; page 151-
158.

Burris Dickinson, "Influence of the Press in Labor
Affairs", *Journalism Quarterly*, Sept., 1932, Vol. IX,
page 269-280.

Wellington Wales, "Labor Writers Stress Peaceful Reporting," *Editor & Publisher*, Dec. 12, 1953, p. 59.

Joseph Dragonetti, "Editor Says Labor Can Win Good
Press By Acting Its Age", *Editor and Publisher*. May 28,
1949, Vol. 82:23, page 9.

Leila A. Sussmann, "Labor in the Radio News: An Analysis of Content," *Journalism Quarterly*, Sept., 1945,
Vol. 22, page 207-14.

Alfred Zacher and others, "A Liberal Newspaper is as
Liberal as Its Labor Policy -- and How Liberal is That?
A Study of the New York Post", *The Masthead*, (issued
by National Conference of Editorial Writers) Vol. 2,
No. 3, Summer, 1950 page 1-10.

"Labor Reporting, How Good Is It Now?" *Business Week*,
Oct., 1951.

For articles bearing on labor and other subjects in
the news see *Journalism Quarterly*, Supplement, Index,
Vol. 1 to 25, issued, December, 1948.

Thesis on Labor Reporting

Arthur T. Jacobs, *Press and San Francisco General
Strike in 1934*, Univ. of Wisconsin, 1935.

Charles O. Voight, Jr., *A Comparative Study of the
Reporting of the San Francisco General Strike of 1934
by San Francisco Newspapers*. Stanford Univ. 1939.

For list of other graduate journalism thesis in American universities, see William F. Swindler's compilation and analysis, *Journalism Quarterly*, Vol. 22,
p.231;-44. Also refers to previous list made by Frank
L. Mott.